ARMIES OF 1812

ARMIES OF 1812

THE GRAND ARMÉE
AND THE ARMIES OF AUSTRIA,
PRUSSIA, RUSSIA AND TURKEY

DIGBY SMITH

SPELLMOUNT

Staplehurst

British Library Cataloguing in Publication Data:
A catalogue record for this book is available
from the British Library

Copyright © Digby Smith 1977, 2002

ISBN 1-86227-165-8

The French Army section first published in the UK in 1977
by Patrick Stephens Ltd

This complete edition published 2002
by
Spellmount Limited
The Old Rectory
Staplehurst
Kent TN12 0AZ

Tel: 01580 893730
Fax: 01580 893731
E-mail: enquiries@spellmount.com
Website: www.spellmount.com

1 3 5 7 9 8 6 4 2

Printed in Singapore by Kyodo Printing Co. (S' pore) Pte Ltd

Contents

Foreword 6
Section 1
The 1812 adventure
Introduction 7
The character of the Grande Armée 7
The casualties 8
The French logistic system 10
The climate 31

Section 2
Uniforms and colours
Grand Duchy of Baden 33
Bavaria 34
Grand Duchy of Berg 38
France 39
Grand Duchy of Frankfurt 57
Grand Duchy of Hessen-Darmstadt 58
Kingdom of Italy 59
Duchies of Mecklenberg-Schwerin and
    Mechlenberg-Strelitz 62
Kingdom of Naples 63
Rheinbund regiments 64
Kingdom of Saxony 66
Grand Duchy of Warsaw 79
Kingdom of Westfalia 83
Kingdom of Württemberg 85
Grand Duchy of Würzburg 90
Uniform glossary 90

Section 3
Orders of battle, maps and casualty graphs
Imperial Guard 99
I Corps 105
II Corps 112
III Corps 116
IV Corps 121
V Corps 127
VI Corps 130
VII Corps 135
VIII Corps 140

IX Corps 142
XI Corps 145
I Cavalry Corps 149
II Cavalry Corps 150
III Cavalry Corps 152
IV Cavalry Corps 153

Section 4
Appendices
French regiments in Russia in 1812 155
Major battles and clashes of the 1812
    Campaign 155
Statement of the Russian and French loss 160
Calculation of Provision, Forage, &c, for the
    support of a large army one week 160

Section 5
The Russian Armies 161
The 1st Army of the West 161
The 2nd Army of the West 164
The 3rd Army of the West 165
The Army of the Moldau (or of the Don) 167
Russian Army Uniforms 170

Section 6
The Austrian Army Corps 184
Colours and Standards 189

Section 7
The Prussian Army Contingent
    (28th Division) 191
Prussian Uniforms 194
Colours and Standards 196

Section 8
The Turkish Army 204

Bibliography 205

Index 207

Foreword

Part of this book appeared originally in 1977 (under my *nom de plume* of Otto von Pivka) and was intended to be Volume I of a two-volume work.

Volume I contained the I–IX and XI Corps and the I–IV Cavalry Corps of the *Grande Armée* .

Man proposes, economics dispose. A cash-flow crisis smothered Volume II and the manuscript has languished in a glass coffin, awaiting a handsome prince ever since. Finally, the handsome prince rode up on his white charger last year in the shape of Jamie Wilson. The strategic decision was taken to combine the two intended volumes into the present work, which contains all the old Volume I, plus the Austrians, Prussians (X Corps), Russians and Turks in similar format to the first volume in order to preserve continuity.

Thus all the troops that fought in Russia in 1812 are represented here, including the major and minor contingents of the states of the Confederation of the Rhine.

There was a Danish contingent nominated to join the invasion, but Napoleon thought it better to leave these troops in Denmark to help to enforce his crumbling Continental System and to guard against any British landing in his rear. The Danish contingent is thus excluded from this book.

Due to limitations of space, only the uniforms, colours and standards of those troops that entered Russia in 1812 are described. The orders of battle included are only valid for the days on which they are dated; Russian orders of battle, in particular, changed frequently during the campaign.

As the reader will see, the cavalry regiments of the Napoleonic 'vassal states' (Bavaria, Prussia, Saxony, Warsaw, Westfalia, Wuerttemberg) were often taken from their national contingents on Napoleon's orders to serve in his Cavalry Corps under French command.

The names of persons and places are spelt as they appear in the original source documents, so variations do occur. This is particularly so with the Russian names which have been transliterated into German, English and French.

The maps of the wanderings of each corps allow the reader to follow any regiment through the campaign with reasonable accuracy, and the graphs of the reductions of the strengths of the corps of the *Grande Armée*, show dramatically how swiftly the combat values of these formations dropped even in the first few weeks of the advance.

A question mark in the text indicates that a detail is unknown.

Digby Smith
Thetford 2002

Acknowledgements

My thanks are due to the following who have assisted me in the compilation of both parts of this book: Mr Andrews and Mr Potts of the Ministry of Defence Library; Herr Berthold Paul, Berlin; Frau Doktor Gretel Wagner of the Lipperheide Kostumsammlung, Berlin; the directors and staffs of the Bavarian Kriegsarchiv, Munich and the Wehrhistorisches Museum in Rastatt / Baden, and Timofey Nikolaievich Shevyakoff in Moscow, who is also bringing out the Russian edition of this work.

Section 1

The 1812 adventure

Introduction

Much has already been written about Napoleon's 1812 adventure and it is not the intention of this book merely to rehash and regurgitate that which has adequately been covered in previous publications.

Almost all works published on the Russian campaign pass rapidly over the period up to the fall of Moscow and then plunge into the drama, misery and pathos of 'The Retreat' to which is devoted the majority of the literary effort. The aim of this book is to re-focus attention on to the early part of the campaign, to that period when the mistakes were made, when plans went wrong, when the *majority* of the appalling losses of the *Grande Armée* occurred. It is often forgotten, or overlooked, that the Retreat from Moscow had its roots in the spring of 1812 and that if things had gone well in the first few weeks of the advance, the Retreat may well never have taken place, or at least its horrific outcome could have been much relieved.

Let us now examine the armies that marched to their deaths in Russia in that fateful year.

The character of the Grande Armée

Many of the regiments which served in Russia had been transferred out of Spain (where they had fought from 1808-1811) specifically to take part in the great expedition. Their place in Spain was infrequently taken by new battalions of young French conscripts and the impression has thus been created that Napoleon's Grande Armée of 1812 consisted largely of veterans. This is unfortunately only partially true. The strength of vast majority of 'ex-Spanish' regiments at the time of marching out of that country in 1811 and early 1812 was about ten to 15 per cent of their strength at the time of entering it. The bitter guerrilla war and, even more so, the terrible ravages of starvation and disease, had wiped out the missing

men. So rather than transferring complete veteran regiments from Spain to Russia, it was a case of moving a seasoned cadre back to its depôt either in France or in one of the states of the Confederation of the Rhine, bringing the regiment up to strength with new young conscripts, and sending the numerically complete but by no means veteran unit off to the east.

Apart from the Imperial Guard, veteran units as such were only to be met with in the armies of Baden, Bavaria, Hessen-Darmstadt, Saxony and Württemberg and even among these the proportion of young conscripts was quite high as Napoleon's insatiable demands for men and matériel far outstripped the relatively modest standing armies which had existed in these states prior to 1800. It must also be mentioned that many of these pre-1800 veterans were, in fact, often 50 or 60 years of age and in fragile health, so within a few weeks of the first whirlwind Napoleonic campaigns, 'natural wastage' would drastically have reduced the fine parade states of these paper armies. Between 1800 and 1809 in all the German states actively engaged in hostilities, the average age of soldiers and officers dropped dramatically.

So it was largely a youthful army which entered Russia in 1812; an army which was never to be allowed to profit from the experience it was to undergo in the next few months. As far as can be assessed, the casualty rate for most units which entered Russia was about 90 per cent, and of these 90 per cent were fatalities. Some units, indeed, vanished without trace. Of course, during the period 1813-1815 a thin trickle of frostbitten survivors made their way back into western Europe but their numbers were pitifully small and they in no way invalidate the staggering loss figures quoted above.

By 1812 Napoleon had converted most of western Europe into an armed camp which was dedicated to the furtherance of his aggressive imperialism. Most of the minor states had been dragooned into the 'Confederation of the Rhine' (*Rheinbund*), an organisation which bore many remarkable similarities to the Warsaw Pact of post-World War 2 Europe. In both cases, the entire military effort of all member states was controlled from one central planning staff; there was extensive standardisation of weapons, tactics, uniforms and rank badges and of the 'official' language (French and Russian respectively). The petty principalities of central Germany, who were too small to provide viable individual military contingents, were concentrated into polyglot 'Rheinbund Regiments'. Larger states (Bavaria, Saxony, Westfalia, Warsaw) provided Divisions or Corps. As with the Warsaw Pact (1956, 1968), Rheinbund troops were used in 1809 and 1813 to hold down their own peoples in favour of the central dictatorship.

The casualties

The appalling casualty rate suffered by the Grande Armée in Russia has already been mentioned, but within the figures is contained an interesting reflection on the society of the times. After reading through many regimental histories with very detailed accounts of the campaign and carefully researched casualty lists for the individual units, it becomes apparent that in almost every case, the officer casualties were usually in the order of 60 per cent of the march-out strength whereas the losses of the soldiers ('enlisted men', 'other ranks') is always in the 90-95 per cent area and often none of the men survived at all.

Possible answers are that, when captured, it was customary for officers to be treated almost as guests by their captors, often being given protection, food, clothing, money and transport to a designated city within Russia. The men, on the other hand, were robbed, beaten, starved and kept in the meanest of conditions, although it must be said that the Russian soldiers endured very similar conditions themselves

and were also often short of food in the later stages of the French retreat.

Apart from the hazards of enemy action, the other (and far greater) danger to any campaigning soldier's life was, and still is, sickness and disease. The ratio of deaths from enemy action and from disease on any campaign is usually in the order of one to three even today, but in the Grande Armée in Russia in 1812 the ratio was more nearly one to ten. This abnormal escalation was brought about by the exceptionally bad logistic arrangements coupled with the almost non-existent medical system. Once committed to a military 'hospital' in Russia, either as the result of wounds or sickness, a man's chances of survival were practically nil. Contamination, disease, dysentery and typhus raged through these overcrowded, undermanned places; there were no medicinal supplies and almost no rations. Hygiene was forgotten and the helpless unfortunates, often after having suffered savage injuries (without anaesthetics) at the hands of their regimental surgeons, lay, mutilated and in deep shock, starving to death in their own and their fellows' vomit and filth, sometimes with corpses to their left and right. If one had money or a faithful servant, this nightmare could be alleviated and, of course, most officers went on the campaign equipped with both. They frequently carried letters of credit from their home towns which they could exchange for gold in Danzig, Warsaw or Wilna, whereas the simple soldier, ignorant, bewildered and unsophisticated, had only himself and was dependent upon the field cashier for his pay, which was usually months in arrears.

Even in the most desolated areas of Russia, money could conjure the most unlikely delicacies from the local Jewish merchant. The price would be exorbitant, of course, but when life itself was at stake, the value for money was good. He who had plenty of money would be likely to survive, paupers (soldiers) starved.

Left *Bavarian cavalry with the IV Corps cross the Niemen under the eyes of Prince Eugène on June 23 1812 (Albrecht Adam).*

Above right *The Niemen crossing: grenadiers and a pontoon vehicle at Pilony on June 30 (Faber du Four).*

Right *The story of Napoleon's 1812 logistics! The heavy and prolonged rainstorms in early June and the lack of proper forage killed over 10,000 weakened horses within a few days (Faber du Four).*

But even those who managed to avoid enemy bullets, their own surgeons and disease had another peril to conquer; lethargy.

The intense, grinding cold of the later stages of the Retreat, coupled with the effects of long-term debilitation brought about by the starvation diet, reduced men to automata. Those with highly developed initiatives, a pronounced self-motivation, ample determination and a fair degree of self-centredness, were those most likely to keep going day after day in the face of all these privations. The officers, drawn from the upper classes, had enjoyed considerable education, training and discipline, usually aimed at 'character building' as much as anything else, whereas the average soldier, conscripted into the army from his family farm or from his village (which he had never previously left) was pitifully ill-equipped for survival in such a hostile environment. The senior non-commissioned ranks, the Sergeant-Majors, Sergeants and even the Corporals were, of course, mostly veterans and better able to look after themselves, but the young conscript privates died like flies.

Even though aided by comrades, many of them just lacked the will to fight on, to keep putting one frozen foot in front of the other, to move away from that tempting, but deadly, bivouac fire. With all the bonds of military discipline and regimental organisation gone, these unfortunates fell easy prey to death in a land which they did not comprehend, among 'comrades' of other, allied, armies who would be as aggressive to them as would the enemy.

International differences became very inflamed in the Retreat; repeated instances are recorded of Germans being driven brom bivouac fires by Frenchmen, of Germans robbing Italians of food, of all possible combinations of the aforementioned crimes. The thin veneer of civilisation was rapidly torn to shreds by the need to survive and cannibalism was a common event. After the Beresina crossing human flesh was more easy to come by than that of beasts.

After all these horrifying privations, the handfuls of survivors staggered out of Russia and found temporary refuge in Poland and Prussia. For many of them, the experience of sleeping in a bed for the first time in months was unbearable! Several have recorded that they could not bear their beds and had to sleep on the floor for the first few weeks.

The tragedy of 1812 did not stop at the borders of Russia however; many of those who succeeded in dragging themselves into the Grand Duchy of Warsaw were in such a state that their death was only a matter of days or weeks away. For some, the unaccustomed warmth of the houses was a veritable death sentence. The intense cold had frozen all germ activity during the Retreat but the bacteria, and the lice, revived in the warm rooms and completed their fatal work. Many of those who returned to Bavaria or Württemberg survived only a few weeks and others who lived lost toes and fingers to frostbite.

In many towns throughout Germany memorials were erected to the memory of the victims of

Italian train vehicles in bivouac during the advance. Note 'Iron Crown' badge on canvas tilt (Albrecht Adam).

Napoleon's insatiable ego of 1812; some have since decayed or been destroyed by bombing but others still exist and may be found by lucky enthusiasts in such cities as Krefeld and München.

1812 left behind it a vacuum in the youth of western Europe which took many long years to fill. It remains a monument in history to the incredible folly of one man, aided and abetted by the compliant silence of his thoughtless underlings.

The French logistic system

The basis of any large-scale military operation is, of course, the logistic apparatus employed. Many myths have grown up around Napoleon and his fabled requisition system which, 'at one sweep, did away with magazines, supply trains and all the impedimenta of a field army'. If this myth was true, why then did things turn out so badly in 1812? The answer is, of course, that it was nothing but a myth. It is an established fact (often conveniently overlooked) that Napoleon in

Bridge building during the advance into Russia (Albrecht Adam).

reality never did do away with magazines; he merely made do without some of them for short periods such as in 1805 and 1809 when, as a calculated risk, he abandoned his slow-moving logistic 'tail' in order to allow his fighting troops to achieve maximum 'kinetic energy' by their rapid marches and thus to surprise his more conventional foes. It was a gamble in 1805 which nearly went wrong when he found himself at Austerlitz — fast running out of rations — but his enemies saved the day for him by accepting the chance of a battle which Napoleon desperately needed and which his genius won.

Looking slightly more closely at the 'requisition myth', it was naturally possible to march through the fertile Danube valley in 1805 and 1809 and to have the troops take what food, fodder, transport, horses and accommodation they needed from the relatively lavish available stocks. The whole French army passed out of any particular area within a few days and the degree of damage to that area was thus relatively limited but, even so, this legalised robbery had its limitations. While a farmer, or a town, could readily be called upon to supply the commodities listed above, even the most willing collaborator was liable to be at a loss if requested to produce 200 musket cartridges, a cannon, a dozen howitzer shells or a spare wheel for a military vehicle. Even at its best, therefore, Napoleon's requisition system was valid only over part of the spectrum of items which were vital to his army. It is no doubt true that he became so used to conquest and victory that, like the Japanese army in the invasion of Malaya in 1942, he actually planned captured weapons, equipment and supplies into his logistic system. The much-maligned 18th Century magazine system was thus a term restricted to the supply of rations and fodder in the field and the resupply of ammunition, weapons and clothing were separate from it and could not be replaced by a haphazard, or systematic, requisition organisation.

The Emperor devoted much thought to the logistic

The IV Corps struggles on into Russia: July 1, between Piloni and Kroni (Albrecht Adam).

preparations for 1812, ordering vehicles and other items in 1811: Napoleon to Lacuée Cessac (head of the Ordnance Department since January 3 1810) at St Cloud, June 1811[1]: 'I have decided on a great expedition. I shall need horses and transport on a large scale. The men I shall get easily enough; but the difficulty is to prepare transport facilities. I shall need an immense amount of transport because I shall be starting from the Niemen and I intend to operate over large distances and in different directions . . . Do not let the questions of expense check you.' Similarly[2], 'other waggon convoys carried tools of all sorts and, apart from furniture, namely ovens, also building materials, prefabricated sections of wooden houses with windows, collapsible windmills — in addition there were whole battalions of artisans, not only bakers, butchers, tailors, cobblers but also masons, carpenters, gardeners . . . also numerous fire engines as if one had foreseen the burning of Moscow.

'There was also the darker side of the picture . . . the disproportionally large numbers of beardless novices, the bad horses of the national French cavalry regiments and the waggon loads of young lads clapped into irons for desertion.'

The Grand Duchy of Warsaw was called upon to provide vast amounts of food and fodder for the Grande Armée as it formed up within its borders in the spring of 1812. This extra burden on a poor agricultural area would have been bad enough in normal times but the Grand Duchy had been heavily taxed with such demands ever since its creation in 1807, and the year 1811 had been particularly bad with an unusually low harvest so the supplies were just not to be had. Almost every sizeable Polish town became a magazine dedicated to the use of the Grande Armée and the civil populace suffered loss and hardship, the effects of which were to be felt for decades to come. The main military magazines were in the fortresses of Thorn, Graudenz, Danzig and Königsberg; Danzig, a free city, was the largest of all[3]:

'The Emperor stayed from June 7-10 [1812] at Danzig. That was the great army depôt, the place where everything had been organised and prepared during the last two years, and to which the Emperor devoted the greatest attention; for it was the strong point which had to supply all his needs.'

Magazines are again mentioned on page 98 of Segur's book[4]: 'From Danzig the Emperor proceeded, on June 12 to Königsberg. At that place ended the inspection of his immense magazines . . . Immense quantities of provisions, adequate to the immensity of the undertaking were there accumulated. No detail had been neglected.

'The active and impassioned genius of Napoleon was then entirely directed towards that most important and difficult department of his expedition. In that he was profuse of exhortations, orders, and even money, of which his letters are proof. His days were occupied in dictating instructions on that subject; at

Ambulance convoy of the IV Corps at Dokscice (Dogschtitze) on July 20. The inscription on the vehicles reads 'Ambu-lanza/della-Guardia/Reale'. Note the condition and variety of the animals (Albrecht Adam).

night he frequently rose to repeat them again. One General received, on a single day, six despatches from him, all distinguished by the same solicitude.

'In one of these, words were remarked: "For masses like these, if precautions be not taken, the grain of no country can suffice." In another: "it will be requisite for all the provision waggons to be loaded with flour, bread, rice, pulse and brandy, besides what is necessary for the hospital service . . . There will be nothing then to expect from the country and it will be necessary to have everything within ourselves."

'But on the one hand [writes Segur] the means of transport were badly calculated; and on the other he allowed himself to be hurried on as soon as he was put in motion.'

Earlier, Segur says[5]: 'He [Napoleon] stopped at Thorn in order to inspect his fortifications, his magazines and his troops. There the complaints of the Poles, whom our allies were pillaging without mercy, and insulting, reached him. Napoleon addressed severe reproaches, and even threats, to the king of Westfalia . . . finally, he might reproach himself as the cause of the disorders which provoked him; for, from the Oder to the Vistula, and even to the Niemen, if provisions were abundant and properly stationed, the less portable foraging supplies were deficient. Our cavalry was forced to cut the green rye, and to strip the houses of the thatch, in order to feed their horses. It is true that all did not stop at that; for when one disorder is authorised, how can others be forbidden?

'The evil augmented on the other side of the Niemen. The Emperor had calculated upon a multitude of light cars and heavy waggons, each destined

The mounted Italian infantry officer carries the packs of the grenadier and his exhausted companion. A scene from July 1812 (Faber du Four).

Bavarian cavalry on the march in July (Albrecht Adam).

to carry several thousand pounds weight through a sandy region, which carts, with no greater weight than some quintals,* found difficulty in traversing. These conveyances were organised into battalions and squadrons. Each battalion of light cars, called "comtoises" consisted of 600, and might carry 6,000 quintals of flour.

'The battalion of heavy vehicles, drawn by oxen, carried 4,800 quintals. There were besides 26 squadrons of waggons, loaded with military equipages; a great quantity of waggons with tools of all kinds, as well as thousands of artillery and hospital waggons, one siege and six bridge equipages.

'The provision-waggons were to take in their loading from the magazines established on the Vistula. When the army passed that river, it was ordered to provide itself, without halting, the provisions for 25 days, but not to use them till it was beyond the Niemen. In conclusion, the greater part of these means of transport failed, either because the organisation of soldiers, to act as conductors of military convoys, was essentially vicious, honour and ambition not lending their support to discipline; or chiefly because these vehicles were too heavy for the soil, the distances too considerable, the privations and fatigues too great; certain it is that the greater number of them scarcely reached the Vistula.

'The army, therefore, provisioned itself on its march. The country being fertile, horses, waggons, cattle, and provisions of all kinds, were swept off; everything was taken . . .

'Some days after, at the Niemen, the embarrassment of the passage, and celerity of the first hostile marches, caused all the fruits of these requisitions to be abandoned with an indifference only equalled by the violence with which they had been siezed.'

*1 quintal = 58.752 kg.

Segur then attempts to justify these excesses of semi-organised brigandry by pleading the speed required of Napoleon's advance[6]: 'Our long and heavy baggage-waggons would have encumbered our march. It was much more convenient to live on the supplies of the country, as we should be able to indemnify the loss afterwards. But superfluous wrong was committed as well as necessary wrong, for who can stop midway in the commission of evil? What chief could be responsible for the crowd of officers and soldiers who were scattered through the country in order to collect its resources? To whom were complaints to be addressed? Who was to punish?

'Moreover some of the leaders set the example: there was a positive emulation in evil. In that respect many of our allies surpassed the French. We were their teachers in everything; but in copying our qualities they caricatured our defects. Their gross and brutal plunder was perfectly revolting.'

Segur also states that[7]: 'The Emperor had written to him "that as the war was to be carried into a barren territory, where the enemy would destroy everything, it was requisite to prepare for such a state of things by providing everything within ourselves". Davout's reply was that he had "70,000 men who are completely organised; they carry with them 25 days provisions. Each company comprises swimmers, masons, bakers, tailors, shoemakers, armourers and workmen of every class. They carry everything they require with them; my army is like a colony; hand-mills follow".'

Thus we see that Napoleon knew of the nature of his intended theatre of war and issued instructions as to the preventive measures to be taken. To issue instructions is one thing, to ensure that they are car-

ried out is another (and much more exacting) task.

Not only road transport was to be used to move these huge quantities of supplies into Russia in the wake of the victorious army, the waterways were also to carry their load. From Danzig (in spite of the ever-present threat of attack from the Royal Navy) convoys of barges were to hug the coast eastward, enter the Frisches Haff and ascend the Pregel river to Vehlau where their cargoes would be transferred to lighter craft to proceed to Insterburg to be transhipped overland to Labiau on the Niemen, then retransferred to river craft and sent further east along that river and the Vilia to Kowno and Wilna. Unfortunately, due to the drought in 1812, the Vilia had shrunk so much that it could not be used and the logistic land transport plans also suffered a setback because the type of waggon used was far too heavy for the light, sandy soil of the area. The theory was that the supplies in the waggons would be consumed then the draught animals slaughtered and cooked on fires built from the demolished vehicles, thus providing more food. In fact, due to total lack of fodder and the hopeless going, the draught animals died first and the contents of the abandoned waggons rotted!

'The army meanwhile, marched from the Vistula to the Niemen. This last river, from Grodno as far as Kowno, runs parallel with the Vistula. The river Pregel, which forms the link between them, was loaded with provisions: 220,000 men repaired thither from four different points; there they found bread and some foraging provisions. These provisions ascended that river with them, as far as its direction would allow. When the army was obliged to quit the flotilla, its select corps took with them sufficient provisions to reach and cross the Niemen, to prepare for a victory and to arrive at Wilna. There the Emperor calculated on the magazines of the inhabitants, on those of the

Cavalry charging the Russian rearguard, July 1812 (Albrecht Adam).

enemy [ie marauder] and on his own, which he had ordered to be brought from Danzig, by the Frischhaff, the Pregel, the Deine, the Frederick canal and the Vilia[8].'

The Grande Armée (325,000 men, 984 guns — 155,400 Frenchmen and 170,500 allies) was now at the Niemen but already the provision system was beginning to fail. Segur states[9]: 'The greatest part of the provision waggons alone were behind.'

'Besides this, Danzig contained so much corn, that she alone might have fed the whole army; she supplied Königsberg. Her provisions had ascended the Pregel in large barges up to Vehlau, and in lighter craft as far as Insterburg. The other convoys went by land from Königsberg to Labiau, and from thence, by means of the Niemen and the Vilia, to Kowno and Wilna. But the waters of the Vilia having shrunk so much through drought as to be incapable of floating these transports, it became necessary to find other means of conveyance[10].'

But even though magazines had been established in the Duchy of Warsaw, not all the troops passing through the area were allowed to use them. In particular, the French commissary officials discriminated against the allied troops as is shown by this following account, written by Lieutenant General von Woellwarth, commander of the Württemberg cavalry to his king, presenting his side of an event which took place because of a predicament into which his Corps was placed by the confused logistic planning of the French commissary department[11].

'At the time of mobilisation of the Royal Army Corps to the north four cavalry regiments [Chevaulégèr-Regiment Nr 1 *Prinz Adam*, Leib-Chevaulégèr-Regiment Nr 2, Jäger-Regiment zu Pferd Nr 3 *Herzog Louis* and Jäger Regiment zu Pferd Nr 4] and two horse artillery batteries were attached to my Division. The march went through the difficult and trackless Thuringian Forest, through Saxony to Frankfurt-on-the-Oder where the Corps spent some weeks in cantonements during the better part of the year.

'The march up to the Oder was carried out in the best order as the national governments were responsible for magazine and food supplies. Only trivial excesses occurred although there were many unfounded complaints. Only Major von Seebach allowed himself to commit an excess in Leipzig, and this was immediately reported to headquarters and investigated and also punished in an Order of the Day.

'Both men and horses, such as could be supplied from the magazines, had the most impressive appearance in the cantonements by the Oder and discipline was extremely good.

'But now begins the first unfavourable epoch for the Army Corps and especially for the cavalry, one regiment of which was taken from my Division at Frankfurt-on-the-Oder and attached to a French Corps. [This occurred on April 15 1812 and it was the Jäger zu Pferd Nr 3 who were brigaded with a Prussian and a Polish cavalry regiment in Thorn under General Montbrun. One of the two horse artillery batteries was also redeployed with French troops.]

'The separation of this regiment from my Division was a sorry portent of events which were to overtake the whole Army Corps.

'Now the III Army Corps moved to Thorn-on-the-Weichsel [Vistula] via Meseriz, Posen and Gnesen and all other Corps on this side of the river were ordered to follow it. On entry into Poland the magazines which were established there were closed to the [our?] cavalry; even in the distant staging posts of the cavalry no provision was made for transitional troops; also, the advancing Army Corps had already consumed most of its supplies and to my Cavalry Division fell the unhappy lot of having to shift for themselves in a Poland already hostile to Germans. As is well known, the Polish peasants have little enough forage and food and that which they had they were forced to give to the French magazines long before our entry into their country.

'The Polish nobleman or gentleman farmer was still required to supply food to many troops but evaded this where possible even to the extent of burying his produce rather than surrender it against a requisition. In these conditions the cavalry was forced, as a matter of life and death, to search for and to possess these goods and to give the nobleman the necessary requisitions for them. No government officials could be found in these far-flung staging posts, and these were really responsible for the supply of the transitory troops. The entire burden of supply lay upon the regimental and squadron commanders and after each day's long march large and small detachments had to be sent out to gather in the necessary food and forage; that duty horses and an impeccable discipline should suffer was an inevitable result.

Under these conditions of supply, which normally are encountered only in a hostile country, we approached the Vistula where the cavalry again went into cantonement for 14 days and I was ordered to establish my Divisional HQ in Pagosz. Here also the French magazines in the area were closed to the [our] cavalry. As War Commissary Crais had been attached to me I sent him to magazines many times which helped not a bit as he was told that the supplies laid up in these magazines were only for the use of passing Guards and French troops. Thus here also supply on a self-help basis was necessary.

'In order to prevent any excesses I published repeated orders which can be seen in the Order Books.

'At about the end of the cantonement around Pagosz begins the second unfavourable epoch for the [our] cavalry.

'On May 30 I received a personal order from the Duke of Elchingen in Thorn: on command of the French Emperor I was to collect enough slaughter cattle for 20 days for the whole Württemberg Army Corps and to arrange this with the Polish government. This requisition had to be completed by June 2 ie within 48 hours within which the cavalry would begin a long march.

'I immediately issued the necessary orders to the regiments and sent Commissary Crais personally to visit the Prefects of the Districts in order to liaise with them over the manner and execution of the requisition.

'Crais could find no Prefects in their homes at all as they had gone to the ends of their Districts to attend a reception of the French Emperor as he was expected to pass through this area on his way to Thorn on this day.

'Prior to this despatch of Commissary Crais to the Prefects, the OverPrefects had already informed OverCommissary Schönlin that they were not in the position to assist with the supply of food for the

Italian line infantry by Smolensk (Albrecht Adam).

troops and would have to give their Districts over to the discretion of the troops.

'The regiments now despatched complete squadrons with their Regimental Quartermasters and the necessary requisitions in order to collect the necessary 800 oxen in 46 hours. Apart from this the regiments were instructed by me to maintain the strictest discipline and also to gather in many days' forage and food supplies during this requisitioning operation for the whole cavalry as I foresaw that on the march which we had before us we would experience the same scarcity in such things as we had already found.

'Before these orders were despatched, on about May 27, I was visited in my room in Pagosz by a French General in the uniform of an Imperial General Adjutant who said that he had been sent to me by the Emperor (the Emperor was still in Dresden) in order to inform me of all the excesses committed by Württemberg's troops; in particular he mentioned the Chasseurs à Cheval [Jäger zu Pferd] commanded by a Colonel called Graf Salm, who permitted unheard of excesses which did not surprise him as he was a brother of M de Salm in Paris.

'I herewith explained to him that this regiment that he had mentioned to me, which was commanded by Graf Salm, was one of my best regiments in matters of discipline and that the excesses he mentioned I had not heard of before.

'Although he laid such emphasis on these excesses he was unable to give me details except that yesterday evening he had arrested four Chasseurs [Jägers] and sent them to Graf Salm who had authorised various requisitions.

'Concerning this I assured him that these excesses would be investigated and punished if necessary and finally I told him exactly how we were treated in matters of food and forage here; that all French magazines were exclusively for the use of the French Guard and not for the Württembergers and that in matters of forage and food we had to shift for ourselves.

'Hereupon he excused himself and rode off. It now occurred to me to find out who this General was and what his direction of march was so I rode after him to the three hours distant Post Station of Pnowrazlaw where I discovered that he was the commander of the Polish Lancers of the French Guard and was in fact General Kraczinsky who was staying at the Station to escort the French Emperor and was not one of his General Adjutants.

'As I had Oberlieutenant [Lieutenant] Münchingen with me I attempted to take him with me to see this General who had been with me earlier this day in order to obtain more details of the alleged excesses of the Württembergers. As we came to him, he received us extremely politely and immediately began to relate to us how after the 1809 campaign he had travelled through the beautiful Württemberg countryside and how he had shot a hare *en route* which had turned out badly as the King of Württemberg had reported this excess and he had been arrested by the French Emperor and punished when he arrived in Paris.

'At the end of the tale I suggested to him that the events concerning the hare had left him with a grudge against the Württembergers but if this were not the case would he please give me exact details of the excesses supposed to have occurred on his march from Posen so that I could report them to HRH the Crown Prince, my commander. He repeated the instance of the four Chasseurs à Cheval who had been arrested yesterday and belonged to Graf Salm's regiment and he asked again if he was a brother of the Salm in Paris. I answered reluctantly that Oberst Graf Salm was a distinguished cavalry officer — 'a rarity in the French cavalry — and anyway I did not know if he was a brother of the Salm in Paris.

'The conversation now became somewhat bitter and just at this moment the King of Naples [Murat] entered the house, which was the Post House, to change horses. Krazinsky ran out of the door to the King's coach and I mounted my horse and rode home as it was late already.

'Scarcely had the regiments begun to carry out their orders to put into action this absolutely exceptional requisition in a friendly country, when on June 1 I received the order to march on June 2 via Thorn to the area of Graudenz so that the entire cavalry should be cleared through Thorn by the afternoon of the 2nd.

'I only executed this order in as far as it was geographically possible; as many squadrons were in the process of gathering in the oxen requisition far behind me, and could only follow after some time. These units were 20-30 hours behind me in order to accumulate the necessary number of beasts.

'In ignorance of this further removal, the nearer requisitioning units had already on June 2 sent over 600 oxen to the Depot in Gniknowo as ordered by the Army Corps; this detail was commanded by Hauptman [Captain] Bezler.

'June 2 was the day that Marshal Ney suddenly heard that the Emperor would pass through Thorn and as a result of this the order had been issued for all units to pass through Thorn on the 2nd.

'By 2 o'clock in the afternoon the entire cavalry

A French line infantry grenadier and a trooper of the élite company, 8th Chasseurs à Cheval, assist a wounded comrade out of the battle for Smolensk (Faber du Four).

Württemberg gunners in action during the battle of Smolensk (Faber du Four).

with its baggage had cleared Thorn and crossed the Vistula and at 4 o'clock the French Emperor arrived. Only Oberstlieutnants [Lieutenant-Colonels] von Palm and Harditsch, who were on distant detachment with their requisitioning units, had to follow on many hours later. The unpleasant circumstances of this whole enforced requisition of cattle gave rise to a great lament by all the nobility and farmers of the area.

'None of them however came to me; they all ran to the Polish general Krazinsky, wailing about the unsurpassed excesses of the Württemberg cavalry who had taken all their fine cattle and driven them off. The Pole Krazinsky was extremely receptive to news of any excesses committed by the Württembergers and was supposed to have advised his countrymen to wait just a couple of hours when the Emperor would arrive and he would seek an opportunity to present their complaints to him. This deplorable behaviour of General Krazinsky was just to be expected. In a few hours the Emperor came to Iznoraslau, two posts before Thorn, where all the noblemen who had had their cattle taken, were presented by General Krazinsky with the explanation that the Württembergers were robbing and plundering in the area (which in fact was nothing other than the execution of the order of the Emperor himself and Marshal Ney to collect 800 oxen in 48 hours which certainly must have appeared as plundering if the co-operation of the civil authorities was withheld and Krazinsky troubled himself to increase this impression to the Emperor).

'This initial impression put the Württembergers at a distinct disadvantage with the Emperor which was always more apparent as the most distant events showed and always proved the disadvantageous posi-

French troops passing through the shattered city of Smolensk
(Albrecht Adam).

tion of the Württembergisch troops in the Emperor's
HQ, as the whole system of supply, as I have already
said, was a permanent excess for the people who were
not informed of the system of supply and did not
want to be informed.

'During the Emperor's stay in Thorn the requisition detachments of Oberstlieutnants Palm and Harditsch with the necessary oxen to complete the requisition arrived and had to pass through Thorn where
they were no sooner sighted by the Guard than all the
oxen and supplies which they had collected were
taken from them by force.

'Scarcely had I entered the cantonments by Gra-
denz than the third unhappy epoch for the cavalry
began as I received the order to form one brigade of
the existing cavalry which from now on would be
known as the 25th Light Brigade and would be under
my command but that I would be detached from the
Württemberg Army Corps and come under the direct

Polish lancers escorting a convoy of Russian prisoners (Albrecht
Adam).

command of Marshal Ney. Simultaneously I received
a marching order to proceed by forced marches from
the Vistula to the Pregel. On this march we had the
unpleasant experience of finding almost all the over-
night bivouac accommodation full of strange troops
and the marching Guard who were supplied from
magazines with food but we had to find our own food
and forage in an area where no more could be found
and so we neared the Pregel fighting continuously for
our night's lodgings and our very existence. We
reached the area of Insterburg on June 15 and found
the whole countryside full of Davout's corps and the
entire Imperial Guard; as the II Corps [Oudinot] had
previously marched through the area it had been so
plundered that the Colonels had the most extreme
difficulty in providing for their regiments on the 16th
which was a rest day.

'I sent Commissary Crais into Insterburg, where a
great magazine had been established in order to get at
least bread for us which we had not seen since the
Vistula, but even this was denied to us and Commissary Crais, who spent the entire rest day in Insterburg, came back empty handed.

'No Württemberg soldier went to Insterburg, no
reports of excesses in the whole area came to me
apart from the story of an officer of the Polish Lancers of the Guard and Lieutenant von Breuning who
got into a violent quarrel as a result of which I
ordered the commander of the *Königs Jägers* to insti-
tute proceedings which resulted in an application being
sent to HRH the Crown Prince who was with the rest
of the Württemberg Army Corps about four miles
[continental miles] behind us asking for satisfaction
for Lieutenant von Breuning. General Krazinsky
managed to turn this even also against us and the
Prinz Neufschachtel [Berthier, Napoleon's Chief of
Staff] was supposed to have explained: "que la caval-
lerie Wirtembergoise avait portée la desastre dans
Insterburg". That this was brought into this area
before our arrival by French troops; this is true; but
that the Württembergers brought disaster into this
area is not true.

A bivouac by Wiazma on August 30. The foreground figures are Württemberg gunners (Faber du Four).

'Desolation and disaster were firmly established in this area before our entry; if excesses were committed by the Württembergers why were not these reported to me as their commander? so that I could assist. In a cantonement three [continental] miles in circumference the commander of the troops cannot supervise everything in a 24 hour period and discover excesses when these are not reported to him. The Brigadiers and Colonels had the sharpest orders from me repeatedly concerning this matter and had been told to maintain the strictest vigilance and to report the slightest excesses to me for investigation.

'It was June 16 when I received the order from Marshall Ney to march with the 25th Light Brigade on 17th so as to reach Cavalri in the Grand Duchy of Warsaw on 20th where the 3rd Army Corps would concentrate on this day; when I reached my goal on the 20th I sent out an officer to find out where the cavalry should bivouac and was told to go to Minkupie where I also found the Württemberg infantry in

Ammunition vehicles fording a Russian river (Albrecht Adam).

bivouac and the HQ of HRH the Crown Prince, where I also set up my personal bivouac. On the evening of the 21st I received the order from Marshal Ney stating that from now on there would not be three light brigades in the 3rd Army Corps but only two and thus the 25th Light Brigade was disbanded and its regiments would be distributed between the two remaining brigades as the 7th and 14th. This distribution is only the result of the general cavalry reorganisation undertaken by the King of Naples so that only two light brigades should remain in each Army Corps the purpose of which was to put the King of Naples at the head of the cavalry. The complete dissolution of the German cavalry was not far away and indeed this highlights a command policy in this present campaign to divide German troops as much as possible and to make as many of their Generals as possible superfluous.'

The inadequacy of the ration and fodder supply was bad enough even in that period when the Grande Armée was stationary and forming up in Warsaw; as soon as it began to advance eastwards in June 1812, the ramshackle logistic façade disintegrated and the troops were left completely to their own devices. In place of an organised and efficient system of provision, the marauding, so much favoured and promoted by Napoleon throughout his earlier German campaigns, was once more recoursed to[12]. '. . . ever since 1805 it had been tacitly understood, that they [the army] should bear with his ambition, and he [Napoleon] with their plundering . . .'

After the sudden, heavy rainstorm on the second day of the crossing of the Niemen, Segur continues[13]: '. . . the insupportable heat of the atmosphere was suddenly changed to a disagreeable chillness. Ten thousand horses perished on the march, and more especially in the bivouacs which followed. A large quantity of equipages [vehicles] remained abandoned on the sands: and great numbers of men subsequently died.'

The extensive looting practised by the Grande Armée in Poland and Lithuania very soon cooled the

Italian Guard sentinel in a rural bivouac (Albrecht Adam).

Italian dragoon horses (Faber du Four).

initial enthusiasm shown by these people to their 'liberators'. One Lithuanian General said to Napoleon's staff[14]: ' "What then do you expect from our zeal? A happy countenance, acclamations of joy, accents of gratitude? — when every day each of us is apprised that his villages and granaries are devastated; for the little which the Russians did not carry away your famishing columns have devoured . . . Your pillagers take all".'

It must also be stated that 1811 had been a bad year for crops in these areas and the Poles and Lithuanians suggested that the French should move south into the still fertile provinces of Volhynia.

The indiscipline of the Grande Armée was already brought to such a pitch by the necessity of their stealing to survive that to try to restore discipline to its normal military level was now beyond contemplation[15]: 'In Prussia, the Emperor had caused the Army to supply itself with provisions for only 20 days. This was as much as was necessary for the purpose of gaining Wilna by a battle. Victory was to have done the rest, but that victory was postponed by the flight of the enemy. The Emperor might have waited for his convoys; but as by surprising the Russians he had separated them, he did not wish to forego his grasp and lose his advantage. He therefore pushed forward on their track 400,000 men with 20 days' provisions, into a country which had been incapable of feeding the 20,000 Swedes of Charles XII.

'It was not from want of foresight; for immense convoys of oxen followed the army, either in herds, or harnessed to provision-cars. Their drivers had been organised into battalions; but being tired out with the slow pace of these heavy animals, they either slaughtered them, or suffered them to die of want. A great number, however, got as far as Wilna and Minsk; some even reached Smolensk but too late; they could only be of service to the recruits and reinforcements which followed us.'

The parade states of many units reflect a drastic drop in the numbers of men under arms even during the first weeks of the advance as hundreds of stragglers would be left behind each day, most of them never to return to their regiment. As one Westfalian infantry officer wrote in his diary: 'What will happen if we catch up with the enemy?' Another contemporary account reads[16]: 'On that same afternoon [July 8] the Italian 15th Infantry Division of General Pino passed us in such a pitiful condition that already some hundreds of men lay dead on the road from hunger and exhaustion.'

Caulaincourt comments[17]: 'The Emperor would gladly have given wings to the entire army. On the 27th [June] he slept at Owzianiskai and on the 28th arrived at Wilna at 9 am. This rapid movement without stores exhausted and destroyed all the resources and houses which lay on the way. The vanguard lived quite well, but the rest of the army was dying of hunger. Exhaustion, added to want and the piercing cold rains at night, killed off 10,000 horses. Many of the Young Guard died on the road of fatigue, cold and hunger.

'His Majesty at once decided to go to Gloubokoje [July 16] . . . [he] spent 12 hours at Swenziany to dictate orders and marched the whole of that night in the hope that, by the rapidity of this movement, he could make contact with the Russian army. In the morning he arrived at Gloubokoje, a fine monastery in a very fertile stretch of country. This astounding march from Wilna to Gloubokoje proved that horses well ridden can cover a surprising distance, for the mounted chargers and the animals laden with heavy packs left Wilna at 6 am, reached Swenziany at 8 pm and by noon the following day were at Gloubokoje, having thus covered 48 leagues.'

After the clash at the Lutchiesa River on July 27, Caulaincourt continues: 'But there were no inhabitants to be found, no prisoners to be taken, not a single

French troops on the march. Note the water waggon (Albrecht Adam).

straggler to be picked up. There were no spies. We were in the heart of inhabited Russia and yet, if I may be permitted the comparison, we were like a vessel without a compass in the midst of a vast ocean, knowing nothing of what was happened around us.

'At last he [Napoleon] decided to give the army a much-needed rest. Part of the cavalry was already worn out, the artillery and infantry were exhausted, the roads were covered with stragglers who destroyed and wasted everything.

'One day, General Belliard, Chief of Staff to the King of Naples, observed in the presence of the Emperor, who was questioning him: "Your majesty must be told the truth. The cavalry is rapidly disappearing, the marches are too long and exhausting, and when a charge is ordered you can see willing fellows who are forced to stay behind because their horses can't be put to the gallop." The Emperor paid no attention to these prudent observations. He wanted to reach his prey; and in his view it was evidently worth paying any price to attain that object, for he sacrificed everything to gain it.

'*Witepsk July 29 1812*. With the exception of the chiefs, the indifference of the administrative officers was complete. The innumerable waggons, the enormous quantity of supplies of all sorts that had been collected at such expense during the course of two years, had vanished through theft and loss, or through lack of means to bring them up. They were scattered along the roads. The rapidity of the forced marches, the shortage of harness and spare parts, the dearth of provisions, the want of care, all had helped to kill the horses. This campaign at express speed from the Niemen to Wilna, and from Wilna to Witepsk, had, without any real result, already cost the army two lost battles and deprived it of absolutely essential provisions and supplies. To ensure that no indiscreet word should be uttered, the Emperor had consulted no-one. Consequently our waggons and all our transport, built for metalled roads and to accomplish ordinary distances, were in no way suitable for the roads of the country we had to traverse. The first sand we came across overwhelmed the horses; for the loads, instead of being cut down in proportion to the weight of the vehicle and the distance to be covered, had been increased in the notion that the daily consumption would sufficiently lessen them. But in working out this scheme of daily consumption the Emperor had not taken into account the distance that would have to be covered before the point was reached when this consumption would begin.

'The men, lacking everything to supply their own needs, were little inclined to pay any heed to their horses, and watched them perish without regrets, for their death meant the breakdown of the service on which the men were employed and thus the end to their personal privations.

'Disorder reigned everywhere: in the town as in the country around, everyone was in want. The Guard was no better provisioned than the other Corps, and thence arose indiscipline and all its attendant evils. The Emperor was angry, and took the Corps commanders and administrators to task with something more than severity; but this did no good in the face of the continued failure to bring up rations. From a spirit of inexplicable and unpardonable meanness the provisioning of the ambulances had been inadequate. Even the personnel was too scanty . . . We had only got as far as Witepsk, we had not fought a battle, and there was not even any lint!

'The King of Naples . . . saw with apprehension the decreasing strength of his regiments, most of which were reduced to less than half their numbers. Forage and stores of all sorts were lacking, for his forces were always in close order and on the alert. Arrangements had not been made for rationing the men during the first few days, and the Cossacks were already hindering them from bringing up stores. The horses were not shod, the harness was in a deplorable state. The forges, like all the rest of the material

Left *Napoleon and Murat watch Bavarian cavalry advancing into battle. Prince Eugène is on the left* (Faber du Four).

Right *Officers of the Italian guard in bivouac* (Faber du Four).

Below right *The ever-increasing regimental baggage trains with their requisitioned waggons, contents and animals* (Faber du Four).

[matérièl?], had been left in the rear. The greater number of them indeed, had been abandoned and lost. There were no nails, no smiths — and no supplies of iron suitable for making nails. ". . . No amount of reasoning, not even the experiences he had met with since the Niemen, nothing could enlighten him [Napoleon] as to the fatality looming ahead . . . He was obsessed once more by his old illusions and returned to his gigantic projects" . . . The staff foresaw nothing. But on the other hand, as the Emperor wanted to do everything himself and give every order, no-one, not even the Chief of Staff [Alexander Berthier, Prince of Neuchâtel], dared to assume the most trifling responsibility. The administration, deprived, as we have seen, of the means of execution and transport, was quite unable to produce the results demanded by the Emperor, or to carry out orders which he gave without troubling himself as to how they should be executed.

'Only ten days had elapsed after our arrival at Witepsk* before it became necessary to send ten or 12 leagues for fodder. The inhabitants who had not fled were everywhere in arms; consequently it was impossible to find any means of transport. Horses already in need of rest were further enfeebled by having to go in search of food, and were exposed, together with the men, to the danger of being caught by the Cossacks or slaughtered by the peasants, as frequently happened.'

After Smolensk, Caulaincourt continues: 'The Russian Army marched in good order, without undue haste, like men intent on abandoning nothing and prepared in case of necessity to stand their ground.' And after Borodino: 'That night the enemy began their retreat in plain view. Orders were given for the army to follow . . . At dawn the following day [Sep-

*Early August 1812.

tember 8] there were only Cossacks in sight. The enemy had taken with them the great part of their wounded: and we had only the few prisoners I have mentioned, 12 guns from the Redoubt . . . and three or four other pieces taken in the line by our troops during their first attack . . . A very small number of stragglers were rounded up; the enemy had not abandoned so much as a cart.'

Later, Caulaincourt says: 'Any honest investigator who would compare the condition of his Corps at the beginning of the campaign with its state at the end, seeking the cause of loss and wastage, would certainly find that it was not the enemy's guns which had done the most damage to our cavalry. The fine state in which some Corps were maintained to the very last moment, compared to the disorder and destruction suffered by others that had seen no longer service, proves that our greatest foe was lack of discipline; and the disorders that followed in its train originated in the negligence of the commanding officers.

'For his headquarters the Emperor had altogether 715 saddle and draught horses in Russia to draw the waggons loaded with provisions of all kinds as well as a great outfit of tents. As his headquarters were always the last to arrive, and that invariably in a place already laid waste because the whole army had already passed by, it was necessary to carry everything with us or seek what we needed from a distance (it must also be observed that the general service of supply did not furnish in all a thousand pounds of bread, a hundred trusses of hay, nor a particle of oats to the Emperor's household throughout the campaign). I have, therefore, had experience of what can be done by method and care in supplementing the provender both in kind and quantity. All persons attached to headquarters were in the same plight, but as none had more than a few horses it was much easier for them to find and provide fodder. It is also an admitted fact that the mounts of the Emperor and his suite made much longer and faster rides than other horses. Yet on reaching Wilna on December 8, during the retreat, only 80 horses had been lost out of the 715 with which we had started the campaign.

'During the retreat horses fell and lay by the roadside chiefly because they were not properly shod to keep their footing on ice, and once down . . . they ended by lying where they fell, and were cut up for food before they were even dead. With proper shoeing and the exercise of a little care, the greater number would certainly have been saved.'

Napoleon was all too keen to lay the blame for the disaster at another's door: ' ". . . Kutusof's retreat was inept as it could be: it's the winter that has been our undoing. We are victims of the climate. The fine weather tricked me. If I had set out [from Moscow] a fortnight sooner, my army would be at Witepsk . . ." ' Even years later Napoleon was to cling to this plaintive line of excuse for his failure in Russia; on September 29 1817 he remarked to Gourgaud: 'My great mistake was in staying too long in that city [Moscow]. But for that, my undertaking would have been successful in the end. . . All our disasters hinge on that fortnight [in Moscow] and on the failure to carry out my orders for the levies of Polish Cossacks.'

Like all egocentric characters, Napoleon sought to attribute the inevitable failure of his Russian adventure, and the vast loss of life, to others than himself. Not for him the realisation that his faulty logistic arrangements had doomed his Grande Armée to virtual destruction within weeks of crossing the Russian frontier. The blame was to be laid in another quarter and at such a time that he was to be excused.

Of the Russian defence plans and of Alexander's comments that the invaders would inevitably be defeated, Napoleon, during his journey in a sledge from Russia to Warsaw with Caulaincourt in November 1812, said: 'Those prophetic proclamations of his [Tsar Alexander's] were all nonsense. If they had wanted to draw us into the interior, they should have retired in the first place and not endangered Bagration's army by spreading their forces over a line which, being too near the frontier, had to be too long. They should not have spent so much money building card-castles along the Dwina [here a reference to the fortified camp at Drissa]. They should not have collected so many stores there. They have been planning from one day to the next without settled scheme. They have never been able to fight to any purpose.' And now a whining note: 'But

for the cowardice and stupidity of Partouneaux [Commander, 12th Division], the Russians would not have captured a single waggon from me at the crossing of the Beresina . . . Everything has conspired to cause my failure. I was not well served in Warsaw . . . The levies were not made; I got nothing from all the resources I should have been able to rely on.'

Napoleon also failed completely to grasp the strategic significance of Britain's involvement in the war in Spain. Caulaincourt says: 'He [Napoleon] would rather have seen the British army in Spain than anywhere else. "If 30,000 English landed in Belgium or in the Pas-de-Calais, and requisitioned supplies from 300 villages — if they were to go and burn the chateau of Caulaincourt — they would do us much more harm than by forcing me to maintain an army in Spain . . . The English are playing into my hands. If the [English] ministry were in my pay, they could not act in a way more favourable to me . . . As it is the war in Spain costs me no more than any other war, or any other compulsory defence against the English." '

This ignores completely the strategic realities: the most hazardous military undertaking (until the advent of airborne forces) was an amphibious invasion into a hostile country. In 1808 the only part of Europe not hostile to Britain, and accessible, was Portugal. There a British landing was unopposed, indeed welcomed and supported. Had the British landed in Metropolitan France, 'requisitioned supplies' and 'burned the chateau', they really would have been playing into Napoleon's hands. As it was, in 1813 when Wellington invaded France from Spain, he was at great pains to ensure that anything that his army needed was paid for in cash on the spot and that the discipline of his men, particularly with regard to their

The battlefield of Borodino (Albrecht Adam).

conduct towards the civil population, was beyond reproach. Compare this with the conduct of the French army in other countries, even those of their allies.

Caulaincourt adds that Napoleon said: ' "I was wrong in not remaining at Witepsk to organise the country, or in not leaving Moscow a week after I entered the city. The reverses I have met with are due solely to that . . . The venture failed by a week's time . . . Everything in the world depends on that. The right moment, timeliness, those are everything." '

Segur comments[18]: 'Napoleon hated contractors. It was his wish that the administration of the army should organise the Lithuanian waggons; 500 were assembled, but the appearance of them disgusted him. He then permitted contracts to be made with the

On the fringe of the battle of Borodino. Note the smouldering match stick to the right of the cannon (Albrecht Adam).

Artillery coming up during the battle of Borodino (Faber du Four).

Jews, who are the only traders in the country; and the provisions stopped at Kowno at last arrived at Wilna; but the army had already left it.

'It was the largest column, that of the centre, which suffered most; it followed the road which the Russians had ruined and of which the French advanced-guard had just completed the spoliation. The columns which proceeded by lateral routes found necessaries there, but were not sufficiently careful collecting and in economising them.'

The responsibility for the calamities which this rapid march occasioned ought not, therefore, to be laid entirely on Napoleon; for order and discipline were maintained in the army of Davout; it suffered less from dearth. It was nearly the same with that of Prince Eugène. When pillage was resorted to in these two Corps, it was always with method, and nothing but necessary injury was inflicted; the soldiers were obliged to carry several days' provisions and prevented from wasting them. The same precautions might have been taken elsewhere. But, whether it was owing to the habit of making war in fertile countries, or to the habitual ardour of constitution, many of the other chiefs thought much less of administering than of fighting.

'Napoleon was, therefore', Segur continues, 'most frequently compelled to shut his eyes to a system of plunder which he vainly prohibited: he was too well aware also, of the attraction which that mode of subsistence had for the soldier [I feel one *must* insert 'French' here!]: that it made him love war, because it enriched him; that it gratified him, by the authority which it frequently gave him over classes superior to his own; that in his eyes it had all the charms of a war of the poor against the rich; [totally irrelevant and fallacious!]; finally that the pleasure of feeling and

proving himself the strongest was under such circumstances incessantly repeated and brought home to him.

'Napoleon, however, grew indignant at the intelligence of these excesses. He issued a threatening proclamation, and he directed moveable [sic] columns of French and Lithuanians to see to its execution. We, too, who were irritated at the sight of the pillagers, were eager to pursue and punish them; but when we had stripped them of the bread, or the cattle which they had been stealing; when we saw them slowly retiring, sometimes eyeing us with a look of concentrated despair, sometimes bursting into tears; when we heard them murmuring that, "not content with giving them nothing, we wrested everything from them, and that we must therefore mean to let them perish of hunger," we, then, in our turn, accused ourselves of barbarity to our own people, called them back, and restored them their prey. In truth, it was imperious necessity which impelled to plunder. *The officer himself only lived on the share which his soldiers allowed him.* [So much for discipline!] A position of so much excess engendered fresh excesses. These rugged men, with arms in their hands, when assailed by so many immoderate wants, could not remain moderate. When they arrived near any habitations they were famished; at first they asked, but, either for want of being understood, or from the refusal or impossibility of the inhabitants to satisfy their demands, and of their inability to wait, altercations generally arose; then, as they became more and more exasperated with hunger, they became furious, and after turning either cottage or palace topsy-turvy, without finding the subsistence they were in quest of, they, in the violence of their despair, accused the inhabitants of being their enemies, and revenged themselves on the proprietors by destroying their property.

'There were some who actually destroyed themselves, rather than proceed to such extremities; others, after having done so: these were the youngest. They placed their foreheads on their muskets, and blew out their brains in the middle of the high road.

'The Emperor was not ignorant of these details [the looting and destruction of property in Lithuania] but he was already committed. Even at Wilna, all these disorders had occurred; the Duke of Treviso [Marshal Mortier], among others, informed him of them: "From the Niemen to the Vilia I have seen nothing but ruined habitations, and baggage and provision waggons abandoned; they are found dispersed on the highways and in the fields, overturned, broken open and their contents scattered here and there, and pillaged as if they had been taken by the enemy: I should have imagined myself following a defeated army.

' "Ten thousand horses have been killed by the cold rains of the great storm, and by the unripe rye which has become their new and only food. Their carcasses are lying encumbering the road: they sent forth a mephitic smell impossible to breathe; — a new scourge which some compared to famine. But the last was much more terrible: several soldiers of the Young Guard have already perished of hunger".

'Up to that point Napoleon listened with calmness, but here he abruptly interrupted the speaker. Wishing to escape from distress by incredulity, he exclaimed, "It is impossible! Where are their 20 days' provisions? Soldiers well commanded never die of hunger."

'A General, the author of this last report, was present. Napoleon turned towards him, appealed to him, and pressed him with questions; and that General, either from weakness or uncertainty, replied, "that the individuals referred to had not died of hunger, but from intoxication". The Emperor then remained convinced that the privations of the soldiers had been exaggerated to him. As to the rest, he exclaimed, "The loss of the horses must be borne with; of some equipages, and even some habitations; it is a torrent that rolls away: it is the worst side of the picture of war; an evil exchanged for a good; to misery her share must be given; my treasures, my benefits will repair the loss: one great result will make amends for all; I only required a single victory; if sufficient means remain for accomplishing that, I will be satisfied."

'The duke remarked that a victory might be overtaken by a more methodical march, followed by the magazines; he was not listened to.

'Thus it was that Napoleon was constrained to shut his eyes to facts. It is well known that the greater part of his ministers were not flatterers. Both facts and men spoke sufficiently [what about the ignored report of the starvation of two men of the Young Guard?]: but what could they teach him? Of what was he ignorant? Had not all his preparations been dictated by the most clear sighted prudence? What could be said to him, which he had not himself said and written a hundred times? It was after having anticipated the minutest details, prepared for every inconvenience, and provided everything for a slow and methodical war, that he divested himself of all these precautions, that he abandoned all these preparations and suffered himself to be hurried away by habit, by

Russian cuirassiers attack Württemberg infantry and jägers during the struggle for the Semenowskaya redoubt. Murat, as usual, forms the glittering centrepiece! (Faber du Four).

the necessity of short wars, of rapid victories, and sudden treaties of peace.

'In the army, the soldiers complained of his [Napoleon's] non-appearance. "They no longer saw him," they said, "except in days of battle, when they had to die for him, but never to supply them with the means of existence . . ."

'The dispersion of the different Corps being indispensible for the sake of procuring subsistence in these deserts, necessarily kept Napoleon at a distance from his soldiers. His Guard could hardly find subsistence and shelter in his immediate neighbourhood; the rest were out of his sight. It is true that several imprudent acts had recently been committed; several convoys of provisions belonging to other Corps were, on their passage, daringly retained at the Imperial headquarters, for the use of the Guard, by whose order it is not known.'

Dysentery, brought on by the rye which formed the major part of the soldiers' diet, was raging and in Witebsk alone 3,000 men were in hospital with it [July]. Davout discovered that roasting the rye prior to eating it considerably reduced the incidence of dysentery.

Segur again: 'Misfortune moreover, had purified the army; all that remained of it could not fail to be its élite, both in mind and body. In order to have got so far as they had done, what trials had they not withstood!

'As we marched from Orcha to Liady, [August 14] the French army formed a long column on the left bank of the Dniepr. In this mass, the I Corps, that of Davout, was distinguished by the order and harmony which prevailed in its divisions. The fine appearance of the troops, the care with which they were supplied,

Bivouac of Italian Guard dragoons after Borodino (Faber du Four).

and the attention that was paid to make them careful of their provisions which the improvident soldier is apt to waste, lastly, the strength of these divisions, the happy result of this severe discipline, all caused them to be acknowledged as the model of the whole army.

'The villages deserted by the enemy, were plundered as soon as we entered them: we passed through them in the greatest haste and disorder. The streams were crossed by fords which were soon spoiled; the regiments which came afterwards passed over in other places, wherever they could. No one gave himself much concern about such details, which were neglected by the general staff: no person was left to point out the danger, where there was any, or the road, if there were several. Each Corps seemed to look to itself alone, each Division, each individual, to

French cuirassiers in action during the battle of Borodino (Albrecht Adam).

be unconnected with the rest; as if the fate of one had not depended on that of the other.

'The army everywhere left stragglers behind it, and men who had lost their way, whom the officers passed without noticing; there would have been too many to find fault with; and besides, each was too occupied with himself to attend to others.'

A contrast is given by a report on how the Russians controlled their stragglers (on August 15 as their rearguard withdrew from Krasnoi): 'The Cossacks were seen striking with the shafts of their lances such of their foot-soldiers as lengthened the line of march, or stepped out of their ranks.'

After capturing Smolensk (August 18) Napoleon realised that the Russians had yet again slipped out of his clutches and had left him master of another pestilential, devastated ruin.

'Out of 22,000 Bavarians who had crossed the Oder, 11,000 only reached the Dwina; and yet they had never been in action. This military march cost the French one-fourth, and the allies one-half, of their army. Every morning the regiments started in order from their bivouacs; but scarcely had they proceeded a few steps, before their disconnected ranks became lengthened out into small and broken files; the weakest, being unable to follow, dropped behind: those unfortunate wretches beheld their Eagles and their comrades getting farther and farther from them: they still strove to overtake but at length lost sight of them and then sank down disheartened. The roads and margins of the woods were studded with them. Some were seen plucking the ears of rye to devour the grain: and then they would attempt, frequently in vain, to reach the hospital or nearest village. Great numbers thus perished.'

Rapp and Sebastiani tried to talk Napoleon into halting at Smolensk to regroup and regather the army because of its disorganised state; the Emperor replied: 'It is dreadful I know; from Wilna half of it

French dragoons guarding Russian prisoners (Albrecht Adam).

consisted of stragglers; now they form two thirds; there is, therefore, no time to be lost; we must extort peace: it is at Moscow. Besides, this army cannot stop now; with its composition and in its disorganised state, motion alone keeps it together. [This is in complete contrast with all the evidence given in the Emperor's previous sentence.] One may advance at the head of it, but not stop or go back. It is an army of attack, not of defence; an army of operation, not of position.'

The attrition of the Grande Armée, largely due to the self-inflicted wounds of the non-existent supply situation, is again illustrated by Segur: 'And yet, his [Napoleon's] column of attack, which was 185,000 strong at his departure from Witebsk, was already reduced to 157,000; it was diminished by 28,000 men, half of whom occupied Witebsk, Orscha, Mohilev and Smolensk. The rest had been killed or wounded or were straggling and plundering in his rear our allies and the French themselves.'

Additionally, there were the following forces at Napoleon's disposal: 'Macdonald with 32,000 men; towards Polotzk St Cyr with 30,000; at Witebsk, Smolensk and Mohilew Victor and 40,000; before Bobruisk Dombrowski and 12,000 and, on the Bug, Schwarzenberg and Regnier [sic] with 45,000. Napoleon also reckoned on the divisions of Loison and Durutte, 22,000 strong, which were already approaching Königsberg and Warsaw; and on reinforcements to the amount of 80,000, all of which would enter Russia before the middle of November. He should thus have 280,000 men, including the Lithuanian and Polish levies to support him, while with 155,000 more he made an incursion of 93 leagues; for such was the distance between Smolensk and Moscow.'

On August 26 Napoleon left Smolensk to march forward to Moscow; by now his army had improvised the logistic services which he had failed to provide. Segur says: 'In the train of each regiment there were a multitude of those diminutive horses with which Poland swarms, and a great number of carts of the country requiring to be incessantly replaced with fresh ones, and a drove of cattle. The baggage waggons were driven by soldiers . . .They were missed in the ranks, it is true; but here the want of provisions, the necessity for transporting everything with them, excused this prodigious train: it required a second army, as it were, to carry or draw what was indispensable for the first'.

Davout's I Corps was still held up as an example: 'Each of these knapsacks, reduced to what was strictly necessary . . . contained two shirts, two pairs of shoes with nails and a pair of extra soles, a pair of pantaloons and half-gaiters of cloth, a few articles requisite to personal cleanliness, a bandage and a quantity

Italian cavalry watch Moscow burn (Faber du Four).

of lint, and 60 cartridges. In the two sides were placed four biscuits of 16 ounces each; under these, and at the bottom, was a long, narrow linen big filled with 10 pounds of flour. The whole knapsack . . . weighed 33 lb 12 oz. Each soldier also carried a linen bag slung in the form of a shoulder belt, containing two loaves of 3 lb each. Thus, with his sabre, knapsack, three flints, turnscrew, belt and musket, he had to carry 58 lb weight, and was provided with bread for four days, biscuit for four, flour for seven, and 60 rounds of ammunition. Behind were carriages laden with provisions for six more days. When the flour-bag was emptied, it was filled with any corn that could be found, and which was ground at the first mill, if any chanced to be met with; if not, by the hand mills which followed the regiments or which were found in the villages . . . It took 16 men 12 hours to grind in one of them the corn necessary for 130 men for one day.'

It will be seen therefore, that the supply of such vital items as food and fodder failed completely to satisfy the demands of the Grande Armée in Russia. We may then assume that the resupply of clothing was even less effective and practically non-existent. Many regimental histories and diaries of this campaign exist and events as important as the arrival of a ration waggon or of a cart full of shoes, uniforms or greatcoats is plainly recorded. The frequency of such recordings only serves to demonstrate that resupply of the fighting troops from their depôts practically never happened. The exceptions shine out in the gloom; both the Bavarians and the Badeners were lucky enough to be found by the odd, lonely waggon trekking through the devastated cemetery that stretched from Poland to Moscow and the Badeners were so reduced in numbers that when a ration waggon finally reached them at the Beresina just before the battle of the crossing, they shared their good for-

tune with their starving comrades of the contingent of the Grand Duchy of Berg.

The French commissary service established magazines of food, equipment, harness and clothing within Russia; stocks being set down in Wilna, Smolensk, Minsk and Borrisow. Unfortunately, when the Retreat began, the collapse of the system was so fast that many of these stocks were captured by the Russians. At Smolensk, the corrupt commissary officials had been selling their supplies to the Russian merchants and now feared exposure of their reduced holdings. They sought to hide their crimes by refusing to issue food and clothing to the starving, frozen wretches clamouring at their doors — the excuse being that they had no requisitions and no means of identifying themselves! Thus, instead of finding the promised food, clothing and shelter at Smolensk, hundreds died in the snow outside the depôt doors and thousands had to stagger on, hungry and in rags when the Russian advanced guard pushed the Grande Armée out of Smolensk and captured the remaining unconsumed stocks.

Talking about the Retreat, Segur says[19]: 'For the space of more than 250 leagues it [Russia] offered but two points where he could rest and halt, the first Smolensk, and the second Minsk. He had made those towns his two great depôts where immense magazines were established.' That these were grossly inadequate soon became evident: 'Thus, after an obstinate combat, and ten days' marching and countermarching, the army, which had brought from Moscow only 15 rations of flour per man . . . was in want of provisions and overtaken by winter. Some men had already sunk under these hardships. In the first days of the retreat, on October 26, carriages, laden with provisions, which the horses could no longer draw, were burned. The order for setting fire to all behind the army then followed; in obedience to it, powder waggons, the

Italian grenadiers on the march. Note the foul weather covers to the peaked bearskins (Albrecht Adam).

Rearguard action at Borowsk, October 26 (Faber du Four).

horses of which were already worn out, were blown up together with the horses.

'In the evening of this long day [the day of the recrossing of the battlefield of Borodino], as the Imperial column was approaching Gjatz, it was surprised to find Russians quite recently killed on the way. It was remarked, that each of them had his head shattered in the same manner, and that his bloody brains were scattered near him. It was known that 2,000 Russian prisoners were marching on before, and that their guard consisted of Spaniards, Portuguese and Poles.'

The Emperor was made aware of these horrifying facts 'but preserved a gloomy silence, but on the ensuing day these murders ceased. These unfortunate people were then merely left to die of hunger.' (It is remarkable that several German eyewitness accounts attribute to the French the order that all Russian prisoners unable to march should be shot.)

'On 5th [November] he [Napoleon] slept at Dorogobusch. Here he found the handmills which were ordered for the expedition, at the time the cantonements of Smolensk were projected; of these a late and totally useless distribution was made.'

At Smolensk, on November 8, Segur says: 'The rest ran to the magazines, and there more of them expired while they beset the doors; for they were again repulsed. "Who were they? To what Corps did they belong? What had they to prove it? The persons who had to distribute the provisions were responsible for them; they had orders to deliver them only to authorised officers, bringing receipts, for which they would exchange the rations committed to their care." Those who applied had no officers, nor could they tell where their regiments were. Two thirds of the army were in this predicament . . . Then only did

these disorganised troops seek their colours; they reformed them for a moment in order to obtain food; but all the bread that could be baked had been distributed: there was no more biscuit, no butcher's meat. Rye flour, dry vegetables and spirits were delivered out to them. It required the most strenuous efforts to prevent the detachments of the different Corps from murdering one another at the doors of the magazines: and when, after long formalities, their wretched fare was delivered to them, the soldiers refused to carry it to their regiments: they fell upon their sacks, snatched out of them a few pounds of flour and ran to hide themselves until they had devoured it. The same was the case with the spirits. Next day the houses were found full of the bodies of these unfortunate wretches.'

Napoleon arrived on November 9 . . . and left on the 14th. He had calculated upon 15 days' provisions and forage for an army of 100,000 men; there was not more than half the quantity of flour, rice and spirits and no meat at all. (A commissary was charged with having made false entries in his account, stating that he had sent on a thousand oxen to meet the retreating army, whereas he had, in fact, sold them to the Jews, who forwarded them to the Russian army.) The commissary saved his life only by crawling for a long time on his knees at the feet of Napoleon.

Apparently, the supplies expected from Germany to stock up the magazines in the city had not arrived as expected and when at last things began to trickle in, it was only the light Lithuanian carts which were able to get there at all. The heavy German and French vehicles remained stuck fast in the sandy soil.

'These were the carriages called comtoises and were the only ones which had traversed the sands of Lithuania: they brought more than 200 quintals of flour and rice; several hundred German and Italian bullocks had also arrived with them . . . it had been found necessary to kill without delay the greater part of the cattle . . . These animals would neither walk any farther nor eat. Their eyes, sunk in their sockets, were dull and motionless. Other misfortunes followed: several convoys had been intercepted, magazines taken, and a drove of 800 oxen had just been carried off from Krasnoi. Regard ought also to be had to the great quantity of detachments which had passed through Smolensk; to the stay which Marshal Victor, 28,000 men and about 15,000 sick had made there; to the multitude of posts and marauders whom the insurrection and the approach of the enemy had driven back into the city. All had subsisted upon the magazines; it had been necessary to deliver out nearly 60,000 rations per day; and lastly, provisions and cattle had been sent forward towards Moscow as far as Mojaisk and towards Kaluga as far as Elnia.

'Many of these allegations were well founded. A chain of other magazines had been formed from Smolensk to Minsk and Wilna. These two towns were, in a still greater degree than Smolensk, centres of provisioning, of which the fortresses of the Vistula formed the first line. The total quantity of provisions distributed over this space was incalculable, the efforts for transporting them thither gigantic, and the results little better than nothing. They were insufficient in that immensity. Thus great expeditions are crushed by their own weight.

'At the same moment, in our rear and our centre, Prince Eugène was conquered by the Wop; the draught-horses which had been waiting for us at Smolensk were devoured by the soldiers; those of Mortier carried off in a forage; the cattle at Krasnoi captured . . .'

The time Napoleon spent in Moscow had been squandered, as Segur points out: 'how [had] it happened, that at Moscow everything had been forgotten; why there was so much useless baggage; why so many soldiers had already died of hunger and cold, under the weight of their knapsacks, which were loaded with gold instead of food and raiment; and, above all, if three-and-thirty days' rest had not allowed sufficient time to make snow shoes for the artillery, cavalry and draught-horses, which would have made their march more sure and rapid?

'If that had been done, we should not have lost our best men at Wiazma, at the Wop, at the Dnieper, and along the whole road . . . But why, in the absence of orders from Napoleon, had not that precaution been taken by the commanders, all of them kings, princes and marshals? Had not the winter in Russia been foreseen? . . . Had not the recollection of the campaign in Poland [1806-07], during a winter as mild as that of our own climate deceived him as well as the unclouded sun . . . of October had astonished even the Russians themselves?'

Italian ration waggons on the way back from Moscow (Faber du Four).

Losses during this phase of the Retreat were heavy: 'The Old and the Young Guard had not more than 9,000-10,000 infantry and 2,000 cavalry: Davout [I Corps] 8,000-9,000; Ney [III Corps] 5,000-6,000; Eugène [IV Corps] 5,000; Poniatowski [V Corps] 800; Junot [VIII Corps] 700; Latour-Maubourg and the rest of the cavalry 1,500; there might also be about 1,000 light horse and 500 dismounted cavalry . . . This army had left Moscow 100,000 strong; in 25 days it had been reduced to 36,000 men. The artillery had already lost 350 of their cannon and yet these feeble forces were always divided into eight armies, which were encumbered with 60,000 unarmed stragglers and a long train of cannon and baggage.'

Another result of past lack of foresight was that none of the surviving horses with the Grande Armée on the retreat had winter studs in their shoes. They thus lost footing on the icy roads and at the hill of Ponari, west of Wilna, practically all remaining vehicles with the army, cash waggons, ammunition and stores vehicles, guns and limbers as well as countless coaches and unofficial carts, were abandoned in one huge traffic jam which became a welter of fallen horses and spilled cargoes.

The climate

Napoleon has been recorded as saying that he was defeated in Russia by 'General Winter'. It is hoped that sufficient evidence has been presented to cast serious doubt on this excuse already but let us now examine the weather in 1812. Up until the crossing of the Niemen (June 23) it had been extremely hot and dry and the shortage of drinking water along the advance route was so severe that men were reduced to drinking their own urine. A sharp change of weather with unseasonable cold and heavy rainstorms followed (June 29-July 4) but this gave way to the previous heatwave and provided only slight relief to the water shortage as well as killing about 10,000 horses who doubtless died of colic, exhaustion and starvation.

The autumn was unusually long, warm and mild for Russia and the first snow did not fall until November 4. Severe cold then set in rapidly and Napoleon, sure that his bridging train was now a useless encumbrance with all the rivers frozen solid, had it destroyed at Orscha on November 19. A sudden subsequent mild spell was, in fact, a major blow to him as, having lost the Beresina bridge at Borrisow, he had to improvise the two fragile, rickety structures at Studienka around which so much human drama was played out.

It is a little known fact that, although these bridges were crowded to capacity during daylight hours, after dark they rapidly became deserted and one Hessian officer records passing repeatedly over them at night in both directions while searching for a comrade and being the only man moving from a bivouac fire.

The last stages of the retreat were conducted in bitter cold (−37.5°C on December 4) but it must be noted that the weather and the terrain are factors with which both contesting armies had to cope so victory went to that side which had made the best preparations to enable it to survive and fight in the environment.

It may be said that the disaster which destroyed the Grande Armée of 1812 was self-inflicted. Its main causes were: Napoleon's obsession with the projected humiliation of Russia which blinded him to an objective consideration of the true factors affecting the enterprise; inadequate logistic arrangements; inefficient use of those logistic assests which *were* provided; extreme lack of discipline in the French Army, caused and aggravated by the failure of the logistics; lack of foresight in making adequate provision for the oncoming winter; and a complete failure on Napoleon's part to admit that his plan to destroy the 1st and 2nd Russian Armies separately, once having

miscarried, really dictated a complete reappraisal of his original aim and a halt to the advance eastwards. Napoleon, of course, attributed the entire disaster to his staying in Moscow for two weeks too long!

Estimates of the march-in strength of the Grande Armée vary, as do those of the total casualties suffered but, even if approximate, these figures are shattering: march-in strength (after Chambry) — 610,000 men, 182,000 horses and 1,372 guns; strength in mid-December — 58,000 men, 18,000 horses and 120 guns; losses — 552,000 men, 164,000 horses and 1,252 guns.

Pride exacted a heavy price!

_____

References in the text

1   *With Napoleon in Russia,* by Marquis de Caulaincourt, Duke of Vincenza, Napoleon's Master of Horse, Ambassador to Russia, page 17.
2   *Schicksale des Grossherzogthums Frankfurt und Seiner Truppen,* by G. Bernays (E. S. Mittler und Sohn, Berlin 1882), page 353.
3   Caulaincourt, page 39.
4   *History of the Expedition to Russia Undertaken by The Emperor Napoleon in the Year 1812,* by General Count Philip de Segur (London 1860).
5   *Ibid,* page 92.
6   *Ibid,* page 94.
7   *Ibid,* page 96.
8   *Ibid,* page 100.
9   *Ibid,* page 102.
10 *Ibid,* page 134.
11 *A short report on the occurrences from the time of marching out of the kingdom until the bivouac by Minkupie, 2 marches away from Niemen,* by Wilhelm von Woellwarth.
12 Segur, page 103.
13 *Ibid,* page 118.
14 *Ibid,* page 132.
15 *Ibid,* page 133.
16 *Tagebuch des Generalmajors Maximilian Graf von Preysing-Moos im Feldzuge nach Russland 1812.*
17 Caulaincourt, pages 49, 57, 62-4, 66, 68, 73, 82, 103-4, 160, 285, 377 and 399.
18 Segur, pages 10, 137, 139, 194, 196, 206, 237, 270, 272.
19 *Ibid,* pages 115, 126, 132, 150, 164, 181, 183, 188.

Section 2

Uniforms and colours

Grand Duchy of Baden

(1st Division, I Corps; 26th Division, IX Corps; 31st Light Cavalry Brigade, IX Corps). March-out strength — 7,666 men; strength December 5 — 400 men.

Uniform: Rank badges and inter-company distinctions as in the French army except as noted below. Cockade: officers' black; NCOs' red within yellow; Privates' company colour.

Generals: Dark blue double-breasted coat; gold buttons, *epaulettes* and embroidery to red collar and cuffs; silver griffons in the red turnback corners; silver, red and yellow sash and *portepée*.

Infantry

(Each regiment of two battalions of six companies.) Black *Kasket* lower in the crown than the Bavarian model; on a *combe* a black crest; below it, covering the combe, red and yellow tassels; lion's head front plate

to combe; front band pierced with the regimental title; chains to edges of black chinstrap. Front plates as follows: 1st Leib-Infanterie-Regiment *Grossherzog:* White metal star of the *Hausorden der Treue.* 2nd 'vacant' *Erbgrossherzog* (and 4th 'vacant' which was in Spain 1808-1814): brass oval plate bearing 'CF' (Carl Friedrich); above this a crown. 3rd *Graf Wilhelm von Hochberg:* as for 2nd and 4th Regiments but in white metal. Above the left-hand chinstrap boss the cockade. Dark blue double-breasted coat; a (collar), b (cuffs) and c (turnbacks) red; white buttons with the Regimental number. The Leib-Regiment had two white loops to a and three to b. White belts and trousers. Black gaiters. **Grenadiers:** White plume to left-hand Kasket boss. **Drummers:** Sleeves edged in white lace with yellow and red worm; six chevrons of this lace (point up) on each sleeve; dark blue swallows' nests trimmed in the lace. Brass drum; white, red and yellow striped hoops. **Officers:** Bicorn with black plume and gold brooch and cords. Long coat skirts; sash and portepée as above; gold gorget. Gold-hilted sword in black sheath. Black, straight-topped boots.

Leichtes Infanterie-Bataillon *von Lingg:* As for the line infantry except: no combe or tassels to helmet; green crest and plume; no front band or plate, only the white metal cypher 'CF'; at the left side of the helmet a white hunting horn. Dark green coat; a, b and c black; black belts; dark green epaulettes. Grey breeches.

Cavalry

Husaren-Regiment *von Geusau* (four squadrons): Black *shako;* gold chinscales, cockade and button and top bands according to rank; yellow/gold *pompon* according to rank; black plume; yellow/gold cords. Dark green *dolman;* red collar and cuffs; yellow buttons and lace. Dark green *pelisse;* black fur; red and yellow sash. Red breeches. White bandoliers. Green *sabretache* edged yellow bearing a crowned 'CF'. Dark

Sabretache, trooper of the Baden Hussars 1800-1812. Dark green with yellow cypher, edging and piping (the crown is that of an Elector).

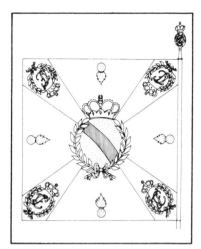

Above left *Grand Duchy of Baden, infantry flag. Gold crowns and grenades, green wreaths, yellow central oval with red stripe, gold cyphers ('FC') and ribbons. It is not known which colours were carried by which regiments. The combinations were: white cloth with dark blue corner piles; dark blue cloth with white corner piles; yellow cloth with white corner piles; yellow cloth with red corner piles; and red cloth with yellow corner piles.* **Above right** *Cartouche, Baden officer, with grand ducal crown. All fittings gilt.*

green *shabraque* edged yellow; in the rear corners the yellow, crowned 'CF'. Yellow trim and tassel to boots. **Trumpeters:** Reversed colours; red plumes. **NCOs:** Yellow chevrons above the cuff; red base and tip to plume. **Officers:** Red base to plume. Gold bandolier edged red. Gold decoration to cuffs and thighs according to rank. Black and gold sabre slings; black portepée with gold tassel; gold sabre sheath.

Artillery

Horse artillery (half a battery — four guns): Black, cavalry-style *Raupenhelm* with brass front plate, bearing the ducal crest within trophies of arms; black crest; white plume. Dark blue coat faced black; red turnbacks; yellow buttons. White bandolier; brass crossed cannon barrels on pouch lid. White breeches. Yellow-trimmed hussar boots (parades) or grey overalls.

Foot artillery (half a battery — four guns): As for horse artillery but lapels and cuffs piped red. Black plumes, belts and gaiters. White breeches.

Artillery equipment painted dark green.

Colours and standards

Infantry: In the centre an oval in gold with a red diagonal stripe, surrounded by green laurel leaves, surmounted by a crown. In each corner the crowned cypher 'CF' within green laurel wreaths, in the centre of each side a gold flaming grenade; from each corner to the centre, a pile. The allocation of flags to regiments is unknown, but the following colour combinations have survived: white cloth, dark blue piles; dark blue cloth, white piles, yellow cloth, white piles;

red cloth, white piles. Flagstaff brown, gilt tip oval in form, enclosing 'CF' and topped by a crown. All flags (two per Line infantry regiment) returned safely from Russia.

The hussars carried no standards.

Bavaria

(VI Corps)

Rank badges

Non-Commissioned Officers

Lance Corporal (*Gefreiter*): Hazelwood stick; blue and white striped sabre strap and tassel.

Corporal (*Unteroffizier* — infantry; *Rottmeister* — cavalry): As above plus bearskin crest to kasket.

Sergeant (*Feldwebel* — infantry; *Wachtmeister* — cavalry): Bearskin crest; malacca cane with silver cord and tassels; blue and white striped mohair sabre strap and tassel.

Sergeant-Major (*Stabsfeldwebel* — infantry; *Stabswachtmeister* — cavalry): As for sergeant but with a red wreath around the blue and silver sabre strap tassel.

Officers

2nd Lieutenant (*Lieutnant*): Gorget; gold with silver crest and lion's head bosses; malacca cane with silver knob; one horizontal lace in the button colour along the collar. Long coat skirts.

Lieutenant (*Oberlieutnant*): As above but two laces on the collar.

Kingdom of Bavaria. **Left** *Infantry 'Leibfahne' (King's Colour). M1786 pattern with 1806 pattern tip ('MJK').* **Centre** *'Regiments' or 'Ordinärfahne'. M 1800 pattern with 1806 pattern tip ('MJK').* **Right** *'Regiments' or 'Ordinärfahne' (regimental colour). M 1808 pattern with 1806 pattern tip ('MJK').*

Captain (*Hauptmann* — infantry; *Rittmeister* — cavalry: As above but three laces on the collar.

Major: As for Lieutnant but with a wide gold/silver lace on top and front of collar.

Lieutenant-Colonel (*Oberstlieutnant*): As for Oberlieutnant but with collar edging as for Major.

Colonel (*Oberst*): As for Hauptmann but with collar edging as for Major.

Brigadier (*Brigadegeneral*) and **Major-General** (*Generalmajor*): Silver laurel leaf embroidery to top and front of collar and cuffs and to each lapel, pocket flap, turnback and cuff buttonhole.

Lieutenant-General (*General-lieutnant*): As above but with an additional silver edging to collar, cuff and lapels.

General: As for Lieutenant-General.

All General officers wore bicorns with elaborate silver embroidery and scalloped edges and a white feather edging. Cornflower blue coats; red collars, cuffs, lapels and turnbacks, all heavily decorated in silver embroidery; silver and light blue waist sash with tassels to the left-hand side; silver and light blue portepée. White breeches and high jackboots. They were permitted to wear their hair queued and powdered if they wished (this had been abolished in the Bavarian army for other ranks in 1805). White leather gloves.

Shabraques were red with a narrow silver edging enclosing a silver laurel leaf design; in the rear corners the royal cypher within a wreath and under a crown, all in gold. Infantry Generals had short, trapezoidal shabraques, cavalry Generals' shabraques were in the long pointed, light cavalry style.

Officers of the General Staff were dressed as for General officers with badges according to rank and no silver embroidery. Silver aiguillettes were worn on the right shoulder. Shabraques were cornflower blue edged in silver and with the royal cypher in gold in the rear corners.

Infantry

The line infantry consisted of 12 regiments each of two field battalions (of one Grenadier, one Sharpshooter and four Fusilier companies) and a reserve battalion (of four Fusilier companies). They wore cornflower blue coats with facings shown on collars, lapels and cuffs in accordance with the following table. All coat turnbacks were red, the button colour also distinguished the regiment. In the first battalions, company distinctions were shown on the helmet; Grenadiers wore a red woollen plume on the left-hand side, reaching to halfway up the crest; Sharpshooters wore a similar plume but in green. In the second battalions the Sharpshooter company plume was green over white. Fusilier companies were distinguished by a woollen crescent (worn above the left-hand chinstrap boss and below the white-light blue-white circular cockade) in the following colours: **1st Battalion:** 1st Company white; 2nd white and yellow; 3rd green; 4th green and yellow. **2nd Battalion:** 5th Company red; 6th red and yellow; 7th blue; 8th blue and yellow. Breeches white. Gaiters black with black leather buttons, although regiments often replaced these by brass or tin for reasons of vanity. Belts white; packs of calfskin; pouches plain black for Fusiliers, decorated with a brass grenade for Grenadiers and with a brass hunting horn for Sharpshooters. Shoulder straps were in the coat colour and edged in the facing colour. **Drummers:** 'Swallows' nests' in the facing colour at the top of each sleeve bearing the royal cypher and edged in the button colour; four chevrons, point up, on each sleeve; sleeve seams, collar, cuffs and lapels edged in braid in the button colour. White drum slings and apron; brass drum with crowned royal cypher and blue and white hoops.

Regimental facings as follows: **No 1** *König:* a (Lapels and cuffs) poppy red; b (collar) poppy red; c (buttons) white; d (remarks) seven white buttonholes on each lapel, four on each cuff, two on each turnback. **No 2** *Kronprinz:* a poppy red; b poppy red; c yellow; d seven yellow buttonholes on each lapel, four on each cuff, two on each turnback. **No 3** *Prinz Karl:* a poppy red; b poppy red; c yellow. **No 4** *Sachsen-Hildburghausen:* a yellow**; b yellow**; c white. **No 5** *Preysing:* a pink; b pink; c white. **No 6** *Herzog Wilhelm:* a poppy red*; b poppy red*; c white. **No 7**

*Edged white.
**Edged poppy red.

Löwenstein-Wertheim: a pink; b pink; c yellow. **No 8** *Herzog Pius:* a yellow**; b yellow**; c yellow. **No 9** *Isenburg:* a yellow**; b red; c yellow. **No 10** *Junker:* a yellow**; b red; c white. **No 11** *Kinkel:* a black**; b red; c white. **No 13** vacant: a black**; b red; c yellow.

Light infantry battalions

(Dark green coats; red turnbacks.) Regimental facings as follows: **No 1:** a (lapels and cuffs) black**; b (collar) red; c (buttons) yellow. **No 2:** a black**; b red; c white. **No 3:** a black**; b black**; c white. **No 4:** a black**; b black**; c yellow. **No 5:** a black**; b yellow**; c white. **No 6:** a black**; b yellow**; c yellow.

Cavalry

There were six regiments of light cavalry called 'Chevaulégèrs', each of six squadrons of 110 troopers. Two squadrons formed a 'division'. Troopers wore moustaches. All regiments wore dark green coats with

Bavarian infantry. **Below left** *A Lieutenant of the 'Herzog Pius' Regiment in early 1812 just before the sash was abandoned in favour of the gorget.* **Below centre** *A Grenadier of the 'Preysing' Regiment with distinctive red plume. Grenadiers in the Bavarian army did not wear the red fringed epaulettes which their French counterparts wore and which were copied by many of the German 'satellite' States.* **Below right** *A Light infantryman with green plume. He carries his rifle in the traditional hunter's manner* (Weiland).

facings shown on cuffs, lapels, turnback edges, pocket flap edging and rear skirt piping. The cavalry kasket had an extra brass strengthening rib to the rear; all ranks wore a white plume on the left-hand side; the chinstrap was covered with brass scales and the front band bore *CHEVLEGERS * REGIMENT*. On the shoulders white metal scales on red backing and piped in white; in the corners of the turnbacks cloth lions and crowns. Breeches white. *Suwarov* boots with steel, buckle-on spurs. Bandoliers and belts white with brass fittings. **Officers:** Silver and light blue bandoliers with gold picker equipment; sabre sheaths steel. **Trumpeters:** Bearskin crests to kaskets. Collars, cuffs and lapels edged in gold or silver according to the button colour. The *Stabstrompeter* (Trumpet-Major) had a double bordering to collar and cuffs. 'Wings' on the backs of the trumpeters' jackets in the facing colour. Brass trumpet; light blue and white cords and tassels.

Regimental facings as follows: **No 1** vacant: a (lapels, cuffs and turnback edgings) red; b (collar) dark green; c (buttons) white. **No 2** *Taxis:* a red; b dark green; c yellow. **No 3** *Kronprinz:* a black**; b black**; c yellow. **No 4** *König:* a red; b red; c white. **No 5** *Leiningen:* a red; b red; c yellow. **No 6** *Bubenhofen:* a black**; b black**; c white.

Shabraque and portmanteaux were red, edged in light blue and white and shabraques had the royal cypher in the rear corners. Harness black with steel fittings. Officers' shabraques had plain silver edging, double for Majors and above. Horses were mainly from Rumania or Galicia and were small (about 14 hands).

Artillery

Foot artillery: Cavalry kasket with red plume. Dark blue coat of infantry cut with red collar, cuffs and turnbacks and black lapels piped red; yellow buttons and shoulder scales; yellow grenades on the turnbacks. Dark blue breeches. Black gaiters. White bandoliers supporting a pistol and a *Faschinenmesser* (straight-bladed sword with brass, lion's-headed hilt). **Officers:** Gorgets and infantry-pattern swords and boots. Officers' shabraques dark blue edged in red; holster covers black bearskin. **Drummers:** As for infantry drummers.

Horse artillery: As for foot artillery but with drooping red horsehair plumes. Tunics of Chevaulégers cut. Cavalry boots. **Officers:** Had *ARTILLERIE * REGIMENT* on their front bands. Black, lacquered leather bandoliers with gold picker equipment. Cavalry sabres. **Trumpeters:** As for cavalry trumpeters with red wings.

Train: Cavalry kasket with no plume. Light grey, single-breasted coat faced light blue; white buttons; grey turnbacks edged light blue with grey lions and

Bavarian Chevaulégèrs fording and swimming a river, possibly the Niemen (Albrecht Adam).

crowns as for the Chevaulégèrs; white metal scale epaulettes; on the upper left arm a blue brassard with a brass plate pierced with the royal cypher. Grey breeches. Black boots. Black bandolier. Infantry sabre; NCOs carried cavalry sabres.

Officers' shabraques were grey with a silver border and light blue outer piping. Horse artillery-style black bandolier with silver picker equipment. Cavalry sabre in steel sheath on white slings. **Trumpeters:** Black bearskin kasket crests; red plumes. Silver edging to collar and cuffs and light blue wings.

Engineers: As for foot artillery but with white buttons.

Apart from the field army there were also the *Leibgarde der Hartschiere* (Archer Lifeguards) and the *Trabanten-Leibgarde* (Yeomen of the Guard) who performed palace duties.

Colours and standards

Only line infantry regiments carried flags in 1812; the light battalions had none and the cavalry regiments, also being light troops, had handed theirs in in 1803 and 1811. The scale of flags was one *Leibfahne* (King's Colour) and one *Ordinärfahne* (Regimental Colour) per regiment; the Leibfahne was carried by the 1st Battalion, the Ordinärfahne by the 2nd Battalion.

All flags taken on the 1812 campaign were lost except those of the 13th Infantry Regiment (who were in Danzig and who brought them back home).

The circumstances of the loss are strangely anti-climatic. When General von Wrede began his withdrawal from Polotzk, his regiments were so weak that, for greater security, he gathered in all the flags and had them sent to the rear in a waggon with the baggage and Weisshaupt's artillery battery (which was short of draught horses). Halfway between Uschatsch

The army of the Grand Duchy of Cleve-Berg in 1812. From left to right (foreground) are infantry Grenadiers in bearskin and shako; two Voltigeurs (one in greatcoat); two Fusiliers (one in greatcoat); mounted Gendarme; trooper, 2nd Lancers; gunner, horse artillery; driver of the Train; foot Gendarme; and gunners, horse and foot artillery. (Background) Grenadier and Fusilier; lancer; two mounted gunners, horse artillery; dismounted trooper, 2nd Lancers; and mounted trooper, same regiment (Peter Schulten; vonder Heid Museum, Wuppertal).

and Kublitschi on October 24 1812 this column was ambushed by the Russians, the small escort killed and all flags captured. These flags covered a span of many years and were of many different patterns; the Leibfahnen dated back in some cases to 1786 and bore the Madonna on the globe on a white field-painted; the blue Ordinärfahne of this era bore the Bavarian crest. The motto on the Leibfahne was *SUB TUUM PRAESIDIUM VIRGO GLORIOSA* and the flags were edged with three rows of light blue and white rombi. Later Leibfahnen (from 1806) bore the Bavarian crest with supporters and the Ordinärfahnen became merely a field of light blue and white rhombi. The tips of these flags were also of various patterns: 1777-1779 — spearpoint in gold with the initials 'CT' (Carl Theodor); 1799-1806 — as above but with the initials 'MJ' (Maximilian Joseph); 1806-1815 — as above but with the initials 'MJK' (Maximilian Joseph König) on one side and a lion holding a sword and shield.

Flagstaffs were brown, nails gilt. Many flags bore blue and white cravattes. All these flags were laid up in the Kazan Cathedral in St Petersburg (latterly Leningrad) and may now have been transferred to the Red Army Museum in Moscow.

Grand Duchy of Berg

(26th Division, IX Corps; 30th Light Cavalry Brigade, IX Corps and Imperial Guard.)

Uniform: Rank badges and inter-company distinctions as in the French army.

Generals: As in the French army but with Berg cockade.

Infantry

French-style shako with oval brass plate bearing a rampant lion; above this a red-within-white cockade; cords, plumes and pompons as for the French line regiments. White coats; light blue collars, cuffs, lapels and turnbacks; yellow buttons bearing the regimental number. The style of cuff also distinguished the regiments: 1st — 'French' with trident-shaped white cuff flap (three buttons) edged light blue; 2nd — 'Polish'; 3rd — 'French' (the three-button flap light blue edged white); 4th — plain round. White trousers, waistcoat and belts. Black, below-knee gaiters edged and tasseled light blue. French musket, sabre and pouch, the latter with an oval brass plate bearing the lion. **Drummers:** Reversed colours and collars, cuffs and sleeves decorated with white lace with a red worm. Brass drum, red hoops.

Cavalry

Chevaux-légèrs: Lancer costume with pink-topped *czapka* (élite company wore black fur *colpacks* and red epaulettes). Dark green *kurtka*, shoulder straps and breeches; pink collar (edged green); pink lapels, cuffs, turnbacks and piping. White bandoliers. Straight-topped, short black boots.

Artillery

As for French foot artillery of the line but with Berg cockade and shako plate. **Train:** As for French equivalent (grey coat, light blue facings) but with Berg cockade and shako plate.

Colours and standards

Infantry: M1808 white, in the centre a golden Napoleonic eagle; in diametrically opposed corners crowned 'N's, in the other corners the regimental and battalion numbers all in gold. Above the eagle the inscription: *ET NOUS AUSSI, CESAR, CONDUIS-NOUS A LA VICTOIRE.* Below the eagle: *BRIGADE D'INFANTERIE DU GRAND DUCHE DE BERG.* All flags were lost in Russia, probably at the Beresina.

The 2nd Regiment of Chevau-Légèrs seems to have received no standard.

France

Rank badges

Officers

Marshal: White, cut feather edging to bicorn. Dark blue coat with rich gold embroidery to collar, cuffs, pocket flaps and lapels; two heavy gold-fringed epaulettes; gold portepée. White and gold waist sash.

General de Division: White, cut feather edging to bicorn. Dark blue coat richly embroidered on collar, cuffs, lapels and pocket flaps with gold. Gold epaulettes with three stars and heavy bullion fringes. Plain single-breasted dark blue coat with gold embroidery on collar, cuffs and epaulettes for field service. Red and gold waist sash; gold portepée.

General de Brigade: As above but less embroidery. Black feather edging to bicorn. Two stars on each epaulette and blue and gold waist sash. From Colonel down the epaulettes follow the button colour (eg gold for line infantry, silver for light infantry).

Colonel: No feather edging to bicorn. No gold embroidery to coat; two plain gold/silver epaulettes with heavy bullion fringes; gold portepée. Regimental uniform.

Major: Shako with gold/silver top band, side chevrons and cords. Otherwise as for Colonel but epaulette straps are silver/gold (ie in reversed colour to the fringes).

Chef de Bataillon: As for Colonel but only the left epaulette is fringed.

Captain: As for *Chef de Bataillon* but the fringes are thinner.

Adjutant Major: As for Captain but the fringe is on the right epaulette.

Lieutenant: As for Captain but with a single red line along each epaulette strap or a red, diamond-shaped figure of eight.

Sub-Lieutenant: As for Lieutenant but with two red lines along each epaulette strap.

Officers of hussars did not wear epaulettes; their rank was shown by one or more strips of gold or silver embroidery above the cuff and on the front of the thigh.

Right *Grand Duchy of Berg, infantry flag. White cloth, gold embroidery and edging, blue shield to crown, gold pike head and cords, brown pike. Lost in Russia.*

Far right *French Eagle.*

Non-Commissioned Officers (NCOs)

Badges of rank took the form of diagonal bars (with the Brandenburg cuff) or chevrons, point up (with the Polish cuff) on the lower sleeve, the exception being the 'Fourier' or Company Quartermaster-Corporal (see below).

Adjutant: As for the Sub-Lieutenant but with two yellow or white lines across the epaulette strap and the fringes worked with gold/silver and red.

Maréchal des logis chef: Gold/silver and red mixed shako cords and epaulette fringes. Two gold/silver bars on red backing.

Maréchal des logis: Gold thread mixed in shako cords and epaulette fringes. One gold/silver bar on red backing.

Fourier: One gold bar on the upper left arm; two red bars on orange backing on the forearms.

Corporal: Two red bars on orange backing.

Years of service in the army were shown by red chevrons, point up, on the upper left arm.

The Imperial Guard

The Old Guard

(All Guards units wore the same button bearing a crowned Imperial eagle, brass unless otherwise stated, and the Old Guard wore pigtails.)

Infantry

Three regiments of *Grenadiers à Pied:* Nos 1 and 2 French, No 3 Dutch; two regiments of *Chasseurs à Pied.*

1st and 2nd Grenadiers: Bearskin caps with white cords; red plume and top patch bearing a white grenade; copper front plate with the Imperial eagle between grenades; cockade. Dark blue long-tailed coat; a (collar) dark blue; b (cuffs) red; c (cuff flaps) white; d ('French' lapels) white; e (turnbacks) red; f (turnback badges) orange grenades; g (waistcoats), h (belts) and j (gaiters) white; k (epaulettes) red; l (sabre knot) red; m (pouch badges) a crowned eagle, in each corner a grenade, all in copper. **3rd Grenadiers:** As above except: no plate to bearskin; white cross on top patch. White coat; a, b, d and e crimson. **Musicians:** Light blue coats faced yellow, facings edged silver.

Sergeants and Sergeant-Majors: As above except: red and gold cords, epaulettes and sabre knot. White gloves. **Officers:** As above except gold cords, epaulettes and sabre knot. Gold gorget with silver eagle. **Drummers:** As for Privates except: red and gold lace edging to all facings; red and gold epaulettes with straps striped red and gold. Brass drum with hoops in red, white and blue triangles. **Pioneers:** As for Privates except: no plate to bearskin; red cords. Red and gold lace edging to facings and to seams of sleeves; crossed axes in red on both upper arms. White apron. Brass badges on red backing on both bandoliers: crossed axes over a bursting grenade over a lion's head. Brown-handled axe. Full beard.

Chasseurs à Pied: As for 1st and 2nd Grenadiers except: no plate to bearskin; red over green plume. Red 'Polish' cuffs piped white; turnback badges — yellow horns on the outer sides, yellow grenades on the inners. Green sabre strap with red knot. The lower ends of the lapels are pointed whereas those of the Grenadiers are square. Pouch badge: only the eagle.

The Middle Guard

Infantry

Fusilier Grenadiers: As for the 1st and 2nd Grenadiers of the Old Guard except: shako with white cords, and side chevrons; brass eagle plate; cockade;

Officers, 3rd French Chasseurs à Cheval, in Hamburg. Dark green coats, red facings, red (left) and grey breeches, white buttons and badges (Suhr).

red pompon and plume. Red epaulette strap with two white lines along it; red half moon; white tassels; white eagles in the turnbacks.

Fusilier Chasseurs: As for the Chasseurs of the Old Guard except: shako with white cords; yellow eagle plate; cockade; red over green plume. Green epaulette strap; red half moon and tassels; white eagles in the turnbacks.

The Young Guard

Infantry

Tirailleurs: Shako with brass eagle plate; cockade; brass chin scales; white cords; red over white plume; green pompon. Short-tailed blue coat with blue lapels*; red collar**, pointed cuffs*, shoulder straps* and turnbacks (with white eagle badges); white pocket and tail piping; yellow buttons. White breeches and belts. Black gaiters and shoes.

Voltigeurs: Shako with brass eagle plate; cockade; brass chin scales; white cords; red over green plume; green (or yellow) pompon. Coat, etc, as for the Tirailleurs except: buff collar**; green epaulettes with yellow half moons; green eagles in the forward turnbacks; green hunting horns in the rear turnbacks.

Flanquer-Grenadiers: Shako with brass eagle plate; cockade; brass chin scales; red cords; red over yellow pompon; white side chevrons. Short-tailed green coat; green collar, shoulder straps and lapels; red pointed cuffs and red turnbacks all piped yellow, as are the vertical pocket flaps; white eagles in the turnbacks; yellow buttons. White belts and breeches. Black gaiters.

Flanquer-Chasseurs: As for the Flanquer-Grenadiers except: no white side chevrons to shako; white cords; yellow over green, carrot-shaped pompon. Green cuffs piped yellow; green hunting horns in the turnbacks.

Cavalry

Grenadiers à Cheval: Bearskin without plate; red top patch with white grenade; yellow cords; red plume; cockade. Coat as for the Grenadiers à Pied but with yellow *contre-epaulettes* and *aiguilette* (right shoulder); g and h white. High, cuffed boots. Brass-hilted *Pallasch* in brass sheath. Dark blue saddle furniture edged yellow. Black harness with brass fittings. **Trumpeters:** White bearskin. Sky blue coat; red lapels; gold edging to facings. Red saddle furniture edged yellow, otherwise as above. Brass trumpet; gold cords; sky blue trumpet banner bearing a crowned eagle within laurel branches on one side, on the other a gold crowned 'N' within laurels; gold fringes.

Chasseurs à Cheval: Colpack with red bag trimmed and tasseled yellow; yellow cords; red plume. Dark green dolman with dark green collar*; red, pointed cuffs*; yellow lace and buttons; red and green barrel sash. Red pelisse with black fur; yellow buttons and lace. Buff breeches. Gold-trimmed hussar boots. White belts. Dark green saddle furniture and shabraque trimmed yellow, the latter bearing the yellow Imperial eagle. Brass-hilted sabre in brass sheath. Black Hungarian harness with brass fittings. **Trumpeters:** White colpack; red over sky blue plume. Sky blue dolman with red collar* and cuffs*. Gold Hungarian knots to thighs of breeches, otherwise as above. Trumpet banner as for Grenadiers à Cheval.

Chevau-Légèrs Lanciers: 1st Regiment (Polish): Czapka with crimson top piped white; white cords and plume; white cockade bearing the white Maltese cross; brass sunburst plate with silver central half circle bearing a gold crowned 'N'. Slate blue kurtka with crimson collar**, Polish cuffs**, lapels**, turnbacks and piping to rear and to sleeves; white buttons and lace; white epaulettes and aiguilette (left shoulder). Slate blue breeches with double crimson side stripes. White belts and gauntlets. Slate blue saddle furniture trimmed crimson, piped white; white corner emblems (crowned 'N' and an eagle). Black Hungarian harness with brass fittings. Brass-hilted sabre in steel sheath. Lances with crimson over white pennants. **Trumpeters:** As above except: white czapka top; red plume; crimson and white cords. White kurtka; crimson and white epaulettes and aiguilette. Crimson breeches and saddle furniture. Brass trumpet; gold cords; crimson trumpet banner bearing the same silver devices as for Grenadiers à Cheval.

2nd Regiment (the Dutch or 'Red' Lancers): As for the 1st Regiment except: red top to czapka. Red kurtka faced dark blue; yellow buttons and aiguilette. Red breeches with dark blue stripes. Dark blue saddle furniture edged red and yellow; yellow crowned 'N' and eagle badges. **Trumpeters:** White czapka top; red plume. White kurtka faced red, facings edged gold. Red and gold cords to brass trumpet. Grey horses. Red trumpet banner with same gold devices as for Grenadiers à Cheval.

3rd Regiment (Lithuanians — raised in the summer of 1812): As for the 1st Regiment but with gold buttons and lace.

Dragoons (*Dragons de l'Imperatrice*): Brass helmet with combe; black horsehair crest; leopard skin turban and red plume. Tunic of the same cut as the Grenadiers à Cheval but dark green with red cuffs

---

*Piped white.
**Piped dark blue.

*Edged yellow.
**Edged white.

The French Imperial Guard cavalry in bivouac. Visible, from left to right, are Chasseurs à Cheval, Dragoons, a Grenadier à Cheval and Chevau-Légèr Lancier. In the left background Napoleon can be seen entering his well-guarded tent (Faber du Four).

and turnbacks; white lapels; gold buttons, contre epaulettes and aiguilette (right shoulder). White belts, breeches and gauntlets. Dark green, heavy cavalry saddle furniture edged yellow; crown in rear corners. Black, heavy cavalry harness with brass fittings. **Trumpeters:** As above except: sky blue plume and tuft to black crest. White tunic faced sky blue; facings edged gold; gold button holes on lapels. Brass trumpet with sky blue and gold cords. Sky blue saddle furniture edged gold. Grey horses. Sky blue trumpet banner with same gold devices as for Grenadiers à Cheval.

Mamelukes: Conflicting details are available as numerous changes occurred with great rapidity. Most popular solution: red 'fez', white turban and horsehair plume; brass crescent front plate. Light blue waistcoat edged red; dark green shirt; red waistsash. Baggy red breeches; black belts. Ivory-hilted sabre in black and gold sheath. Turkish saddle and black harness; dark green shabraque edged red, piped white. **Kettledrummer:** As above except: white feather plumes; gold decoration to 'fez' and turban. Red waistcoat with gold braid and edging; light blue shirt decorated gold; light blue waistsash. White breeches. Green shabraque edged and decorated gold. Green drum banners bearing the crowned Imperial eagles and decorated and fringed gold. Grey horse with red ceremonial Turkish harness.

Gendarmes d'Élite: Uniform as for the Grenadiers à Cheval except: white plume and cords; black peak (edged white) and white chinscales. Red lapels and cuff flaps; white buttons, contre-epaulettes, aiguilette (left shoulder) and grenade badges on turnbacks. Yellow waistcoat, breeches, gauntlets, Pallasch hilt and sheath and yellow belts edged white. Dark blue, heavy cavalry saddle furniture edged white.) **Trumpeter:** As for Gendarmes except: red plume. Red coat faced dark blue, facings edged white. Red outer trim to saddle furniture. Red banner to brass trumpet with silver cords and devices. Grey horses. **Kettledrummer:** As for trumpeter except: white, fringed epaulettes. Dark blue drum banners decorated with the crowned Imperial eagle; trimmed silver, edged red.

Artillery

Horse Artillery of the Guard: Black busby with red plume on left side and red bag on right side; red cords. Blue dolman with red lace and trim and yellow buttons. Blue pelisse with red lace; yellow buttons and black fur; red and yellow barrel sash. Blue hussar breeches with red thigh knots and side stripes. Hussar boots with red trim and tassel. White belts with brass fittings. Brass-hilted sabre in brass sheath, white strap. Blue sabretache edged red with yellow metal motif of crowned Imperial eagle on crossed cannon barrels. **Officers:** Gold braid and white fur on the pelisse. **Trumpeters:** White busby with sky blue bag and plume (with white tip). Sky blue dolman, pelisse and breeches; red and gold braid; yellow buttons; black fur. Sky blue sabretache with gold edging and same badge as before.

Foot Artillery of the Guard: Black bearskin with

black, brass-edged peak; brass chinscales; red top patch with yellow grenade; red plume and cords for parades. Blue coat of Grenadier cut with blue collar, cuff flaps and lapels edged red; red turnbacks with blue grenades; red cuffs; red epaulettes; yellow buttons. Blue trousers. Long gaiters with yellow metal buttons. White belts. Infantry equipment with sabre.

Artillery Train of the Guard: As for the Artillery Train of the line except: red plume and cords to shako. Red epaulettes; grey waistcoat braided red in hussar-style. Red Austrian knots on the thighs of the breeches. Hussar boots with red trim and tassel.

Artillery Park of the Guard: As for the Artillery Park of the line but with the Guard distinctions mentioned above.

Engineers of the Guard (one company): Polished steel helmet with brass frontal eagle, combe, peak and neck shield trim and chinscales; black fur 'sausage' crest; red pompom and plume to left-hand side. Dark blue coat; black collar, cuffs, cuff flaps and lapels all piped red; red epaulettes and red turnbacks with dark blue grenades; yellow buttons. Dark blue breeches. White belts. Black gaiters.

Marines

Marines of the Guard (one battalion): Shako with brass eagle and anchor plate; orange top and bottom bands and cords; red pompon and plume. Dark blue dolman; dark blue collar edged orange; orange cuffs,

chest lacing and edging; brass scale epaulettes (without fringes); brass buttons. Wide, dark blue trousers with orange side stripe and Hungarian thigh knots. Black bandoliers with square brass buckle plate bearing an anchor. Curved sabre (cutlass?) in black and brass sheath; orange fist strap. Dark blue greatcoat.

Line regiments

Infantry

From one to six battalions per regiment each of six companies (one battalion became the depôt or training unit and had only four Fusilier companies). One Grenadier, one Voltigeur (or light) and four Fusilier companies. The company was 140-strong and was divided into two platoons. Inter-company distinctions are shown below.

Uniform: Dark blue, short-tailed coat, with red collar and cuffs; white lapels and turnbacks (piped red); dark blue cuff flaps; yellow buttons. White breeches. Black gaiters. White belts.

Grenadiers: Red trim to top, bottom and side chevrons of shako; red ball pompon with red tuft on top; red plume and cords for parades; flaming grenade stamped on chinstrap bosses. Red grenade badges on turnbacks; red epaulettes; red sabre knot.

Fusiliers: Smaller shako than the Grenadiers and with a white, lenticular disc bearing the company number (1-4) and edged in the company colour (1 —

'Shako' of lambskin, officer, Lithuanian Tartars of the Guard. Dark green bag edged gold; gold turban; crimson and gold tassel.

Czapka of a field officer, 1st (Polish) Lancers of the Guard (probably privately made).

green; 2 — sky blue; 3 — orange; 4 — violet); five-pointed stars stamped on chinstrap bosses, white cords for parades. Blue, five-pointed star badges (or crowned 'N') on turnbacks; shoulder straps in blue, piped white or red. No sabres, except for NCOs.

Voltigeurs: Shako size as for Fusiliers with yellow top, bottom and side trim; yellow or green ball pompon and tuft; green plume with yellow tip and green cords for parades; hunting horn stamped on chinstrap bosses. Yellow collar; green epaulettes with yellow half-moons; yellow hunting horns on each turnback.

Light infantry

(Dark blue *habit-veste* with white piping and buttons.)

Carabineers (Grenadier equivalent): Red plume; white cords. Red collar edged white; red grenades on turnbacks; red epaulettes. Red sabre knots.

Chasseurs (Fusilier equivalent): Green plume; white cords. Red collar edged white; white hunting horns on turnbacks; green epaulettes with red half-moons.

Voltigeurs: Green plume tipped yellow; green cords. Yellow collar edged red; yellow hunting horns on the turnbacks; green epaulette straps; yellow half moons; red fringes. Green sabre knots.

Musicians

A decree of January 19 1812 standardised all French regimental musicians' coats as a dark green, single-breasted coat with red epaulettes, cuffs, collars and turnbacks and the usual company emblems. It was heavily trimmed with dark green lace bearing alternate crowned 'N's and Imperial eagles in dark green on yellow ovals. Of course, there was no time for much of the army to be issued with this new uniform and the bewildering galaxy of 'regimental taste' decorated the vast plains of the Russian Empire.

Cavalry

Carabiniers (1st and 2nd Regiments): Brass helmet and combe; steel trim and front plate with gold crowned 'N'; red crest; steel chin scales. Brass cuirass trimmed with steel; brass rivets; dark blue cuff edged white; brass shoulder chains on brown leather straps; brown waist belt. White coats; sky blue collar and turnbacks edged white, white grenade in each turnback corner; red cuffs and white cuff flaps trimmed white for the 1st Regiment, sky blue with sky blue flaps trimmed white for the 2nd Regiment; red epaulettes. Buff leather breeches. High jacked boots. Buff bandolier edged white; white metal fittings. Buff sabre belts; brass sabre hilt and sheath; black pouch with brass grenade badge. Sky blue saddle furniture with white lace and grenades. **Trumpeters:** White (1st Regiment) or sky blue (2nd) crests and

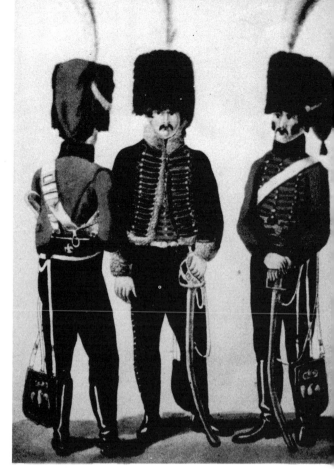

French hussars in Hamburg — troopers of the 7th Regiment. Red dolman with yellow buttons, dark green collars, cuffs and breeches, red cords and sabretache, dark green pelisse, red busby bag.

white (1st) or red (2nd) epaulettes; red bugle cords. Grey horses.

Cuirassiers: Steel helmet with black fur turban; brass combe and chinscales; black horsehair tuft (aigrette) and trailing crest; black leather peak edged in brass; white plume for parades. Steel cuirass; brass rivets; red cuff edged white; brass shoulder scales on red backing. Dark blue, single-breasted coat; white buttons; white bandolier; red epaulettes; blue collar.

Regimental facings as follows: **1st Regiment:** a (collar, turnbacks and pocket flap edging) red; b (cuffs and cuff flap trim) red; c (cuff flaps) red. **2nd:** a red; b red; c blue. **3rd:** a red; b blue; c red. **4th:** a, b and c orange. **5th:** a and b orange; c blue. **6th:** a orange; b blue; c orange. **7th:** a, b and c yellow. **8th:** a and b yellow; c blue. **9th:** a yellow; b blue; c yellow. **10th:** a, b and c pink; **11th:** a and b pink; c blue. **12th:** a pink; b blue; c pink. **14th** (ex-2nd Dutch Cuirassier Regiment): a and b lilac; c blue. Dark blue saddle furniture with white edging and grenades. **Trumpeters:** Imperial livery with regimental facings; white aigrette and crest. Grey horses.

Dragoons: Helmet as for cuirassiers but in brass and with brown fur turban; red plume for parades. Green coat; white buttons; green collar and shoulder straps edged in the regimental facing colour. (19th Regiment had white plume for parades and white epaulettes.) Green grenades in the turnbacks. White bandolier and belts with brass fittings. White breeches. Black boots. Mid-green saddle furniture with white lace and regimental number. **Trumpeters:** White aigrettes and crests, often the old reversed colours instead of the new Imperial livery. Grey horses.

Regimental facings as follows: **2nd:** a (lapels and turnbacks) scarlet; b (collar) green; c (cuffs) scarlet; d (cuff flaps) green; e (horizontal pocket flaps). **5th:** a scarlet; b green; c scarlet; d green; f (vertical pocket flaps). **7th:** a, b, c, d carmine; e. **12th:** a, b carmine; c green; d carmine; f. **13th:** a, b, c, d pink; e. **17th:** a pink; b green; c pink; d green; f. **19th:** a, b, c, d yellow; e. **20th:** a yellow; b green; c yellow; d green; e. **23rd:** a yellow; b, c, d green; f. **28th:** a, b, c, d orange; f. **30th:** a, b orange; c green; d orange; f.

Chasseurs à Cheval: Fusilier shako (Grenadier shako or brown fur busby with red bag for élite companies), with squadron pompons as follows: 1st — red; 2nd — sky blue; 3rd — orange; 4th — violet. Each squadron had two companies, the second company in each squadron had a white centre to the lenticular pompon or a white ring around the spherical pompon. White rhombic front plate with eagle over regimental number; steel chin scales with five-pointed star badge on boss. Dark green coat either single-breasted or with dark green lapels edged in the regimental facing colour; green hunting horns on the turnbacks; white buttons; green shoulder straps (red epaulettes for the élite company). Green breeches with white side piping and thigh knots. Black hussar boots with white top trim and tassel. White bandolier and belts (except 5th, 8th and 27th Regiments which had buff leatherwork); black cartouche. Brass-hilted sabres in steel or black leather scabbards. White or buff gloves. Sheepskin shabraque with dog's tooth edging in facing colour.

Regimental facings as follows: **1st:** a (collar) scarlet; b (collar edging) green; c (cuffs and turnbacks) scarlet. **2nd:** a green; b, c scarlet. **3rd:** a scarlet; b green; c scarlet. **4th:** a yellow; b green; c yellow. **5th:** a green; b, c yellow. **6th:** a yellow; b green; c yellow. **7th:** a pink; b green; c pink. **8th:** a green; b, c pink. **9th:** a pink; b green; c pink. **11th:** a green; b, c crimson. **12th:** a crimson; b green; c crimson. **16th:** a sky blue; b green; c sky blue. **19th:** a orange; b green; c orange. **20th:** a green; b and c orange. **23rd:** a green; b, c dark orange. **24th:** a dark orange; b green; c dark orange. **25th:** a madder red; b green; c madder red. **28th:** a peach blossom pink; b green; c peach blossom pink. **Trumpeters:** Reversed colours were worn by trum-

Officer, French horse artillery, in Hamburg. Dark blue uniform and saddlecloth with red piping and trimmings, gold lace and buttons, and gold and red edging to saddlecloth (Suhr).

peters of the 1st, 5th, 7th and 19th Regiments, those of the 16th Regiment wore uniforms completely in the facing colour.

Hussars: Fusilier shako with rhombic plate in the regimental button colour; cockade and company pompons as for the Chasseurs à cheval. Élite companies wore brown fur busbies (11th Regiment white) with regimental plumes on the shakos for parades (and cords and chin scales in the button colour). White leather work. Brass-hilted sabres with steel scabbards. Sabretache of various patterns; usually with regimental number and Imperial eagle. Hussar boots with trim and tassel in the regimental lace colour. Trumpeters often wore white busbies if in élite companies. Sheepskin shabraque with dog's tooth edging.

Regimental distinctions as follows: **5th:** a (dolman) sky blue; b (collar) sky blue; c (cuffs) white; d (pelisse) white; e (breeches) sky blue; f (buttons) yellow; g (shako plume) white; h (barrel sash) red/yellow; j (braid edging to collar, cuffs, dolman front, bottom and rear seams, pelisse edging) yellow; k (side seams

and thigh knots on breeches) none; l (busby bag) sky blue; m (trim and tassel of busby bag) yellow; n (fur trim to pelisse) black; o (trumpeter's dolman) white with sky blue cuffs; p (trumpeter's pelisse) sky blue; q (other points) plume 2/3 black over 1/3 yellow; light blue shakos; r (dog's tooth edging to shabraque) blue. **6th:** a, b, c red; d, e royal blue; f yellow; g black with red tip; h red/yellow; j yellow; k red; l red; m yellow; n black; o dark green (?); p dark green (?); q black plume; red shakos; r blue. **7th:** a green; b, c red; d green; e red; f yellow; g black; h red/yellow; j yellow; k red; l red; m yellow; n black; o all red; p red; q plume 1/3 red over 2/3 white; light green shakos; r red; **8th:** a green; b, c red; d green; e red; f white; g black; h red/white; j red and black; k red; l red; m white; n black; o all red; p red; q plume black; red shako; r red. **9th:** a red; b, c, d, e light blue; f yellow; g black with white tip; h red/yellow; j yellow; k red; l red; m yellow; n black; o buff yellow; p red; q plume 1/3 yellow over 2/3 black; r red; **11th:** a royal blue; b, c red; d, e royal blue; f yellow; g black; h red/white with a central vertical blue line in the white; j yellow; k red; l red; m yellow; n white; o, p white with gold trim; q plume black; r blue shabraque with yellow edging.

Chevau-Légèr-Lanciers: The 1st-6th Regiments wore brass, dragoon-style helmets with brown fur turban; black peak and neck shield and black crest; brass chinscales; red crest for trumpeters and for the élite companies. Their coat was a green Spencer of line infantry cut but with Polish cuffs, lapels, collars and turnbacks in the regimental facing colour. In the turnback corners a green crowned 'N'. Élite companies had red epaulettes; others green shoulder straps trimmed in the facing colour; buttons yellow. Breeches were green with regimental side stripes; white belts; black cartouche with brass crowned 'N' (flaming grenade for élite companies); similar badges on the square brass belt plate. Hussar-style boots with yellow trim and tassel. Hussar-style sabre; white sabre strap (with red tassel for élite companies). Officers' helmets had leopard skin turbans. **Trumpeters:** Imperial livery with chevrons, point up, on each sleeve. Lance pennants red over white. Green horse furniture with yellow or white lace and regimental number; white sheepskin shabraque with dog's tooth edging in regimental facing colour.

Regimental facings as follows: **1st:** scarlet. **2nd:** orange. **4th:** crimson. **5th:** sky blue. **6th:** red. The 8th Regiment wore black czapkas with brass front rayed plates with steel crowned 'N' in the centre. Dark blue kurtka and breeches (see Duchy of Warsaw for details) with regimental facings shown on Polish

French Line infantry sapper. Near regulation dress with carbine slung and with service chevrons above his sapper badge (Suhr).

cuffs, lapels, collar, turnbacks, piping and breeches side stripes; silver buttons. Regimental facings dark blue, yellow piping.

Artillery

Foot artillery: Fusilier shako with yellow plate and chinscales; red pompons, tuft, (red plume and cords for parades). Blue line infantry coat; blue collar, lapels and cuff flaps, all trimmed red; red cuffs, epaulettes and red turnbacks with blue grenades; yellow buttons. Blue breeches. White belts.

Horse artillery: Grenadier shako with yellow plate and chinscales; red pompon (red plume and cords for parades). Blue coat of line infantry cut; blue collar and lapels; red Polish cuffs and red turnbacks with blue grenades; red epaulettes; yellow buttons; white bandolier and belts; black cartouche with yellow crossed cannon barrel badge. Blue breeches with red side stripe. Hussar boots with red trim and tassel. Hussar sabre with brass hilt; white fist strap and steel scab-

bard. Officers had dark blue sabretaches with red trim and yellow central motif of regimental number over crossed cannon barrels over a flaming grenade.

Artillery Train: Fusilier shako (but with the eagle on a white lozenge plate); white chinscales; red pompon. Light grey coat of line infantry cut; dark blue collar, lapels, cuffs and cuff flaps all trimmed red; dark blue turnbacks with light grey grenades; light grey shoulder straps trimmed red; white buttons. Light grey breeches with red side stripe. Straight-topped riding boots. White belts with square brass buckle plate bearing a flaming grenade over crossed cannon barrels over a unit number. **Train of the Artillery Park:** As for the Artillery Train but without the red piping. **Equipment Train:** As for Artillery Park Train but all facings light grey with dark blue edging and with Polish cuffs. **Bridging Train:** As for Artillery Park Train but all facings black with red edging.

Text continued on page 53.

The battle of Borodino. A French cuirassier (10th Regiment) and his horse, both wounded, leave the battlefield past a group of Bavarian Chevaulégèrs tending a mortally wounded officer.

Captions to colour plates 1-11

1 Grand Duchy of Baden, Foot Artillery. *This plate clearly shows details of the officers' sash and cartouche and of the two gunners' helmet plates (Augsburger Bilder).*

2 Grand Duchy of Baden, infantry. *Left to right: infantry officer, walking out dress; note silver sash with red and yellow stripes; Private, Leib-Regiment. Although this unit did not go to Russia, the helmet is of interest as it shows the black crest and the red and yellow fringes hanging down over the combe of the lion's head boss on the combe front. Line regiments had yellow metal helmet fittings and instead of the star shown here they had an oval plate. The Line infantry had no white laces to collars or cuff flaps. Jäger: the Kasket front plate is the crowned cipher 'CF' (Carl Friedrich); he carries his rifle slung in the traditional, hunter's way and instead of a sabre he has a sword-bayonet or 'Hirschfänger'. Garde-Grenadier —this unit was not in Russia (Knötel).*

3 Grand Duchy of Baden, cavalry. *Two regiments are shown on this plate, the Garde du Corps who did not go to Russia, and the hussars who won immortality with their desperate charge to save the dwindling bridgehead on the east bank of the Beresina river on November 27 1812. The officer (centre) has a red base to his dark green plume (portraits of officers of this regiment also show black plumes) and grey fur to his pelisse; the trooper (far right) has his plume in its foul weather case. His pelisse fur is black (Augsburger Bilder).*

4 Bavarian artillery and train. *Another of the 'Augsburger Bilder' series which shows two gunners of foot artillery but without their red plumes and with what appear to be gold fringes to their shoulder scales — strictly unauthorised! The drivers of the artillery train in the centre background are as described in Müller-Braun, but the mounted officer of horse artillery should be wearing a black lacquered bandolier and not a white one. Note his black gauntlets. Medals, when awarded in this era, were worn all the time and not just a strip of ribbon as is the case in everyday wear now.*

5 Bavarian Chevaulégèrs. *This plate from the Augsburger Bilder series depicts men of the 4th Regiment König, and shows the officer pattern saddle furniture well. The officer is an Oberlieutenant as· shown by the two gold stripes on his collar. The embroidery on his bandolier is also clear and the lid of his cartouche bears the crowned Bavarian crest. Unfortunately, his skirt ornaments are reduced to small, unrecognisable blobs. The light blue edging to the trooper's shabraque is so faded that the diamond shapes are almost invisible. Usually trumpeters rode greys but the man on the grey here is an ordinary trooper. The original dark green paint of the officer's tunic has now become almost dark blue.*

6 Bavarian infantry. *This group is from the 3rd Infantry Regiment Prinz Karl as shown by the white piping to the red lapels and cuffs and the yellow buttons. The Sergeant (Feldwebel) can be rec-*

ognised by the bearskin crest to his kasket, the malacca cane hanging from his coat button and his light blue and white sabre knot. The drummer is portrayed with the chevrons on his sleeves point down, whereas Müller and Braun — a most reliable source — give them as being point up. The light blue and white stripes on the drum hoops are almost invisible. The Fusilier is shown in summer marching order. Note the jaunty manner in which the kasket is worn cocked to the left.

7 Grand Duchy of Berg, Fusilier, 1st Line Infantry Regiment. *This excellent rear view shows the pouch lid badge — an oval bearing a rampant lion. The equipment is standard French pattern. A plate by an unknown artist.*

8 French Imperial Guard cavalry. *From left to right: Corporal, Chasseurs à Cheval; Elite Gendarme (background); Grenadier à Cheval (rear view); and Dragoon — a much more credible figure than that on plate 9 (Augsburger Bilder).*

9 French Imperial Guard cavalry. *This plate is one of a series of plates produced in national groups (each of about five plates) in the city of Augsburg in the period 1806-1812. Like other contemporary sources, they must be treated with caution and evaluated in the light of later research. For instance, a cuirassier is shown and it is well known that there were none in the Imperial Guard; this man must therefore be from a line cavalry regiment. The Mamelukes (both standing and mounted in the background) appear to be authentic as does the Elite Gendarme. The Dragoon with white facings seems again to be from a line regiment. From Charackteristische Darstellung der vorzüglichsten europaischen Militairs, by J. M. Voltz. The series of plates is commonly known as the 'Augsburger Bilder'.*

10 French Imperial Guard infantry. *Left to right: background — unidentified infantryman in shako; Pioneer, Grenadiers (note arm and belt badges); the red and yellow lace sleeve seams are missing — perhaps they were only worn on parade uniform; Elite Gendarme (dismounted section) rear view; (background) Port Aigle with much simplified flag! Chasseur of the Guard — note green epaulettes. Officer, Grenadiers in summer parade dress; note that the white cuff flap has erroneously been coloured yellow and that no portepée is shown on the sword. The silver eagle is missing from the gold gorget (Augsburger Bilder).*

11 French Horse Artillery. *This is one of a famous series of plates drawn by the brothers Cornelius and Christian Suhr in Hamburg. From 1806 to 1814 they faithfully recorded the uniforms of the many contingents of troops which passed through that city and their work is regarded as authentic and very reliable. Inevitably, what the uniform regulations dictated should be worn and what the troops actually wore in the field often differed. Thus we see here (from left to right): officer in pelisse, colpack and grey (campaign) overalls; note the rank chevrons over the cuffs, the ornate bandolier and the apparently 'shaggy' sabretache; gunner in shako, surtout and dark blue overalls with black leather reinforcing; and gunner in frock coat.*

1 *Above* Grand Duchy of Baden, foot artillery. 2 *Below left* Grand Duchy of Baden, infantry. 3 *Below right* Grand Duchy of Baden, cavalry.

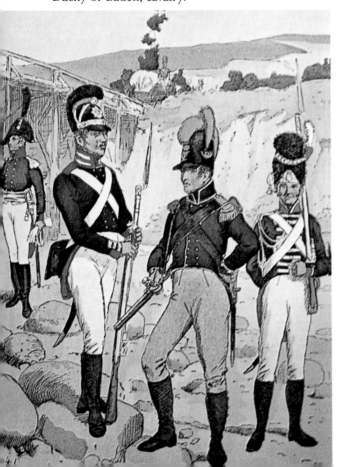

4 *Left* Bavarian artillery and train.

5 *Below left* Bavarian Chevaulégèrs.

6 *Below* Bavarian infantry.

7 *Right* Grand Duchy of Berg, Fusilier, 1st Line Infantry Regiment.

8 *Far right* French Imperial Guard cavalry.

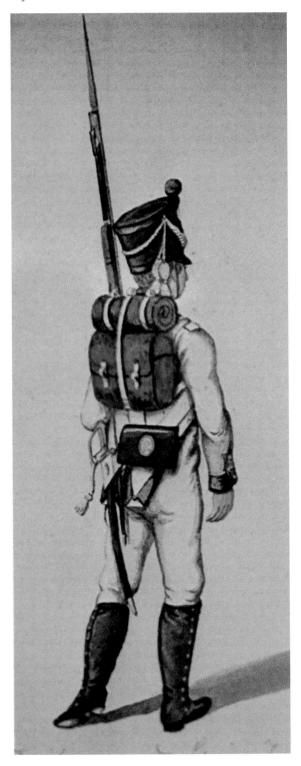

9 *Above* French Imperial Guard cavalry.
10 *Right* French Imperial Guard infantry.
11 *Below* French horse artillery.

Eagles and colours

Napoleonic Eagles were ruthlessly destroyed after Waterloo and it is difficult to be precise as to their appearance but from surviving relics the following picture emerges.

On December 5 1804 Napoleon presented over 1,000 Eagles to all regular line Corps on a scale of one per battalion or squadron. Units present included line and light infantry, artillery, cuirassiers, carabiniers, dragoons, chasseurs à cheval, hussars, two battalions of pontonniers, the gendarmerie legions, the maritime sections, the Fleet, the Imperial Guard and the foreign regiments (Swiss and Irish). All old colours were gathered in and burned.

The infantry, foot artillery, marine artillery, pontonniers and veterans received Eagles with square colours (80 cm each side).

The carabiniers, cuirassiers and hussars received square standards (60 cm each side).

The chasseurs à cheval, dragoons, horse artillery, artillery train, baggage train and gendarmerie received guidons with rounded points on the fly side, the cloth 60 cm high, 60 cm wide in the centre and 80 cm long at the two points.

The Eagles were the same design for all colours: 18-20 cm high, gilt, head turned to its right, beak partly open showing the tongue, wings partially extended, the left claw resting on a thunderbolt. This stood on a rectangular plinth about 10-12 cm long, 6 cm high and 5 cm wide. On the long side of the plinth appeared the regimental number 4-4.5 cm high.

The pikes were about 180 cm long, dark blue (dark green for chasseurs à cheval and some dragoon regiments) and ended in a brass shoe.

The colours and standards bore the same basic devices: in the centre a white lozenge, the corners touching the centres of each side; opposing pairs of corners were red and blue (the upper staff corner being blue). The lozenge was bordered in gold-painted laurel leaves. In each corner was the regimental number within a laurel wreath all in gold. Within the white lozenge, in gold, was the regimental designation on the obverse: *L'EMPEREUR/DES FRANCAIS/AU — me REGIMENT/D'INFANTERIE/DE LIGNE (or DE DRAGONS, D'INFANTERIE/LEGERE, D'ARTILLERIE,* etc). The Eagles of the Guard bore on the obverse: *GARDE / IMPERIALE/L'EMPEREUR/DES FRANCAIS/AU —er REGIMENT/DES GRENADIERS /À PIED* and in each corner was (instead of the number) a badge (grenade, horn, anchor). On the reverse, within the white lozenge (in gold) was *VALEUR ET/DISCIPLINE/-e BATAILLON (ESCADRON* for

French infantry colours. The colour of the 111th Line Infantry Regiment. This 1804 pattern flag is one of the few surviving examples in relatively good condition. It is now in the collection of Prince Rainier of Monaco (by gracious permission of His Serene Highness, Prince Rainier).

French infantry colours. The 1811 pattern tricolour flag of the French army. From the staff, the colours are blue, white and red. The embroidery on this example is silver, but for Line regiments would be gold.

cavalry). There were no tassels or fringes to these colours which were fixed to the staff by two rows of gilt nails. A tricolour cravatte with gold fringes and laurel wreaths at each end was tied around the pike just under the Eagle. The ends of this cravatte reached to about halfway down the flag.

In the Eagles described above, the laurel leaves along each side of the lozenge all faced the same way (from the centre of each vertical side they ran points up in the upper half, points down in the lower half). In Eagle colours issued between 1805 and 1811 these laurel leaves pointed from the outer edges of the flags and met in the centre of the sides of the lozenge. Those regiments which fought in all the decisive battles against Prussia and Russia in 1806 and 1807 (Jena and Auerstädt, Friedland and Eylau) had gold laurel wreaths presented to them by the City of Paris when they returned to France. These wreaths were affixed around the necks of the battalion (squadron) Eagles. By 1808 Napoleon, disturbed at the heavy losses of Eagles at Eylau (12 from the 14^e, 18^e, 24^e, and 28^e Ligne, the 10^e Leger and four cuirassier regiments), directed that only one Eagle per regiment should be retained. The Eagles of the 2nd, 3rd and 4th, etc, battalions/squadrons were to be returned to the magazines and these units then received *Fanions* with lance tips. The colours of the Fanions were: 2nd Battalion white; 3rd red; 4th blue; 5th green; 6th yellow. They bore regimental inscriptions and were frequently far more ornate than officially permitted.

Battle honours could be worn on the colours; the complete permissible list was: Ulm, Austerlitz, Jena, Eylau, Friedland, Eckmühl, Essling and Wagram. The Guard could also wear 'Marengo' and the 84^e de

Ligne also carried the motto: *Un contre dix — Gratz 1809* but this was ordered to be removed in 1811. By 1812 it was the rule that units not already in possession of Eagles should 'earn' them in battle; thus the 127e de Ligne (a German regiment) was awarded theirs for their conduct at Smolensk.

Foreign Regiments (Régiments Etrangér) in French service

1st Regiment (the old *La Tour d'Auvergne*: Shako with brass eagle plate and chinscales. Dark green Spencer, lapels*, cuffs* and waistcoat; red collar*, cuff flaps* and turnbacks*. Dark green breeches. White belts. Short black gaiters. Badges of rank and inter-company distinctions French. White buttons with the peripheral inscription *RÉGIMENT ETRANGÉR*; in the centre the figure 'I'.

2nd Regiment (the old *Regiment Isenburg*): As above but sky blue coat, lapels, waistcoat and cuffs; yellow collar, cuff flaps and piping; white buttons with the central number '2'. Sky blue breeches.

3rd Regiment (the old 'Irish Legion'): Uniform as for 1st Regiment except: yellow collar, lapels, cuffs and piping; green cuff flaps; red turnbacks; white waistcoat; yellow buttons with the central number '3'. White breeches.

4th Regiment (the old *Regimente Preusse*): As for 1st Regiment except: red turnbacks and piping, yellow buttons with the central number '4'.

The Croatian Regiments (*Chasseurs Illyriens*) (9th,

*Piped white.

11th and 13th Divisions): By the terms of the Peace of Schönbrunn in 1809 a large area of Austrian Croatia passed into French possession and with it six of the 17 Grenz-Infanterie regiments. In 1810 these units were reorganised into three regiments in French service and uniformed as follows: Shako with brass rhombic plate and chinscales; French cockade; company pompon and cords. Dark blue single-breasted coat and shoulder straps*; facings shown on collar, pointed cuffs and turnbacks. French badges of rank and inter-company distinctions. Long, plain Hungarian-style breeches. Facings: **1st Regiment** (*Liccaner*) the old 1st: red. **2nd** (*Ottochaner*) the old 2nd: crimson. **3rd** (*Oguliner*) the old 3rd: light yellow. **4th** (*Szluiner*) the old 4th: dark brown. **5th** (*1st Banalisten*) the old 10th: light blue. **6th** (*2nd Banalisten*) the old 11th: dark green.

By 1812 these six new regiments had been reduced to three by combining the 1st and 2nd, 3rd and 4th

French Napoleonic Eagle.

and 5th and 6th into new units. A decree of January 19 1812 gave them the following uniform: French shako with white rhombic plate bearing a hunting horn (or eagle plate); cockade, etc, as before. Dark green coats of French light infantry pattern with yellow collars (the 3rd Regiment had light blue piping to their collars); dark green lapels*; yellow pointed cuffs, turnbacks and trim to hussar-styled black gaiters. Dark green breeches*. White belts and waistcoat. Officers had silver epaulettes, portepée and trim and tassel to hussar-style boots.

Regiment d'Illyrie: Shako with white rhombic plate and chinscales; cockade; red pompon and plume. Dark blue light infantry coat, lapels**, pointed cuffs**, turnbacks**, breeches** and shoulder straps**; red collar and swallows' nests**; white buttons bearing on the periphery *EMPIRE FRANÇAIS* and in the centre *RÉGIMENT d'ILLYRIE*.

The Portuguese Legion

(6th Division, II Corps; 10th and 11th Divisions, III Corps.) Three infantry regiments, two cavalry regiments. Rank badges and inter-company distinctions as in the French army.

Infantry

Portuguese shako with raised front; brass chinscales and front band pierced with the regimental number; above this a grenade or horn for élite companies; company cords and plumes. Dark brown coat; red collar, lapels, turnbacks, cuffs and cuff flaps. Fusiliers had dark brown shoulder straps edged red. Dark brown breeches and short white gaiters or white trousers with red side stripes. Élite companies had turnback badges in yellow and brass pouch badges. White belts. These units are poorly recorded and it seems likely that regiments were distinguished by differently styled cuffs and possibly by lapels in the coat colour piped red and white instead of red turnbacks. **Officers:** Silver epaulettes; bicorns; red waist sashes; gold gorgets; gold-trimmed hussar boots; gold portepée. **Drummers:** Red plumes and cords; white bars on sleeves; brass drums with blue hoops.

Cavalry

Black leather helmet with black combe and crest; black fur turban; yellow, oval front plate, chinscales and side struts. Elite companies wore black fur colpacks with red pompoms. Dark brown coats, lapels and shoulder straps; red collar, piping to lapels and shoulder straps; red turnbacks; yellow buttons; white waistcoats. Brown breeches. Plain hussar boots. Red horse furniture edged white; white sheepskins edged

*Piped in the facing colour.
**Piped white.

red; black harness with yellow fittings. Swords in black and yellow sheaths. Grey overalls with red side stripes or white breeches were also worn. White bandoliers. **Officers:** Red bandoliers edged silver; white gauntlets; silver epaulettes; black sword belts; gold portepée.

Colours and standards

No really reliable information is available but it seems that the cavalry had no standards and the infantry colours were white with a central gold device surrounded by gold trophies; gilt spearpoint tip; gold cords; brown staff.

Spain

The Regiment Joseph Napoleon (2nd and 3rd Battalions, 2nd Division, I Corps; 1st and 4th Battalions, 14th Division, IV Corps): This infantry regiment was formed by a decree of February 13 1809 from Spanish prisoners of war in France. It was disbanded on November 25 1813. All uniform details French. Shako with tricolour cockade; brass eagle plate and chinscales; company pompon, plumes and cords. White coat, buttons, waistcoat, breeches and belts; light green collar, lapels, pointed cuffs and turnbacks. Black gaiters.

Switzerland

The Swiss Regiments (9th Division, II Corps): These four infantry regiments were taken into French service on September 12 1806. Each had three battalions organised on standard French lines. In Russia they formed the 'Red' 9th Division together with the 123ᵉ de Ligne (a Dutch unit). On April 15 1814 the survivors were released from their oath of alliegance to Napoleon and returned home or took service with the army of Louis XVIII.

All uniform detail French except where otherwise noted. Apparently the regiments wore the old style uniform habit-veste with long skirts. Shako with brass eagle plate; tricolour (French) cockade on top left-hand side, above this the company pompon and plume; company cords; black leather chinstrap. Red coat, cuff flaps* and shoulder straps*, facings to collar*, lapels* and cuffs*, white turnbacks; yellow buttons. White waistcoat, breeches and belts. Black, below-knee gaiters. **Grenadiers:** Bearskin cap with brass eagle plate; cockade and red plume; white cords; brass chinscales; red epaulettes; yellow eagles on turnbacks. **Voltigeurs:** Yellow collar* and epaulettes; green plume with yellow tip; green cords. **Drummers:** Company uniform; gold lace to facing

*Piped white.

French foreign regiments: Napoleon's expansionist policies created more 'Frenchmen' than the conjugal activities of his original metropolitan subjects! Several regiments of the 'French' army were absorbed as formed units from other armies and retained their essentially foreign character. Shown here are troopers of the Belgian 27th Chasseurs à Cheval (left) and Piemontais 21st Dragoons (Fieffe).

colours; swallows nests in the facing colour edged white; five gold lace chevrons (point down) on each sleeve. Brass drum with sky blue hoops. **Sappers:** Bearskin cap without eagle plate; white cords; red plume with black tip. Gold fringed epaulettes; yellow eagle turnback badges; four pairs of crossed axes in gold on each sleeve. White apron. Gilt-hilted sword with cock's head boss. Brown-handled axe. Beard. **Officers:** Company uniform (Grenadier officers with gold cords and white plumes with red tips); gold gorget with silver eagle. Gilt-hilted sword in black and gold sheath; black portepée. Gold-trimmed hussar boots. White gloves. Fusilier officers had gold top and bottom bands to shakos, Voltigeur officers a gold top band only. Swords were carried on white bandoliers.

Regimental facings were as follows: **1st:** a (facings) yellow; b (piping) sky blue. **2nd:** a royal blue; b yellow. **3rd** a black; b white. **4th** (a) sky blue; b black.

Each regiment had its own artillery company, presumably in blue uniforms.

Eagles

One per regiment; 1804 pattern, ie a central white lozenge with opposing pairs of corners red and blue, embroidery gold. In the lozenge the following inscriptions: obverse: *L'EMPEREUR/DES FRAN-ÇAIS/AU 1ᵉ (2, 3, 4) REGIMENT/SUISSE;* on the reverse: *VALEUR/ET DISCIPLINE/1ᵉ BATAILLON.* In the gold wreaths in each corner the regimental number. The dark blue pike was surmounted by a gilt Eagle.

The infantry battalion of the Prince of Neuchâtel: Raised by decree of May 11 1807. Alexander Berthier received the principality in March 1806, it having been taken from the King of Prussia. Until May 1812 the battalion served in Spain; it was then refitted in Besançon and sent to Russia. On August 25 it reached Smolensk and stayed there until October 15 (strength 483 men) then advanced and joined Imperial headquarters. 1,027 men marched off for Russia; in January 1813, 21 survivors returned to Königsberg.

Organisation, rank badges, etc, French. Shako with brass lozenge plate bearing the Imperial Eagle (some sources show crowned shields bearing the Eagle); above this the French cockade under the company pompom and plume; cords for parades; white chin scales. Short skirted 'Spencer' in a deep yellow with scarlet collar, cuffs, scalloped cuff flaps, lapels and turnbacks; yellow shoulder straps edged red; white buttons with the central inscription *'BATAILLON DE NEUCHÂTEL'* and peripheral inscription *'EMPIRE FRANÇAIS';* yellow five-pointed star on turnbacks. White belts and breeches. Below-knee black gaiters. **Grenadiers:** Bearskins for parades, otherwise as for French line with yellow grenades on turnbacks. **Voltigeurs:** Deep yellow cuff flaps; yellow hunting horns on turnbacks. **Drummers:** Company uniform; dark blue coats; red facings edged with the green and yellow Imperial livery lace; green and yellow lace bars on sleeves. Brass drums, dark blue hoops. **Sappers:** Bearskin with red cords and plume. On each upper sleeve red, crossed axes. White apron. Silver crossed axes and flaming grenade badges on bandoliers. Beards, axes. NCOs' shakos had silver top bands. **Officers:** Silver shako trim; silver gorget with gold eagle; silver portepée and epaulettes.

Artillery company: Red top band and pompon to shako; red cords. Dark blue Spencer, lapels*, cuff flaps* and turnbacks*; deep yellow collar and cuffs.

*Edged deep yellow.

Contemporary water colour of the 127th, 128th and 129th 'French' Line Infantry Regiments raised in the Hanseatic towns of Hamburg, Bremen and Lübeck and in the Duchy of Oldenburg. Dark blue coats, white lapels, waistcoats and breeches, white cuff flaps, red collars, cuffs and turnbacks, brass shako eagles. Usual French inter-company distinctions. The Voltigeur Corporal has yellow hunting horns in his turnbacks.

Grand Duchy of Frankfurt

One infantry regiment of two battalions; organisation, equipment, rank badges and inter-company distinctions as in the French army. Together with a regiment of Würzburgers it was part of the *Division Princiere* (34th Division), XI Corps. March out strength 1,710 all ranks; 209 survived to reach Danzig in 1813.

Uniform: French shako; white metal front plate bearing a crowned wheel; above this a red within white cockade, white loop and button; cords and plumes for parades. Dark blue coat and collar; red lapels*, pointed cuffs*, turnbacks* and pocket pip-

*Piped white.

ing; dark blue shoulder straps piped red. Dark blue waistcoat and breeches. White belts and gaiters (under the trousers). **Drummers:** Collar, lapels, cuffs and turnbacks edged with white lace having a red zig-zag along it. Same lace to trouser side seams and thigh knots. Brass drum; red and white striped hoops. **Officers:** Silver shako trim; pompon. Silver gorget with golden crest; silver epaulettes and portepée; silver and black sabre slings.

No flags were carried.

Grand Duchy of Frankfurt. Although this plate by Knötel is primarily dedicated to the 1st Battalion of Frankfurt's troops in Spain, it shows well the uniform also worn by the junior battalions in Russia in 1812. The shield-shaped shako plate and the officer's gorget bear the wheel badge of the city of Mainz. From left to right the figures are a Fusilier, Grenadier, Oberst (Colonel) and Grenadier drummer.

Grand Duchy of Hessen-Darmstadt

(4th Division, I Corps; 34th Division, XI Corps; 30th Light Cavalry Brigade, IX Corps.)

Uniform: Rank badges as for the French Army; cockade red within white.

Generals: As in the French Army with silver and red sash.

The Guard
Infantry

Leibgarde-Regiment (two battalions each of four musketeer companies): French shako; white metal front shield bearing a rampant lion; above this the cockade, with white loop and button; above this a pompon surmounted by a red tuft. The pompon was in the company colour (1 — white; 2 — black; 3 — blue; 4 — red; 5 — yellow over white; 6 — black over white; 7 — blue over white; 8 — red over white). Black plume for parades; white metal chinscales and lion's head bosses. Dark blue coat with red collar, lapels*, cuffs and turnbacks; dark blue cuff flaps*; dark blue, fringeless cloth epaulettes edged red; white buttons. Dark blue breeches. Short black gaiters edged red. White belts. NCOs had red plume tips and their epaulettes were edged white. **Drummers:** Red plumes and cords; red swallows nests. Brass drums with red and white striped hoops. **Officers:** As for the men except: bicorns; black plumes with red bases. Silver and red waist sash. Hussar-style boots trimmed silver.

Garde-Fusilier-Bataillon (from March 1 1812 part of the 'Provisional Light Infantry Regiment', 34th Division, XI Corps): As for Leibgarde-Regiment except: a hunting horn in the corners of the skirt turnbacks; facings scarlet; buttons white. Officers wore cavalry-style *cartouche* and curved sabres on black bandoliers worn crossed on the chest. All belts black.

Cavalry

Garde-Chevau-Légèrs: Black leather helmet; black crest and plume; brass fittings and crowned frontal badge 'L'. Bright green tunic; red collar with black frontal patches; black lapels and cuffs; red turnbacks; white buttons and lace decoration to collar, lapels, skirts and cuffs. Dark green overalls with red stripe. Black bandolier. Green shabraque; black vandyke edging; white piping and rear cypher 'L', under a crown; green round portmanteau edged red. **Trumpeters:** As for the men but no white lace button holes

*Piped white.

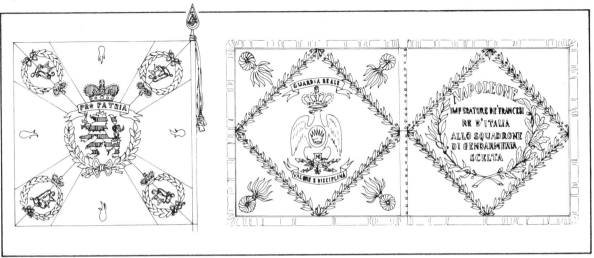

Above left *Grand Duchy of Hessen-Darmstadt, infantry flag. Red and white striped lion on blue ground, green wreaths, gold cyphers, crowns, pike tip and grenades, red and silver cords, black pike.* **Above right** *Kingdom of Italy, standard, Elite Gendarmes.*

on the lapels (which were edged in white lace). Brass trumpet; red and white cords. **Officers:** As for the men but red base to black plume; silver epaulettes; black and silver bandolier; red and silver portepée.

Line regiments

Infantry

Leib-Regiment (two battalions each of four musketeer companies) (4th Division, I Corps): As for Leibgarde except: black leather chinstrap edged with cloth in the facing colour (light blue). Turnbacks red.

Leib-Fusilier-Bataillon (from March 1 1812 part of the 'Provisional Light Infantry Regiment'): See Garde-Fusilier-Bataillon above.

Artillery

As for the line infantry except: pompon red. Collar, lapels and cuffs black piped red; turnbacks red; buttons yellow. **Trumpeters:** Lapels, collar and cuffs bordered white (within the red piping). Brass trumpet; red and white cords. **Drivers:** Black 'corsican' hat edged white with the rear brim only turned up; red pompon; white loop and button at top of brim. Blue single-breasted coat; black collar and cuffs; red turnbacks; white buttons, bandolier and breeches. Sabre in brown sheath. High, jacked boots.

Artillery equipment painted light blue.

Colours and standards

Leibgarde: Four *Leibfahnen:* white, in the centre a light blue disc bearing the rampant, red and white striped Hessian lion, crowned and holding a sword; around this disc green laurel wreaths tied with a red ribbon; above it a golden scroll bearing *PRO PATRIA*

under a crown; in each corner a crowned laurel wreath enclosing *LLX* (Landgraf Ludwig X) in gold; in the centre of each side a bursting silver grenade. White pike; gilt spearpoint tip bearing *LLX*; silver, red and blue cords and tassels.

Leib-Regiment: One white Leibfahne and three *Ordinarfahnen.* The Leibfahne: as above except that from each corner a red and black pile ran towards the centre; in the middle of each side a gold bursting grenade. Brown pike. The Ordinarfahnen: as above except black cloth, red corner piles and red bursting grenades. Brown pike. All flags returned safely.

Kingdom of Italy

(IV Corps. 27,397 Italians with 8,300 horses, 740 draught oxen, and 58 cannon and draught animals 1,000 men survived; all cannon and draught animals were lost).

Uniform: Rank badges, etc, as for the French army.

Generals: As in France but dark green coats with silver buttons and lace.

The Guard

(14th Division.) (Cockade green within red within white.)

Infantry

Grenadiers: As for the Grenadiers of the French Imperial Guard but dark green substituted for dark blue and the buttons and grenadier cap plate were white (the plate bore a grenade flanked by 'R' and 'I').

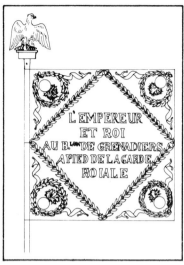

Kingdom of Italy, infantry colour.

Italian dragoons (Albrecht Adam).

Carabiniers: As for the Chasseurs à Pied of the French Imperial Guard but with dark green coats and white buttons. **Vélite Grenadiers:** As for the Carabiniers but white uniform; dark green facings and yellow buttons. **Vélite Carabiniers:** As for Vélite Grenadiers but pointed lapels and cuffs. **Chasseurs à Pied:** French shakos; white top band, eagle plate and cords. Dark green coats and lapels; red collar and cuffs; white piping; yellow buttons; green epaulettes with red half moons and fringes.

Cavalry

Guards of Honour: Brass helmet with combe in the form of an eagle; black crest; white plume; white metal 'turban' and chinscales; black peaks; front badge a crowned 'N'. Dark green coat (as for Dragoons of the French Imperial Guard); company facings; silver lace and buttons. White belts, breeches and gauntlets. Dark green horse furniture edged white; white crown in the rear corners; black harness. Sabre in steel sheath. High, jacked boots. Facings as for company as follows: **1st** (*Milan*): pink; **2nd** (*Bologna*): yellow; **3rd** (*Brescia*): buff; **4th** (*Romagna*): scarlet: **5th** (*Venice*): orange. **Dragoons of the Guard:** Completely as for the Dragoons of the French Imperial Guard but with white buttons and aiguilette.

Line regiments

Infantry

(15th Infantry Division, IV Corps.) French shako; rhombic plate in the button colour. White uniforms with facings as follows: **2nd Regiment:** a (collar) white**; b (lapels) red*; c (cuffs) white**; d (cuff flaps) red*; e (turnbacks) white**; f (buttons) yellow; g (shoulder strap piping) red. **3rd:** a, b, c, d, e red*; f yellow; g red. **Voltigeurs:** As above but dark green coats. **Grenadiers:** Bearskins with brass plate bearing a grenade for parades; otherwise shakos and as for Fusiliers.

Light infantry

As for line infantry but dark green coats, cuff flaps and breeches; yellow buttons. Carabiniers had bearskin caps and red epaulettes and sabre knots. **1st Regiment:** a, c red; e white**; h (waistcoat) dark green. **3rd:** a, c, e, h white.

Dalmatian Regiment: As for the light infantry; brass rhombic shako plate (bearing 'RDI' under the Italian crown). Dark green coat; red facings; yellow buttons.

Cavalry

Dragoni Regina: As for French line dragoon regiments with green plume and pink a, b, c, e and piping. **Chasseurs à cheval:** Single-breasted, dark green tunics and Hungarian breeches; white buttons and lace bars across the chest. White lace thigh knots and side stripes; white belts. **2nd Regiment:** Plain French shako with only the Italian cockade at the top front surmounted by a dark green plume with red tip; a, c and e red. **3rd Regiment:** Black fur colpack with cockade and red plume at top front; a, c and e red.

*Piped white.
**Piped red.

Artillery

Foot artillery: Peakless shako with red cords and plumes and brass, crossed-cannon barrels badge. Dark green coats and waistcoats; dark green a**, b**, c**, e** and shoulder straps; red d; white f; red grenades in turnbacks. Dark green breeches. Black gaiters. White belts. **Drivers:** As for artillery but single-breasted tunics.

Horse artillery: Black czapka; red plume; cockade; gold chinscales. Dark green dolman; yellow buttons; red collar, pointed cuffs and lace. Dark green breeches; red thigh knots, side stripes and hussar boot trim. White belts. Sabre in black and gold sheath. **Drivers:** As for artillery but dark green collar and cuffs piped red.

Engineers: As for foot artillery but French shakos. Red epaulettes; black, pointed cuffs edged red.

Colours and standards

Infantry colours: As for French 1804 pattern: central white lozenge; top pike and bottom fly corners dark green, opposite corners red; embroidery gold. Example: inscriptions (obverse): *L'EMPEREUR/ET ROI/AU B^{LON} DE GRENADIERS/A PIED DE LA GARDE/ROIALE*; (reverse): *GARDE ROIALE/VAL-*

Above *Before Borodino, September 6. Italian dragoon (lying) and artilleryman (seated)* (Albrecht Adam).

Below *Italian or French dragoons in a straw-hutted bivouac. The relatively good condition of the horses indicates that this is early in the campaign* (Albrecht Adam).

EUR/ET DISCIPLINE. Flaming grenades within the corner wreaths. Brown pike surmounted by a golden eagle as for the French model but with the head turned in the opposite direction.

Cavalry standards: As above but smaller (56 cm square) and fringed in gold.

Duchies of Mecklenburg-Schwerin and Mecklenburg- Strelitz

(Mecklenburg-Schwerin, 5th Division, I Corps.) March-out strength, March 1812 — 1,700 men; strength July 25 — 1,363; September 10 — 843 (was part of Wilna garrison from July 23-September 21; strength October 10 — 700; November 6 — 300; December 9 — 40; 41 reinforcements arrived, thus up to 81; December 21 — 35 men.

Uniform: Rank badges and inter-company distinctions as in the French army. Cockade yellow within blue within red.

Generals: As in the French army but golden waist sash mixed with red and blue.

Infantry

Contingents-Regiment (also known as the 7th Rheinbund-Regiment): French shako; brass chinscales and front badge (reversed 'FF' — Friedrich Franz); company pompon (white for the four musketeer companies) and cords. Dark blue double-breasted coat; red collar, cuffs, turnbacks; dark blue cuff flaps and shoulder straps; white buttons. White belts and trousers or grey trousers with red side stripe. Short black gaiters. **NCOs:** Blue tips to pompons and to white plumes; red, white and blue mixed shako cords. **Drummers:** Red plumes and cords. Brass drum; red, yellow and blue striped hoops. **Pioneers:** Bearskin caps; red plumes. Brass crossed axe badge on pouch. Beards. **Officers:** Silver top band to shako;

Below left *Sleeve of a Corporal's tunic, Mecklenburg-Schwerin Garde Grenadiere. Dark blue, red cuffs and piping, white buttons and lace. The rank stripes are edged red. Note the holes in the sleeve at elbow level — wounds? (Exhibit, Museum für Deutsche Geschichte, Berlin).* **Below right** *Italian Guard (left and right) with unidentified figure (captured cossack?) (Albrecht Adam).*

Above left *Duchy of Mecklenburg-Schwerin, infantry flag. 1st Battalion — white cloth; 2nd — dark blue. Gold borders and tip, white pike.*
Above right *Kingdom of Naples, early pattern infantry colours. White lozenge, crimson and black corners, gold lettering, wreaths, numbers and borders. Royal crest has a gold crown and blue mantle with white and purple edges.*

silver peak edging and chinscales; gold sunburst plate with ducal crest. Junior officers had silver pompon and black plume, field officers gold pompon and white plume. Turnback badges according to company in silver as on the men's pouches. Sash as for Generals; similar coloured portepée. **Grenadiers:** Pouch badge: brass grenade (NCOs' plumes and pompon tips white). **Voltigeurs:** Pouch badge: brass hunting horn (NCOs' plumes and pompon tips white).

Artillery

As for infantry (Fusiliers) but black facings and plumes.
(Mecklenburg-Strelitz, Infanterie-Bataillon (four companies) (3rd Division, I Corps).)

Uniform: As for Mecklenburg-Schwerin Contingents-Regiment except as under. Yellow buttons. Officers had dark blue plumes with red base; gold oak leaf top band to shako; gold front plate of Strelitz crest with supporters. Gold epaulettes. Sabre on waistbelt. Gold, yellow and blue waist sash with oval gold buckle. Grey breeches. This contingent formed the 3rd Battalion of the 7th Rheinbund-Regiment.

For the Russian campaign this unit was attached to the 127ᵉ de Ligne (a regiment raised in Hamburg) as part of the 3rd Division of Davout's I Corps. The 1st and 2nd Companies went to Moscow, the 3rd and 4th stayed in Widsy, Lithuania.

Colours

The Mecklenburg-Strelitz battalion carried no flag. The 1st Battalion of the Contingents-Regiment carried a white flag: in the centre the crowned arms of Mecklenburg on an oval shield, supported by a black ox and a gold griffon and resting on a trophy of arms; on the oval shield appeared the crests of Mecklenburg, Rostock, Schwerin (town), Schwerin (county), Ratzeburg, Stargard and Werle; the oval shield was surrounded by gold palm and laurel leaves and the flag was edged with gold laurel leaves; in each corner was the crowned cypher (reversed 'FF'). Staff white; gilt tip bearing the crowned 'FF' within a spearpoint. The flag of the 2nd Battalion was of the same design but dark blue. Both flags went to Russia and returned safely.

Kingdom of Naples

The Neapolitan contingent formed the 33rd Division under General Francesci (later General Destrées) in Marshall Augereau's XI or Reserve Corps. The Division had 6,000 men.

Uniform: Cockade carmine within white; rank badges and inter-company distinctions French; NCOs' sabre knots carmine and white.

Generals: As in France.

The Guard

Infantry

Vélites à Pied: Bearskins (no front plate); green cords and plume (1st Regiment with a red tip); carmine top patch with gold grenade. White coats, belts, breeches; carmine a**, b**, c**, d** and e; gold but-

**Piped white.

tons and gold lace bars to collar (2), lapels (7) and pointed cuffs (3); carmine epaulettes. **Officers:** White plumes; gold cords and epaulettes; gold gorget, sword knot and trim to hussar pattern boots. **Drummers:** Carmine and white lace edging to facings and to carmine swallows nests; seven such lace chevrons (point up) on each sleeve and similar edging down sleeve seams. Brass drum; carmine and white dog-toothed hoops. **Voltigeurs:** As for Vélite but buff shakos with green pompons and cords; buff collars.

Marines of the Guard: French shako with crowned, brass, shield-shaped front plate; cockade; red pompon and cords; brass chin scales. Dark blue coat and breeches. Black, below-knee gaiters. Red a*, b*, c* and d; red epaulettes with white half moons; gold g. Buff belts edged white. **Drummers:** Lace, etc, as above.

Cavalry

Gardes d'Honneur (*Guardia d'Onore*): Polish lancer costume; carmine top to black czapka; white plumes, cords; gold sunburst plate bearing a crowned 'JN'. White kurtka; a (collar*), b (cuffs*), c (lapels*), d (turnbacks) and e (piping) carmine; f (shoulder straps) white piped carmine; g (buttons) silver; h (breeches) carmine with double white side stripes. Black gauntlets. White belts. Sabres in steel sheaths. j (saddle furniture) carmine edged white with white crowned corner cypher 'JN'. **Trumpeters:** As above except: carmine base to plume. Kurtka in reversed colours and carmine and white striped lace edging to collar (top and front) and cuffs (top and back). **Officers:** As for the men but silver epaulettes and aiguilette; gold bandolier edged silver.

Vélites à Cheval: Shako with gold top band; chin-scales; sunburst plate with crowned 'JN'; gold cords; white plume. Kurtka in dark blue and of the same design as for *Guardia d'Onore* but with yellow facings, buttons and lace decoration. Dark blue h with double yellow side stripes. Dark blue j with yellow edging and cypher. **Trumpeters:** Kurtka is reversed colours with lace as for *Guardia d'Onore*. **Officers:** As for the men but gold epaulettes and aiguilette; gold bandolier edged dark blue.

Line regiments

Infantry

French shako; brass, shield-shaped plate, bearing 'JN' as for Marines; pompon and cockade but no cords. White coat, shoulder straps, belts and breeches; yellow buttons. Facings on a** b**, c**, d**, scalloped cuff flaps** and e as shown below. Black, below-knee gaiters.

*Lace decoration in the button colour.
**Piped white.

5th Regiment *Calabria*: dark green; **6th** *Napoli*: orange; **7th** *Africa*: yellow (this regiment was largely composed of negroes.) **Grenadiers:** Bearskins; red cords, plume, top patch and epaulettes. **Drummers:** Lace, etc, as above. **Musicians:** Single-breasted coats in reversed colours with drummers' lace bars across chest and white plume with red base. **Pioneers:** Grenadier distinctions; red crossed axes under a flaming grenade on both upper arms. White aprons. Axes with brown hafts. Beards.

Artillery

Horse artillery: Black colpack with red bag edged and tasseled yellow; red pompon and plume. Dark blue dolman and breeches with yellow lace and buttons; dark blue and red sash. **Officers:** As above except gold pompon; white plume; gold decoration (according to rank) to cuffs and thighs and to collar. **Trumpeters:** As above except red dolman and breeches; dark blue collar, cuffs and breeches decoration. Carmine and white striped lace to collar and cuffs; white over red plume.

Colours and standards

Initially the pale blue pikes were given a plain steel lance tip but by 1812 this was replaced by a prancing bronze horse on a Corinthian column. The size and design of colours and standards was very similar to the French 1804 pattern but with the unit designations in Italian: *GIUSEPPE/NAPOLEONE/RE DELLE DVE SICILIE/AL-ᵐᵒ REGGIMENTO/D'INFAN-TERIA/LEGGERA (DI LINEA* or *CACCIATORI A CAVALLO)*. By 1812 this early designation had, of course, changed to *JOACHIM/MURAT/etc.*

The central lozenge was white and opposing pairs of corners were black and purple, black being in the top pike corner. Embroidery and fringes were in the regimental button colour. Cravattes were attached to the pike head; they were light blue, with silver fringed ends bearing in silver a crowned 'G' (by 1812, 'J') above two rows of purple and silver dicing. They reached about one third of the way down the flag. On the reverse of the colour, the central badge was the Neapolitan crest on a blue and ermine crowned mantle, edged in a double row of purple and silver dicing. In the heart shield of the crest was the golden Imperial eagle on a blue ground.

Rheinbund regiments

4th Rheinbund-Regiment

(Part of the 'Division Princiere', later in 34th Division, XI Corps.) Composed as follows: Sachsen-Gotha-Altenburg: eight companies (1,100 men); Sachsen-

Coburg-Saalfeld: two companies (400 men); Sachsen-Meiningen: two companies (300 men). These individual contingents were equally divided between the two battalions.

Uniform (same for all three contingents): Rank badges and inter-company distinctions French. French shako with crowned, oval brass plate within laurels bearing the ducal Saxon crest; company pompon; cords and plumes; black within yellow cockade. Royal blue coat and cuff flaps; red collar, lapels, cuffs, turnbacks (and piping to Fusiliers' blue shoulder straps); yellow buttons. White belts, waistcoat and breeches. Below-knee black gaiters. Royal blue breeches with a red side stripe were also worn. The coat was in the Prussian style. **Drummers:** Collar, lapels and cuffs edged yellow; red swallows nests edged yellow. Brass drum with red and white triangles to hoops. **Officers:** Gold shako trim, cords, epaulettes and portepée. White gauntlets. Riding boots.

Sachsen-Weimar: One battalion (800 men) attached to the 4th Rheinbund-Regiment as a light battalion. Rank badges, etc, as in the French Army. Shako with German-style brass hunting horn under black within yellow cockade; yellow pompon; white cords; yellow chinscales. Dark green, Prussian-style coat with two rows of yellow buttons; green collar, cuffs and cuff flaps; yellow collar patches and turnbacks. Black belts. Grey breeches. Black, below-knee gaiters. White trousers (over the gaiters) were also worn.

No flags were carried.

5th Rheinbund-Regiment

Part of the 'Division Princiere', later 34th Division, XI Corps.)

1st Battalion: Composed of the contingents of Anhalt-Bernburg, Anhalt-Dessau and Anhalt-Köthen (800 men in all). Rank badges, etc, as in French Army. French shako with white rhombic plate bearing the arms of Anhalt; green cockade; company pompon; cords and plumes. Dark green single-breasted coat and cuffs; pink collar, shoulder straps (Fusiliers), turnbacks and piping to coat front; white buttons. Grey breeches. Black, below-knee gaiters. Black belts. **Officers:** Silver shako trim, epaulettes and portepée. Sword on black bandolier. Dark green coat turnbacks and no piping to coat.

Flags: One flag, white, on both sides the Anhalt crest (red half-eagle and black, yellow and green Saxon stripes, within a red surround under a crown; across the shield a white ribbon bearing *ANHALT*. Silver spear point tip bearing the same badge, black pike. This flag was brought safely back from Russia.

2nd Battalion: Composed of the contingents of the principalities of Lippe-Detmold (500 men) and Schaumburg-Lippe (150 men). Rank badges, etc, French. French shako with white rhombic plate bearing a crowned, eight-pointed star under a white within green cockade; white chinscales; company pompon; cords and plumes. White coat, white lapels*, shoulder straps* and cuff flaps*; dark green

*Piped dark green.

Below left *5th Rheinbund Regiment, Anhalt contingent. White cloth, red eagle and surround, black and yellow bars, green diagonal, gilt tip and crown.* **Below right** *5th Rheinbund Regiment, 'Lippe' Battalion. White cloth, gold tip, fringes and inscription. The crests are: (top row, left to right) Schwalenberg, Ameide, Lippe and Sternberg; (bottom row, left to right) Saxony, Zerbst, Anhalt and Bernburg.*

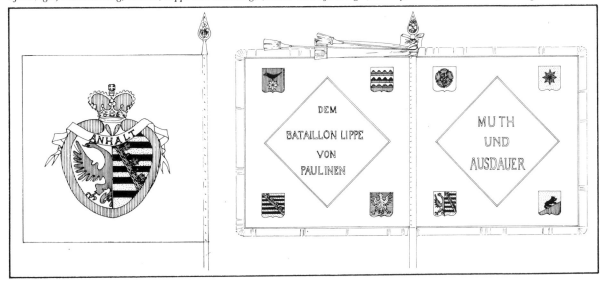

collar, cuffs, turnbacks and piping. White buttons, breeches and belts. Short black gaiters. **Drummers:** As above except a green bar across the top of the sleeves. Brass drum; green and white striped hoops. **Pioneers:** Bearskins; grenadier badges; buff apron and gauntlets; beards. **Officers:** Silver shako trim, epaulettes and portepée; gold gorget with silver crest. Sword on white bandolier with oval gold plate bearing a silver hunting horn. Riding boots.

Flags: One flag, pale yellow silk, fringed gold. In the centre of each side a gold edged lozenge; obverse a badge in each corner; top fly-Schwalenberg, top staff Ameide; bottom fly — Saxony, bottom staff — Zerbst; in the central lozenge *DEM/BATAILLON LIPPE/VON/PAULINEN*; Reverse: top fly — Lippe, top staff — Sternberg; bottom fly — Anhalt, bottom staff — Bernburg; in the central lozenge *MUTH/UND/AUSDAUER*. Gold spearpoint tip enclosed reversed 'L's. White cravatte with gold fringes; gold cords and tassels; brown pike. The flag was brought back safely out of Russia.

6th Rheinbund-Regiment

(Part of the 'Division Princiere', later 34th Division, XI Corps.)

1st Battalion: Composed of the contingents of Schwarzburg-Rudolstadt (331 men) and Schwarzburg-Sondershausen (319 men). Rank badges, etc, French. French shako with brass front plate (rhombic with 'FSR' under a crown for Rudolstadt; octagonal with 'FSS' under a crown for Sondershausen); blue within white cockade; company cords; pompons and plume; brass chinscales. Dark green double-breasted, Prussian-style coats with green shoulder straps (Fusiliers) and green cuff flaps for Sondershausen, plain red cuffs for Rudolstadt; red collar and turnbacks; yellow buttons. Black belts. Grey breeches. Black, below-knee gaiters. **Officers:** Gold shako trim and cords. Gold epaulettes; silver and crimson portepée; dark green turnbacks. Grey breeches with narrow red side stripe. Gilt-hilted sabre in steel sheath on gold slings. Gold trim and tassel to hussar-style boots.

2nd Battalion: 400 men of the principality of Waldeck; 450 men of the principalities of Reuss-Gera, Reuss-Greiz, Reuss-Ebersdorf, Reuss-Lobenstein and Reuss-Schleiz. Rank badges, etc, French.

Waldeck: French shako; brass chinscales and rhombic plate bearing the Waldeck crest; black within yellow within red cockade; company cords; pompon and plume. White coat and belts; dark blue collar, lapels, cuffs, turnbacks and shoulder straps; yellow buttons. Grey breeches. Black, below-knee gaiters. Brass pouch badges: a crowned, eight-pointed star between the letters 'F' and 'W'. **Officers:** Gold shako

trim and cords; gold epaulettes and portepée. Sword on white slings.

Reuss: French shako with oval brass plate bearing an 'R'; other details as for Waldeck. White coat, single-breasted; white shoulder straps and belts; yellow buttons; light blue collar, cuffs and turnbacks. Light blue Hungarian breeches with black, yellow and red mixed lace decoration to thighs and side seams. Short black gaiters. **Officers:** Gold shako trim; gold epaulettes and portepée. Gilt-hilted sabre in black and gold sheath on white bandolier. Hussar boots with gold trim and tassel.

No flags were carried.

Kingdom of Saxony
(VII Corps)

Uniform: Badges of rank and inter-company distinctions as in the French Army. Officers had black bases to their plumes; NCOs had black tips and gold top bands to shakos.

Generals: As for French Generals but the pattern of the gold embroidery was slightly different. Saxon cockade white. White waistcoat and breeches for everyday wear, red for parades. Silver and crimson waist sash.

Shako of a Sergeant of Fusiliers, Saxon infantry. Gold top band, shield and chinscales, white cord. The cockade is missing (Exhibit, Museum für Deutsche Geschichte, Berlin).

Above left *Kingdom of Saxony, infantry flag Regiment 'Von Low'. Black border with green oak leaves, brown acorns and white diamonds. White cloth, gold cypher, shield edge and tip, 'steel' grenades, red and yellow flames. Reverse — as for cavalry standard but with white corner shields bearing 'RS' in black. Lost in Russia.* **Above right** *Kingdom of Saxony, Garde du Corps standard. White cloth, gold and blue borders and fringes, gold embroidery and pike tip, red pike. Both this and the standard of the 'Zastrow' Kürassiers were lost in Russia.*

The Guard

Cavalry

Garde du Corps: Brass helmet with combe; sealskin turban; black crest; white plume. Buff *kollet* (short tunic); a (collar) blue; b (cuffs) blue; c (lapels) none; d (turnbacks) blue; e (buttons) yellow; f (lace) blue, red and yellow; brass shoulder scales; g (breeches) and belts white. High jacked boots. **Trumpeters:** As above except red crests and plumes. Red kollets; blue facings. Silver trumpet with blue and white cords and tassels.

Line regiments

Infantry

French shako with crowned front shield in brass bearing 'FA' (Friedrich August); white cords, plume, cockade. White coat, waistcoat, breeches and belts. Short black gaiters. Regiments were distinguished by their facing colours (collars, cuffs, lapels, turnbacks and shoulder strap piping) and their buttons as follows: *König:* ponceau, yellow. *Vacant von Niesemeuschel:* ponceau, white. *Prinz Anton:* dark blue, yellow. *Von Low:* dark blue, white. *Prinz Friedrich August:* dark green, yellow. *Prinz Clemens:* dark green, white. **Drummers:** Red plumes and cords. A bar of lace (usually in the facing and button colour) across the top of each sleeve. Brass drum; drum hoops in the facing colour and white. **NCOs:** Gold top band to shako. Silver and crimson sabre knot. **Officers:**

Elaborate gold top band to shako (clover leaf design); silver shako cords. Gold gorgets with silver crest; epaulettes in the button colour; long coat tails. Riding boots. Swords with silver and crimson portepée.

Light infantry (1st and 2nd Regiments): As above except: green cords and plumes. Dark green coats; black facings (dark green lapels) edged red; yellow buttons with the regimental number. Grey breeches with red side stripe. Black belts. **Officers:** No gorgets. Sabre on black slings. Gold-trimmed hussar boots.

Cavalry

Kürassier-Regiment *vacant von Zastrow:* As for the Garde du Corps except: white coats; yellow a, b and d; white, black and yellow f. Black *Kürass* (front plate only) with yellow trim. **Trumpeters:** As for Garde du Corps but yellow coats faced white, edged in regimental lace. White, yellow and black trumpet cords. Shabraque yellow edged in regimental lace.

Chevaux-légèrs (sic): French shakos as for the infantry; white cords and plumes. Red coats with facings on collar, cuffs, lapels and turnbacks as follows; all buttons yellow: *Prinz Albrecht:* dark green. *Prinz Johann:* black. *von Polenz:* light blue. Red shabraques edged in the facing colour, laced yellow. **Trumpeters:** Reversed colours. Red shakos with gold top band and red plume. Brass trumpets with cords as follows: *von Polenz* and *Prinz Albrecht:* red and white. *Prinz Johann:* red and white. Trumpeters of *Prinz Johann:* buff coats faced red.

Text continued on page 78.

Captions to colour plates 12-22

12 French 'Aigle-Garde', Garde Nationale. *This plate is of extreme interest as it shows many details of the Eagle's escort. The Eagle is shown without its colour — apparently a frequent occurrence as the painted silken emblems were very fragile and soon wore out. The detail of the Eagle bandolier's embroidery is of interest, as are the halberds and pennants carried by the two flanking escorts (both long-serving Sergeants!). The inscription on the pennants seems to be 'NAPOLEON' and both escorts carry a brace of pistols in the large holsters slung on their left chests* (Suhr).

13 French Line dragoons (7th Regiment) and chevaulégèrs. *Three finely detailed officers (from left to right): dragoon in surtout; dragoon in service dress (the red base to the white plume is unusual); and chevauléger in surtout (4th Regiment)* (Suhr).

14 French foreign troops. Officer and trumpeter, 1st Lancers of the Vistula Legion. *A plate from Fieffe's book showing a regiment which became the 7th Chevaulégèrs Lanciers of the French line cavalry. Note that the trumpeter has silver lace around his collar and lapels. The cut of the officer's shabraque is most suspect; it should be much longer in the rear points.*

15 French foreign troops. The Regiment 'Joseph Napoleon' and the 'Bataillon Septinsulaire'. *The red paint on the Grenadier of the Regiment 'Joseph Napoleon' (also known as the 'Regimental Espagnol') has faded since being painted in 1854 to the dark brown seen here on this plate from Fieffe's book. The 'Bataillon Septinsulaire' wore French Light infantry style uniform and the gaiters, here shown white, should be black. The battalion did not serve in Russia.*

16 Grand Duchy of Hessen-Darmstadt. *Left to right: trooper, Chevauxlégèrs; the red portion of his collar appears very dark; the badge on front of the helmet is a crowned 'L' in brass (Ludwig — the Grand Duke); the cuff flap buttons have been omitted by the artist; Fusilier, Leibregiment (light blue facings); Fusilier, Leibgarderegiment (red facings). The company pompon should have been in reversed colours, ie, red over white, and the artist has omitted the white metal shako shields bearing the rampant Hessian lion. The other figure in the background appears to be from one of the same two infantry regiments* (Augsburger Bilder).

17 French Foreign Troops. Ex-Dutch regiments of the Imperial Guard. *In 1810 Napoleon added the Kingdom of Holland and much of north Germany, including parts of Berg, Westfalia and the Hanseatic towns of Hamburg, Bremen and Lübeck, to Metropolitan France. Dutch units became the famous 2nd (Red) Lancers and the 2nd Grenadiers of the Imperial Guard on September 13 1810. Although the style of this plate from Eugene Fieffe's book* Geschichte der Fremdtruppen im Dienste Frankreich *is unmistakably post-Napoleonic, the basic details are fairly accurate. A point to note is that the czapka should be heavier and possibly slightly taller. The 2nd Grenadiers became the 3rd Grenadiers on May 18 1811, when a newly raised French 2nd Regiment ousted them.*

18 The Portuguese Legion. *This formation of infantry and cavalry was raised for French service from Portuguese prisoners after the 1808 campaign. Napoleon's famous 'requisition system' is doubtless to blame for the tatty state of the uniforms shown here! From left to right: Chasseur à Cheval (mounted); Grenadier (rear view); Fusilier; Voltigeur (?) — note cap badge but absence of epaulettes, cords and plume; Voltigeur Corporal (seated, foreground); officer, élite company, Chasseurs à Cheval (mounted in colpack); Fusilier officer; Chasseur à Cheval (mounted)* (Augsburger Bilder).

19 Kingdom of Italy, Sergeant Sapper of Line infantry, officer of Light infantry in surtout. *This plate was painted from life by the Suhrs in Hamburg and such minor details as the red grenades in the top corners of the Sapper's apron, the red backing to the brass grenade and crossed axes belt badge and the silver embroidery to the collar of the officer's surtout are thus all the more interesting. The pigtail dates the plate to 1806-07 but the uniforms shown here were valid for 1812.*

20 Kingdom of Italy, infantry. *This group is taken from a large plate by Enrico Adam entitled* L'Infanteria Del Regno D'Italia *and published in Vienna and Milan. Close examination of the plate only increases the initial, confusing impression, as the minute details clearly show the eagles on the headwear facing both ways on various figures! The mystery is compounded by the fact that the facings and pipings on the various infantry regiments do not correspond to the tables given for this army either by Knotel in his* Uniformkunde *or by Lienert and Humbert. The figures (foreground, left to right): officer and Grenadier of the Line infantry in undress frock coats; Grenadier of Line infantry (rear view); Carabinier, 1st Light Infantry Regiment; two Grenadiers of the Line infantry. In the background are Vélite Grenadiers of the Royal Guard and, behind them, horse and foot artillery and Élite Gendarmes.*

21 Kingdom of Italy, Prince Eugène, Viceroy. *Adam has left us a portrait of this competent warrior, shown here with a surprisingly modern moustache. On his left (mounted, rear view) is an Italian General; in front of the Viceroy (rear view) an officer of the Vélite-Grenadiers of the Royal Guard (note gold buttons bearing an eagle); to the right foreground (left to right): officer, Vélite Carabiniers; officer, Grenadiers of the Line; officer, Fusiliers of the Line; officer, Grenadiers of the Guard (green collar and lapels); officer, foot artillery of the Guard. From the plate* L'Infanteria Del Regno D'Italia *by Enrico Adam.*

22 Duchies of Mecklenburg-Schwerin and Mecklenburg-Strelitz. *Left to right: Grenadier, Schwerin infantry regiment. Note the Prussian-style double-breasted coat and the French badges; officer, Schwerin artillery — the uniform differed from the infantry mainly in the black facings and silver front plate to shako; officer, Strelitz infantry battalion — this man's shako had gold oak leaf decoration to the top and the front plate is the great crest of the Duchy; apart from this and the gold buttons and epaulettes, the uniform was as for the Schwerin infantry regiment* (Knötel).

12 *Above* French 'Aigle-Garde', Garde Nationale.

13 *Above* French Line dragoons (7th Regiment) and Chevaulégèrs.

14 *Below* French foreign troops — officer and trumpeter, 1st Lancers of the Vistula Legion.

15 *Below* French foreign troops — the Regiment 'Joseph Napoleon' and the 'Bataillon Septinsulaire'.

16 *Above* Grand Duchy of Hessen-Darmstadt.

17 *Above left* French foreign troops — ex-Dutch regiments of the Imperial Guard.

18 *Left* The Portuguese Legion.

19 *Right* Kingdom of Italy, Sergeant Sapper of Line infantry and officer of Light infantry in surtout.

20 *Far right* Kingdom of Italy, infantry.

21 *Above* Prince Eugène, Viceroy of the Kingdom of Italy. **22** *Below left* Duchies of Mecklenburg-Schwerin and Mecklenburg-Strelitz. **23** *Below right* 5th Rheinbund Regiment.

24 *Above* The contingents of Schwarzburg and Reuss.

25 *Above* Kingdom of Saxony, trooper, Prinz Clemens Chevauxlégèrs.

26 *Below* Kingdom of Saxony, officer, Garde du Corps.

27 *Below* Kingdom of Saxony, officer of hussars, parade dress.

Uniforms and colours

28 *Far left* Kingdom of Saxony, drummer of Fusiliers, infantry regiment 'Prinz Friedrich August'. **29** *Left* Kingdom of Saxony, officer, Light infantry. **30** *Right* Kingdom of Saxony, sergeant, horse artillery.

31 *Below* Grand Duchy of Warsaw, Voltigeur and Grenadier, 12th Infantry Regiment. **32** *Below right* Grand Duchy of Warsaw, Legion of the Vistula.

33 *Above* Grand Duchy of Warsaw, Line infantry.

35 *Below* Grand Duchy of Warsaw, 9th Uhlans.

34 *Above* Grand Duchy of Warsaw, officers of hussars.
36 *Below* Kingdom of Westfalia, officer, horse artillery of the Guard.

Captions to colour plates 23-36

23 5th Rheinbund Regiment. *Left to right: officer and Fusilier, 1st Battalion. This unit was made up of the contingents of Bernburg, Dessau and Köthen and the survivors of the Spanish wars 1808-1811 were brought home to act as the cadre for a new regiment destined to be destroyed in Russia. Some sources show a pink piping down the front of the jacket; Fusilier, 2nd Battalion (Lippe-Detmold and Schaumburg-Lippe), the dark green facings and piping are difficult to distinguish (Knötel).*

24 The contingents of Schwarzburg and Reuss. *Left to right: Fusilier and officer, Schwarzburg; officer and Sergeant, Reuss. The latter figure appears to be wearing a grey coat; it should in fact be white. The shako plate on the Schwarzburg Fusilier should be a rhombus (Augsburger Bilder).*

25 Kingdom of Saxony, trooper, Prinz Clemens Chevaux-légèrs. *This man is shown on outpost duty and the plate illustrates the use of the first strap on the sabre of a cavalryman. He wears grey overalls and the light green of the facings has faded almost to yellow on this Sauerweid plate. The cropped horse tail was referred to as 'the English style'.*

26 Kingdom of Saxony, officer, Garde du Corps. *This man is a Rittmeister (Captain) and officer status is shown by the gold oak leaf wreath around the helmet, the black base to the plume, the gold epaulettes, bandolier, waistbelt and edging to facings and the silver and crimson portepée. This regiment distinguished itself at the capture of the great redoubt at Borodino, a fact not popular with Napoleon who would have preferred a French regiment to have had this honour (Alexander Sauerweid).*

27 Kingdom of Saxony, officer of hussars, parade dress. *A fine plate by Alexander Sauerweid, clearly showing all details of both uniform and harness. The silver, inverted clover leaf braid to the shako top was common to all Saxon officers. Rank is indicated by the silver decoration above cuffs and on the thigh fronts. The Saxon hussar horses came wild, in herds, from southern Poland and were difficult to handle.*

28 Kingdom of Saxony, Drummer of Fusiliers, Infantry Regiment 'Prinz Friedrich August'. *The plumes and cords, together with the white trousers over the gaiters, and the pack and rolled greatcoat suggest 'battle dress', that is to say, the uniform worn by Napoleon's troops when actually going into action in a set piece battle. The detail of the drummers' braid at the shoulder — white, edged in the facing colour and with a row of black and yellow diamonds along the centre — is particularly interesting.*

29 Kingdom of Saxony, officer, Light infantry. *The silver shako cords, green plume and elaborately decorated dark green breeches indicate parade dress; on the march an oilskin cover would hide the gold trim on the shako and grey breeches and plain boots would be worn. The sabre was carried by most Light infantry officers to establish a link with the speed and dash of the Light cavalry whose role they filled for the infantry.*

30 Kingdom of Saxony, Sergeant of Horse Artillery. *Badges of rank are the gold shako top bands, the gold bars over the cuffs and the crimson and silver tassel (not clearly shown here) on the sabre first strap. The white breeches, the red plume and cords suggest parade dress (Sauerweid).*

31 Grand Duchy of Warsaw, Legion of the Vistula. *This unfinished plate could cause utter confusion among uniform specialists unless its defects are known! The anonymous artist had not coloured the Grenadier's (central figure) epaulettes red. The Grenadier officer (left) wears French style silver epaulettes and portepée and the Voltigeur (right) should have a green sabre knot. The Vistula Legion was one of Napoleon's favourite formations and often closely associated with the Imperial Guard.*

32 Grand Duchy of Warsaw, Voltigeur and Grenadier, 12th Infantry Regiment. *This plate is interesting for the deviations it shows from the regulations: the Grenadier's bearskin without a peak or front plate (Bakrynowski Collection).*

33 Grandy Duchy of Warsaw, Line infantry. *From left to right: Voltigeur, marching order with black oilskin foul weather cover to czapka; Fusilier officer, marching order; Fusilier private, marching order with foul weather cover to czapka. Note the white shoulder straps and cuff flaps (possibly the artist's omission as they should be blue) and the lack of a sabre (Frauendorf).*

34 Grand Duchy of Warsaw, Officers of Hussars. *Left — officer, 10th Hussars, parade dress (rear view); right — officer, 13th Hussars, undress uniform (Bakrynowski Collection).*

35 Grand Duchy of Warsaw, 9th Uhlans. *This informative plate shows interesting aspects of the uniform of an arm of the cavalry which, originating in Poland, was avidly copied in almost all other European armies. From left to right: mounted officer, centre companies, rear view in Kurtka (parade and service dress); officer in undress uniform (stable cap, frock coat, embroidered waistcoat and dashing breeches and boots!); trooper, centre companies, drill order with pennant wrapped around lance and in a black cover; trooper, élite company, in Kurtka and colpack. Some sources give the cuff piping for this regiment as white and not red as shown here. A Polish plate.*

36 Kingdom of Westfalia, officer, Horse Artillery of the Guard. *The similarity between Westfalian uniforms and those of equivalent arms of the French army is, in some cases, striking. This officer is in parade dress (Sauerweid).*

Uhlans *Prinz Clemens*: As for Chevaux-légèrs but facings light green. Lances with red shafts, pennants varying according to squadron: crimson over white, red over white, green over white, white with a red triangle against the pike. **Trumpeters:** As for Chevau-légèrs. Brass trumpets, red and blue cords. Red shabraque edged light green, laced yellow.

Husaren-Regiment: Shako with white cords and plume. Light blue dolman, pelisse and breeches; white lace and buttons; black collar, cuffs and fur; red and white sash; blue sabretache with white edging and crowned 'FA'. **Trumpeters:** Light blue shako; red plume; white cords; gold top band. Red dolman and pelisse with light blue collar, cuffs, lace and

R. Knötel

Left *The Saxon Kürassier Regiment 'vacant von Zastrow' storming the Rajewsky Redoubt during the battle of Borodino. Together with the Saxon Garde du Corps and remnants of the 14th Cuirassiers of the Grand Duchy of Warsaw, they took this vital feature, a fact often conveniently overlooked by French historians (Knötel).*

Below *Grand Duchy of Warsaw, Eagle, 11th Infantry Regiment. Silver with gilt crown, white cravat and silver fringes.*

cords. Light blue breeches. No epaulettes: officers' ranks were indicated by silver chevrons over the cuffs and silver thigh decorations. Blue shabraque edged black, laced white.

Artillery

Foot artillery: Shako with red cords and plume. Dark green coat; red facings; yellow buttons. Buff leatherwork.

Horse artillery: Colours as for Foot artillery, style as for Chevaux-légèrs; brass shoulder scales. Chevaux-légèrs' horse furniture. **Trumpeters:** Green shakos; red plumes and cords; gold top bands. Red coats faced green; yellow edging to collar and cuffs. Brass trumpets with green, yellow and red cords. Green shabraque, edged red, laced yellow.

Ingieneur-Corps: As for Foot artillery but with silver buttons. **Train:** Shako with white cords and plumes. Light blue coat with black facings edged red; white buttons; black bandoliers.

Colours and standards

Infantry: Each line regiment carried one *Leibfahne* (sovereign's colour) and one *Ordinärfahne* (regimental colour). All Leibfahnen were white with an edging varying in design and colour according to regiment. The Ordinärfahne was in the colour of the Leibfahne edging with a border in the regimental button colour as shown below: *König*: a (Leibfahne edging and Ordinärfahne) red; b (Ordinärfahne edging) yellow. *Vacant von Niesemeuschel*: a crimson; b white. *Prinz Anton*: a dark blue; b white. *Von Low*: a grass green; b white. *Prinz Friedrich August*: a green; b yellow. *Prinz Clemens*: a dark blue; b yellow.

Light infantry, artillery and Train carried no colours.

Pikes were red, the tips gilt spearpoints bearing the crowned *FAR*. Gold cords and tassels hung from the tip to about half-way down the flag.

On the obverse was the crowned golden cypher *FAR* on a shield and within palm and laurel branches; in each corner the Saxon crest; on the reverse the Saxon crest on a crowned ermine coat and in each corner a white shield bearing 'RS'.

Cavalry: Garde du Corps and Kürassier regiments each carried four white standards with distinctive regimental edging: *Garde du Corps:* gold and blue; *Zastrow:* yellow.

Chevaux-légèrs regiments had one white *Leibestandarte* and three red *Ordinärestandarten*, all edged in a regimental colour: *Prinz Albrecht*: green and brown; *Prinz Johann*: black and green; *Von Polenz*: light blue and gold; *Prinz Clemens Uhlanen*: as for Chevaux-légèrs: green and violet. Within each cavalry regi-

ment the Leibestandarte had a white cravatte, the standard of the 2nd Squadron red; 3rd blue; and 4th yellow. Hussars carried no standards.

On the obverse of the standards was the crowned cypher *FAR* in gold within laurel branches and on the reverse the Saxon crest on a crowned ermine coat.

Most flags were lost in Russia, either at Kobryn or late in the retreat.

Grand Duchy of Warsaw

(The V Corps, X Corps, Imperial Guard and various Light Cavalry Brigades.)

Uniforms: Rank badges and inter-company distinctions as in the French Army; musicians, trumpeters and drummers were dressed at the whim of the regimental commander and thus cannot be described in detail within the confines of this book. Cockade white (with silver Maltese cross for officers).

Generals (service dress): As for French generals but with Warsaw cockade and special zigzag silver lace; silver buttons with the Polish eagles. Dark blue kurtka, crimson facings and breeches. Silver-trimmed boots.

Guards

Within the army of the Duchy there were no Guards. Serving with the French Imperial Guard were the 1st (Polish) and 3rd (Lithuanian) Lancers and the Lithuanian Tartars of the Guard. See section on France for further details.

Cavalry

1st (Polish) Lancers: Slate blue uniform; crimson facings; white lace and buttons (silver for officers).

3rd (Lithuanian) Lancers: As above but with yellow (gold) lace and buttons. This unit was raised in July 1812 in Lithuania and was almost destroyed at Slonim on October 18 1812.

Lithuanian Tartars: Black lambskin 'shako' with front badge of three stars over a crescent in brass and one star beneath it; green bag to right side with red tassel; yellow turban. Green shirt and voluminous trousers (with double crimson side stripes); crimson waistcoat edged and decorated yellow. White belts and gauntlets. Green over crimson lance pennants. Officers wore very elaborately decorated uniforms. This unit was only one squadron strong and was badly mauled at Wilna on December 10-12 1812 (having been raised in July of that year). In 1813 they were combined with the 2nd Chevau-Légèrs attached to the Young Guard.

Line regiments

Infantry

All regiments dressed the same (except the 13th Regiment) and were distinguished by the number on their buttons.

Fusiliers: Black felt czapka with white metal eagle over a brass plate pierced with the regimental number; cockade; white cords; pompon in the company colour; black plume; brass chinscales. Dark blue coat, collar*, shoulder straps*, turnbacks* and trousers (white for parades); white half lapels*; crimson cuffs; dark blue cuff flaps; brass buttons. White belts and gaiters. Black pouch bearing the regimental number in brass. French equipment. NCOs' czapka cords and sabre knots were white and crimson and their czapka top bands were yellow or gold. **Grenadiers:** As above except: bearskin caps with brass plate bearing the Polish eagle, regimental number and flanking grenades; brass chinscales; red plumes, cords and top patch bearing a white cross. Red epaulettes and sabre knot. Brass grenade pouch badge. **Voltigeurs:** As for Fusiliers except: yellow top band, pompon and cords to czapka; yellow plume with green tip. Green epaulettes with yellow half moon. Green sabre knot. Brass hunting horn pouch badge. **Drummers:** Red cords, pompon and epaulettes. White kurtka with crimson cuffs and piping. Brass drum; crimson and white striped hoops. **Offic-**

*Piped crimson.

ers: As for their company except: silver hat cords. Gold gorgets with silver eagle; long coat skirts; gold epaulettes. Silver portepée. White breeches. Gold-trimmed hussar boots. Mounted officers had dark blue shabraques edged gold and black bicorns.

13th Regiment: As above except: white coats, trousers, cuffs and buttons; light blue collar, cuff flaps, lapels, turnbacks and cuff piping (drummers in reversed colours). The 18th-21st infantry regiments were raised in Lithuania in July 1812, the *Chasseurs à Pied Lituaniens* was completed only in November 1812 and almost all these new units were destroyed in the Retreat.

Cavalry

Chasseurs à Cheval (Regiments 1, 4, 5): Black shakos; white eagle plate and cockade; white cords; brass chinscales (élite companies wore black busbies with red plume and cords). Dark green coat; yellow buttons; facings shown on collar, cuffs, turnback piping and trouser stripes as follows: **1st Regiment:** red; **4th:** crimson; **5th:** orange; yellow metal epaulettes (red fringes for élite companies). White belts; pouch with regimental number. White sabre knot (red for élite companies). Dark green breeches with twin side stripes in the facing colour. **Officers:** As above but all wore busbies with bags in the facing colour; gold cords. Gold hunting horns in the turnback corners. White breeches (or green). Gold-trimmed boots. Black and gold bandolier and pouch.

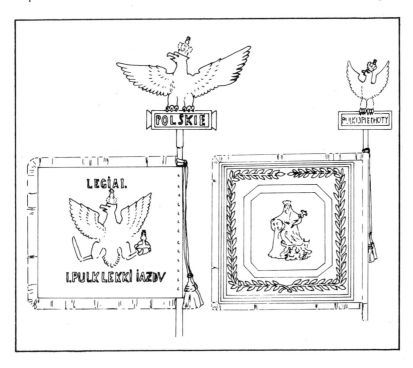

Far left *Grand Duchy of Warsaw, standard, 1st Chasseurs à Cheval. Crimson cloth, silver embroidery, fringes, cords and eagle.*

Left *Grand Duchy of Warsaw, 13th Infantry Regiment. Crimson and silver (probably a captured Italian flag from the 1800 campaign).*

Right *Grand Duchy of Warsaw, driver, Military Train. According to the regulations, the czapka was worn by this corps and on the upper left arm was a brass plate bearing the Polish eagle and the number of the battalion (Bakrynowski Collection).*

Lancers: Black czapka; white eagle plate; cockade; white cords; black plume. Dark blue kurtka lined dark blue; yellow metal buttons bearing the regimental number; white belts. Dark blue breeches striped as shown in the following list. Rank badges as for Chasseurs à Cheval. **Lance pennants: 2nd, 3rd and 16th Regiments:** red over white; **7th-16th:** a blue triangle next to the pike, top section red, bottom section white; **17th-21st:** blue over white.

Facings as follows: **2nd Regiment:** a (collar) red; b (collar piping) white; c (lapels) dark blue; d (lapel piping) yellow; e (cuffs) red; f (cuff piping) white; g (trouser stripes) yellow. **3rd:** a and e crimson; b, d and f white; c dark blue; g yellow. **6th:** a and f white; b, d, e and g crimson; c dark blue. **7th:** a, e and g yellow; b, d and f red; c dark blue. **8th:** a, b, d, f and g red; c dark blue; e yellow. **9th:** a and g red; b, c and e dark blue, d and f white. **11th:** a, c and g crimson; b, d and f white; e dark blue. **12th:** a and g crimson; b, d and f white; c and e dark blue; **15th:** a, c, e and g crimson; b, d and f white. **16th:** a, d, e and g crimson; b and f white; c dark blue. **17th:** a, d, e and g crimson; b and f white; c dark blue. **18th:** a, d, e and g crimson; b and f white; c dark blue. **19th and 20th:** a, b, d, e, f and g yellow; c dark blue. **21st:** a, b, d, e, f and g orange; c dark blue. The 17th-21st Lancer regiments were raised in Lithuania in 1812 and their czapka plates bore the mounted warrior badge instead of the Polish eagle.

Hussars (everyday uniform): **10th Regiment:** Light blue shako with white (silver) cords and decorations according to rank. Dark blue dolman and pelisse; crimson collar; gold lace and buttons; black fur; white (silver) and crimson sash; black sabretache with silver eagle and number. Light blue breeches. Black belt and bandolier. Hussar boots with yellow (gold trim). Élite company: black astrakhan busby with light blue bag. Saddle furniture crimson edged yellow (gold). **Trumpeters:** Fox fur busby. Blue dolman. Crimson breeches. Yellow boots. **13th Regiment.** As above except: silver (white) lace and buttons; white fur trim to pelisse. **Trumpeters:** Fox fur busby. Crimson dolman. Light blue breeches. Red boots.

Krakus: Crimson 'beret' with white radial stripes and black astrakhan headband. Dark blue *Litewka* coat with crimson collar and cuffs and white piping. Dark blue overalls with twin crimson side stripes. Black belts. Crimson, cossack-style cartridges on each side of the chest, edged white.

Kürassiers: As for French Kürassier regiments with red facings and yellow buttons bearing the number '14'. Dark blue shabraque edged yellow. **Trumpeters:** Red crest; white plume. White coat faced red; red epaulettes; red and yellow lace bars across chest. Brass trumpet; red cords.

Polish regiments serving with the French Army

Infantry

The 4th, 7th and 9th Infantry Regiments served in Spain in French pay and in 1812 wore French infantry uniforms (the 4th Regiment even wore the tricolour cockade). The 7th and 8th Lancer Regiments of the French Army were, in fact, recruited from Poles and these regiments had originally been the cavalry of the Legion of the Vistula. They wore Polish-style uniforms in the following colours: Kurtka, czapka and breeches dark blue; buttons and facings white. **7th Regiment:** a (collar), b (cuffs), c (skirt turnbacks), d (piping) and e (lapels) all yellow. **8th:** a dark blue; b, c, d and e yellow.

Legion of the Vistula: (four regiments of infantry): French shakos with brass sunburst plate having at its centre a silver semi-circle bearing an 'N' (the same plate decorated the czapkas of the 7th, 8th and 9th Lancers of the French army). Dark blue kurtka (or French Spencer) with yellow collar, cuffs, lapels and turnbacks; white buttons with the regimental number. Otherwise as for French line infantry.

Artillery

Foot artillery: Shako with brass front plate bearing a flaming grenade and crossed cannon barrels all under a white eagle; brass chinscales; red cords, pompon and plume; cockade. Dark green kurtka; black facings edged red; brass buttons; red epaulettes. Dark green or white trousers. White gaiters. **Officers:** As for infantry officers but in artillery colours.

Horse artillery: Black busby; red pompon and cords; brass chinscales. Dark green kurtka; black facings piped red; yellow grenades on collars and turnbacks; brass scale epaulettes with red fringes; red aiguillette. White belts. Dark green breeches. Short boots. **Officers:** As for Officers of Chasseurs à Cheval but in artillery colours.

Train: Dark blue czapka; white eagle plate; cockade; red pompon and cords. Blue kurtka faced yellow; white buttons; on the left arm an oval brass plate bearing an eagle, the number of the division and the vehicle. White belts. Blue breeches with yellow stripes. Red sabre knots. **Engineers:** As for the Foot artillery (but the buttons bearing a trophy of arms); gold grenades on the collars.

Colours and standards

Infantry: As in the French army. Eagles were carried at a scale of one per regiment by the 1st Battalion; the other battalions carried Fanions in varying colours with plain steel or gilt lance tips. The Eagles

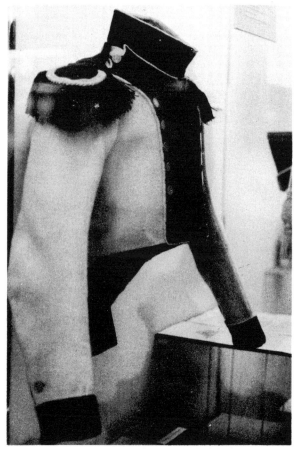

Tunic of a Fusilier private, 5th Westfalian Infantry Regiment. Dark blue facings and epaulettes, brass buttons bearing '5' within a French ring (Exhibit, Museum für Deutsche Geschichte, Berlin).

were in traditional Polish style, in silver and set upon a plinth, bearing *WOYSKO POLSKIE* on one side and the regimental designation on the other (eg *PULK 1^{szy} PIECHOTY* — 1st Infantry Regiment). Below the Eagle was a cloth, about 90 cm square, white or crimson in colour and bearing a silver Polish Eagle holding a gold orb and sceptre and crowned in gold; above the Eagle the regimental designation and below the Eagle the battalion designation, both in silver. The pike was brown.

Cavalry: Basically as above but the cloth was much smaller — about 50 cm square and fringed silver. One was issued per regiment. Colours and standards were decorated with cravattes in varying colours and heavily embroidered in silver and gold.

Details of losses are confused as the Russians took many Napoleonic colours back into Russia in 1830 and these were mixed up with others actually captured in 1812.

Kingdom of Westfalia

(The VIII, X and XI Corps and IV Cavalry Corps.)

Uniform: Rank badges, inter-company distinctions, weapons and equipment as in the French army. Westfalian cockade blue within white.

Generals: As in the French army.

The Guard

Infantry

Grenadier-Garde: Black bearskin bonnet (for parades); red cords, plume and top patch with gold grenade badge; brass chinscales; cockade. White, long-skirted coat with red a* (collar), b* (cuffs), c* (lapels) and d (turnbacks). Gold buttons. Red epaulettes; yellow grenade badges on turnbacks. White breeches and gaiters. Red sabre knot. Ammunition pouch badge (brass): central lozenge with crowned 'JN'; flaming grenades in the corners. For field wear a shako with brass lozenge plate bearing a crowned 'JN'; brass chinscales; cockade; red pompon.

Jäger-Garde: Shako with white eagle; white cords and plume; cockade; white chinscales. Dark green coat with lemon yellow a**, b**, d and e. Dark green c. White buttons. Green epaulettes and breeches with white Hungarian thigh knots. Short black gaiters with

*Gold/yellow bars of lace.
**Silver/white bars of lace.
***Red bars of lace.

white trim and tassel. Pouch badge a white bugle. Green sabre knot.

Jäger-Carabiniers: Shako with yellow eagle plate; red cords; green plume with red tip; brass chinscales; cockade. Dark green coat with dark green a***, b***; red c and e. Dark green epaulettes with red half moons. Dark green waistcoat and breeches with red Hungarian thigh knots and side stripes. Short black gaiters, red trim and tassel. Black belts. Red flask cord. Brass-hilted *Hirschfänger* in brown sheath. Rifles.

Cavalry

Garde du Corps, *Service Dress:* Steel helmet with brass combe and trim; black crest; white plume; 'JN' on brass front plate; brass chinscales. Royal blue coat with a*, b*, c*, d and e (piping) all red. Gold trefoil on right shoulder. Blue waistcoat and breeches. High, jacked boots. Gold buttons.

Chevau-légers Garde: Black helmet with brass combe, front plate, chinscales and trim; black crest; red plume. Dark green jacket with red a*, b*, d and e; yellow bars across chest; yellow buttons; brass scale epaulettes; yellow aiguilette. Dark green waistcoat and breeches, yellow Hungarian thigh knots and side stripe. Hussar boots with yellow trim and tassel.

Artillery

Artillery of the Guard: Shako with brass lozenge plate bearing crowned crossed cannon barrels; red cords, pompon and plume; brass chinscales. Dark

Below left *Kingdom of Westfalia, infantry flag. Dark blue cloth, white lozenge, gold embroidery and tip, dark blue pike (after Hewig).*
Below centre *Kingdom of Westfalia, standard, 1st Hussars. Dark blue triangles, white diagonal cross, gold eagles, numbers and crown, gilt tip. The standards of both hussar regiments were burned in 1813.* **Below right** *Kingdom of Westfalia, standard, Leibgarde zu Pferde. Dark blue cloth, white diagonal cross, gold eagles, fringes, embroidery and tip.*

blue coat with red a, b, d and epaulettes. Blue breeches with red Hungarian thigh knots and side stripes. Seven red bars across chest; yellow buttons. Hussar boots with red trim and tassel. Buff gauntlets and bandolier.

Guard drummers and trumpeters wore reversed colours.

Line regiments

Infantry

(1st-8th Regiments): Regimental identity was shown only by the number on the brass buttons. Grenadiers of the 1st Regiment wore bearskins on parade as for the Grenadier-Garde. Shako with brass lozenge plate bearing the crowned eagle over the pierced regimental number; cockade; cords, pompons and plume according to company. White coats with dark blue a, b, c, d; white e; epaulettes according to company (Fusiliers had dark blue fringed epaulettes with white half moons). White waistcoats and breeches. Short black gaiters. Drummers had red swallows nests at the shoulders and their collars, cuffs and lapels were edged in a regimental lace as follows: **1st Regiment:** Green with two red stripes along it. **2nd:** Dark

Side view, helmet of the Westfalian Garde du Corps (Exhibit, Museum für Deutsche Geschichte, Berlin).

blue edged orange. **3rd:** White with light blue diamonds along its length. **4th:** Yellow with red edging. **5th:** Red with yellow edging. **6th:** Light blue edged black and with black 'chain' pattern along it, the inside of the chain links white. **7th:** White with light blue eagles. **8th:** Orange edged black.

Light infantry (1st-3rd Battalions): Shako with white eagle plate and chinscales; green plume; cockade. Dark green coat with light blue a, b, d and e; white buttons. Dark green breeches. Short black gaiters. Black belts.

Cavalry

1st Kürassiers: Steel helmet with brass combe; black crest and brown fur turban; white plume; brass front plate with crowned 'JN'. Dark blue coat with crimson a, b, d and e; white buttons. White breeches. High, jacked boots. Steel Kürass with crimson cuff. **2nd Kürassiers:** As for 1st Regiment but orange facings. **Trumpeters:** Reversed colours, no Kürass.

1st Chevau-Légers: Helmet as for Chevau-Légers Garde but with white metal fittings. Dark green coat with orange a, b, d and e; white buttons. Dark green breeches with orange Hungarian knots and side stripes. White trim to hussar boots. Buff bandoliers. **Trumpeters:** Black fur colpack with green bag and white plume; light blue coats faced red laced white. **2nd Chevau-Légers:** As for 1st Regiment but with buff facings.

1st Hussars: Shako with white eagle plate; green plume; white cords and chinscales; cockade. Green dolman, pelisse and breeches; white buttons and lace; red collar and cuffs; red and white sash; black fur. Black belts and sabretache with silver '1'. **Trumpeters:** Reversed colours. **2nd Hussars:** As for 1st Regiment but light blue dolman, pelisse and breeches; grey fur; red collar and cuffs; white plume; silver '2' on sabretache.

Artillery

Artillery Regiment: As for French line artillery except that the collar was red and that Westfalian cockade, cap plate and buttons were worn. **Train:** Shako with red pompon; white lozenge plate bearing crowned 'JN'; white cords and chinscales. Grey coat with red a, b, d and e; grey c and shoulder-straps; white buttons. Red waistcoat with white lace and buttons. Grey breeches with white Hungarian knots and side stripes. Plain hussar boots. Buff bandoliers.

The Gendarmerie: Bicorn with silver edging; red plume; cockade. Long-skirted dark blue coat with red a, b, c and d; white buttons and aiguillette. White breeches and high jacked boots for mounted Gendarmes, dark blue breeches and black gaiters for foot Gendarmes.

Württemberg artillerymen spike the guns they can no longer move due to lack of horses, and throw the barrels into the River Dnieper at Smolensk (Faber du Four).

Colours and standards

Line infantry 1808 pattern: Square, dark blue with a central white lozenge; in each corner a golden laurel wreath enclosing heraldic devices; the lozenge was edged in gold laurel leaves and the central inscriptions were in gold in French. **Line infantry 1810 pattern:** As above but the inscriptions were in German. Pikes were black with gilt spearpoint tips; cravattes in various colours were attached to the pike.

Standards: There were four patterns: M1808, M1812, M1812 (Guards) and M1813. All were 60 cm square. **M1808:** Dark blue with white diagonal cross; on the obverse the cypher '*JN*' and the Westfalian eagle in gold; on the reverse the Westfalian crest; regimental inscriptions in French. **M1812:** As above but with German inscriptions. **M1812 Guards:** As M1808 embroidered and fringed gold with German inscriptions. This pattern was only issued to the

Garde du Corps. Inscription: *DER KÖNIG/VON WESTPHALIEN/AN SEINE/LIEBGARDE ZU PFERDE.* Pikes and cravattes as for infantry colours.

Losses in 1812: 1st Battalion, 6th Infantry Regiment at Wereja, October 10; 4th Infantry Regiment at Wilna, November 6 — one flag.

Kingdom of Württemberg

(25th Division, III Corps.)

Uniform: Cockade red within black within yellow. **Rank badges: Corporal:** Gold or silver (button colour) to front and bottom of collar and top and back of cuffs; **Feldwebel:** As for Corporal plus a cane with a gold knob and tassel, silver and red portepée; **Unterlieutenant** (all epaulettes in the button colour):

Fringed epaulette on the left shoulder, 'contre epaulette' on the right; **Oberlieutenant:** As above but on opposite shoulders; **Hauptmann/Rittmeister:** Two fringed epaulettes; **Major:** Two epaulettes with bullion fringes. All officers wore (on parade) silver waist sashes with red and yellow stripes; silver, red and yellow portepée and a helmet of different design from that of the men. NCOs and officers carried brown canes with gold knobs.

Generals: As in the French army with national devices.

Infantry

Black leather kasket with black combe and crest, front and rear peaks and chinstrap; brass chinstrap bosses, peak edging and front plate bearing the Württemberg arms over a front band; cockade over left boss, above this a white plume. Dark blue coat and lapels; facings on collar cuffs, shoulder straps and turnbacks as shown below. White breeches and belts. Black, below-knee gaiters.

1st Regiment *Prinz Paul:* a (facings) yellow; b (piping) yellow; c (buttons) yellow. **2nd** *Herzog Wilhelm:* a and b orange; c white. **4th:** a pink; b and c white. **6th** *Kronprinz:* a white; b red; c yellow. **7th:** a and b red; c yellow. **Officers:** Taller kaskets than the men, with larger, gilt front plates; bearskin crests and black base to white plume; gilt chinscales and scalloped gilt edging to rear of helmet. Long coat skirts; silver, red and yellow waist sash and portepée. Swords. White breeches and riding boots. **Drummers:** As for privates but swallows nests in the facing colour edged and decorated with white lace in a 'Volkswagen' design '\/'. Brass drum, yellow, red and black striped hoops, red Kasket plume.

Light infantry (1st and 2nd Battalions): As for the infantry except: black, bell-topped shako with brass rhombic front plate (bearing the arms of Württemberg) and chinscales; cockade on top left hand side; no plume. Dark green coat; light blue facings; white piping; yellow buttons. Buff belts. Dark green breeches. Boots (all ranks). Officers carried sabres in steel sheaths on black bandoliers with gilt crowned 'FR' (*Friedrich Rex*) breast badge.

Jägers (1st and 2nd Battalions): As for the light infantry except facings black; piping white; buttons (1st Battalion) yellow, (2nd) white. Officers wore black gauntlets. Black belts. Dark green plumes (buglers with red tips).

Cavalry

Officers had Bavarian style *Raupenhelme* with front plates, peak trim and chinscales in the button colour; bearskin crests and white plumes with black base on left side. Soldiers' kaskets were similar to those of the infantry. Crowned 'FR' on helmet plates and brass plate to ammunition pouches. Beneath the helmet plate a band bearing *FURCHTLOS UND TREU* (fearless and faithful).

Chevauxlégers-Regiment N^r 1 *Prinz Adam:* Yellow over black crest to combe (soldiers only); white plume. Dark blue coat and lapels*; a (collar), b (cuffs), c (turnbacks**), d (buttons) and e (sash) yellow. f (breeches) and g (belts) white. Black harness with white metal fittings. Dark blue horse furniture, edged red for soldiers; gold with red piping for officers. Corner cyphers a crowned 'FR' in red/gold. Yellow

*Piped in the facing colour.
**Piped red about one inch in from the outer edge.

Left *Kingdom of Württemberg cavalry. This plate shows the two Jäger zu Pferd regiments, Nr 3 'Herzog Louis' with lemon yellow facings, and Nr 4 'König' with pink facings (centre). The differences between officers' and soldiers' helmets is clearly brought out. This Knötel plate is dated 1808, ie, before the regiment 'König' received its collar lace.*

Right *Kingdom of Württemberg, infantry flag (the standards of the Chevaulégers regiments were identical in design but smaller than the flags; colours were yellow for the 1st Regiment and red for the 2nd). Yellow fringes, gilt tip, gold cypher ('FR') and crowns, black pike.*

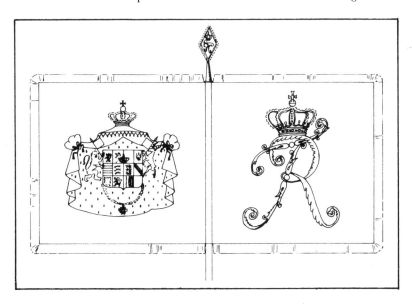

metal shoulder scales on red backing. High jacked boots. **Officers:** As above plus waist sash as for the infantry. Gilt-hilted sabre in steel sheath on black slings. Black portepée strap with silver tassel, black bandolier with gold fittings. **Trumpeters:** Red over black crests. Yellow coats; regimental facings and buttons.

Leib-Chevauxlégèrs-Regiment N^r 2: As above except; brick red a***, b and e; white d, f and g. Soldiers' kaskets had drooping, black horsehair crests; black plumes. White shoulder scales. Red horse furniture edged blue.

Jäger-Regiment zu Pferd N^r 3 *Herzog Louis*: Yellow over dark green crest (soldiers); white helmet fittings and buttons. Dark green coat, lapels*, breeches, collar* and cuffs*; yellow turnbacks (piped black) and piping. Black belts and gauntlets. Dark green horse furniture edged yellow; yellow 'FR' crowned cyphers.

*Piped in the facing colour.
***Two white buttons and lace loops on either side of the collar.

Sabres in steel sheaths. Black harness with white fittings. Otherwise as above (facing colour yellow). **Jäger-Regiment zu Pferd N^r 4** *König*: As for N^r 3 except: green crests, pink collar***, white piping.

Artillery

1st Horse Artillery Battery: All ranks wore Bavarian-style Raupenhelme with brass front plate (with oval, crowned, arms of Württemberg), peak edging, chinscales and side struts; black crest; white plume. Light blue coat, lapels and breeches; black collar, cuffs and sash; white buttons, shoulder scales and piping; one white lace loop to collar, two to cuffs; yellow turnbacks edged black about one inch in from the outer edge. White belts and sabre slings. Steel-hilted sabre (white knot). Plain hussar-style boots. **Trumpeters:** As for cavalry. **2nd Horse Artillery Battery:** As for 1st Battery except: no lace decoration to collars; yellow buttons and shoulder scales.

Foot Artillery, 1st and 2nd Batteries: As for Horse artillery except: yellow buttons; black shoulder straps

Württemberg artillery passing Smorgoni on July 23 1812 (Albrecht Adam).

edged yellow; black turnbacks. Black, below-knee gaiters. Officers had gold grenades in their turnbacks. **Drummers:** As for the infantry. **Train:** Shako with brass, rhombic plate and cockade to top left-hand side. Single-breasted, light blue coat; black collar, cuffs, shoulder straps (edged yellow) and turnbacks; yellow buttons.

Artillery equipment was painted light brown. All cannon were lost in Russia.

Colours and standards

Infantry colours (one per battalion): On the obverse the crest of Württemberg on a crowned ermine coat with supporters; on the reverse the crowned golden cypher 'FR'. All flags edged in yellow fringes. Colours: **1st Regiment:** lemon yellow; **2nd:** orange; **4th:** pink; **6th:** quartered blue and white;

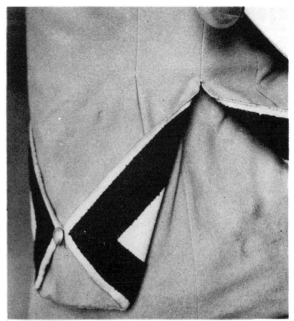

Right *Coat tail detail of a gunner, Württemberg horse artillery. Light blue, yellow and black* (Exhibit, Wehrgeschichtliches Museum, Rastatt/Baden).

Below *Württemberg artillery during the Retreat* (Faber du Four).

Württemberg artillery at Beschenkowiczi on July 29. Note the ammunition chest on the gun trails (Faber du Four).

7th: quartered blue and red. Black pikes; diamond shaped gilt tip enclosing the crowned 'FR'.

The colours of the 1st, 2nd, 4th and 6th Regiments were destroyed in a barn fire in Russia.

Cavalry standards: Only the two Chevauxlégèrs regiments carried standards at a scale of one per squadron. Design details as for infantry colours; those of the 1st Regiment were yellow; the 2nd Regiment red.

Grand Duchy of Würzburg

Three battalions of infantry as 1st Rheinbund-Regiment in the 34th Division, XI Corps. March-out strength — 2,040; entered Russia in November; strength November 27 — 957 (plus 782 sick); strength December 26 — 700.

Infantry

Rank badges and inter-company distinctions as in the French army; cockade red within blue within yellow. French shako; brass rhombic plate bearing 'F' (Ferdinand); above the plate a crown; over this a cockade then the company pompon (and plume if élite company); brass chinscales. White coat, shoulder straps*, turnbacks*, waistcoat, trousers, belts, piping

*Piped red.

to lapels, cuffs and cuff flaps*; red cuffs, lapels and collar; yellow buttons. Black, below-knee gaiters. **Officers:** Golden gorgets with silver ducal crest; gold, red and blue portepée (and sash for parades).

Artillery

Regimental Artillery Company (four light guns): Dark blue coats, otherwise as above.

Flags

(One per battalion): Yellow cloth, edged with red, blue and white triangles; on the obverse the crowned initial 'F' in red within green laurel branches tied with a red ribbon; on the reverse the ducal crest on an ermine coat under a crown, within laurel branches. Gilt tip (spearpoint) bearing a crowned shield; on one side the 'F', on the other the red-white-red Austrian badge. Pike painted in red and white spirals. No flags were lost in Russia.

Uniform glossary

Aigrette: A tuft of hair or feathers such as worn at the front of the combe (qv) of a French cuirassier's helmet.

Aiguilette: A shoulder cord, originally thought to have been introduced by a Walloon cavalry regiment in 1567-73 which, having defected from the side of

Above *Grand Duchy of Würzburg, infantry flag. Yellow cloth, red, blue and white border triangles, green wreaths with red ribbons and berries, red 'F' and mantle, gold crowns, gilt tip, red and white pike.*

Left *Helmet of a trooper, Württemberg Leib Chevauxlégers Regiment. White metal fittings. The motto on the helmet front band reads 'Furchtlos und Treu' (fearless and faithful).*

the notorious Spanish Duke of Alba to join the rebels, was threatened with the reprisal that any man captured would be hung like a common thief. The regiment retorted that they would provide their own noose and nail and they wore these items around their right shoulders. This later became a badge of honour due to the regiment's fighting record and is now a decoration, highly stylised and ornate in gold and silver, worn by Generals and other military dignitaries.

Bandolier: A leather belt, usually worn over one or both shoulders, on to which would be hung a pouch, cartouche (qv), carbine or sabre. For officers this item was heavily decorated in gold or silver lace and adorned with pickers (qv).

Bearskin (bonnet or cap): Cylindrical headdress of bearskin worn by foot and mounted grenadiers, usually with a coloured top patch (Calot), front plate, chinscales and peak.

Boites: Cartridges.

Boots: a (hussar) Below knee-length boots, higher at

Text continued on page 97.

Captions to colour plates 37-46

37 Kingdom of Westfalia, 1st and 2nd Hussars. *From left to right: officer, 1st Hussars, parade dress; the silver pompons at the base of the green plume appears to be missing; officer, 2nd Hussars, parade dress; the portepée would be silver; trooper (mounted) 1st Hussars, parade dress. After giving excellent service in Russia, both these regiments went over to the allies in 1813 and formed the 1st and 2nd Hussars of the Austrian-German Legion* (Knötel).

38 Kingdom of Westfalia, Jäger-Carabinier of the Guard. *This unit was one battalion strong and was formed, as could be expected from the uniform and the way the rifle is carried, from hunters* (Sauerweid).

39 Kingdom of Westfalia, Garde-Jäger. *This beautifully clear plate by Alexander Sauerweid shows a wealth of detail. The eagle shako plate could well be mistaken for a French item. Note the company number in the dark blue and white pompon. This regiment suffered heavily at Borodino from artillery fire.*

40 Kingdom of Westfalia Garde-Grenadiere, parade dress. *This finely detailed plate by Sauerweid gives an excellent, and unusual, rear view showing the pouch and coat tail decoration. On the march this regiment wore shakos with red pompons and a single-breasted tunic. Note the unusual cuff decoration.*

41 Kingdom of Westfalia Private, Garde du Corps, Gala uniform. *This unit had two forms of dress, the one shown (worn when on duty in the royal palace) and a royal blue coat faced red which was for everyday wear. When King Jérôme was sent home from Russia in disgrace by the Emperor for failing to catch and destroy the southern Russian army at the start of the campaign, he initially set off homewards with his entire Guard (Grenadiers, Jägers, Carabiniers, Chevaulégers and artillery as well as the Garde du Corps). As soon as Napoleon heard of this, he immediately instructed Jérôme to retain only the Garde du Corps (126 men) with him and to send the other regiments back to join VIII Corps* (Sauerweid).

42 Kingdom of Westfalia. *Left to right: driver, artillery train — a rather decorative uniform for a service that was usually clothed in a very drab fashion; trooper (mounted) Chevauléger-Lanciers of the Garde — the helmet and shabraque cyphers are the crowned 'JN' (Jérôme Napoleon), note the pistol on the bandolier. Wounded*

officer of kürassiers, undress uniform; karabinier private of Light infantry — these Grenadiers of the Light infantry wore the red badges of their line counterparts; the facings shown as dark blue should, in fact, be light blue; Grenadier of Line infantry: by 1812 all Line infantry should have been wearing dark blue facings; yellow was the colour previously worn by the 5th and 6th regiments (Knötel).

43 Kingdom of Württemberg; officers. *This plate is one of the extensive series produced by Professor Knötel prior to the Second World War. The series is highly regarded for its painstaking research, authenticity and accuracy. From left to right: Garde-Füsilier officer, officer of the Horse Grenadiers and one of the Leibjägers: none of these three units went to Russia but the officer of the Garde-Füsiliers shows well the shako worn by the Württemberg Jägers (except that the cockade of the Jägers was at the top left side of the shako); officer of Horse Artillery — this man is from the 1st Battery as his lace decoration to the facings shows. Note silver, red and yellow waist sash.*

44 Kingdom of Württemberg, Horse Artillery. *Foreground (left to right): Corporal (Unteroffizier), 2nd Battery, campaign uniform; NCO's distinctions are the yellow lace to collar and cuffs, the two chevrons on the upper left arm are for service; gunner (Kanonier), 1st Battery, parade dress; background: two mounted gunners, apparently both 1st Battery, campaign dress* (Knötel).

45 Kingdom of Württemburg, cavalry. *Left to right: background — unidentified mounted figure; foreground (seated) — trooper, Leib-Chevauxlégers-Regiment N^r 2, still wearing the old pattern helmet with drooping, horse hair crest. Unfortunately the label across the peak of his helmet has erroneously been painted over black; (standing) — trooper, Jäger-Regiment zu Pferd N^r 4, König: the pink collar is almost completely obscured by the white lace and button decoration; trooper, Chevauxlégers-Regiment N^r 1 Prinz Adam (without plume to helmet); trooper, Jäger-Regiment zu Pferd N^r 3 Herzog Louis* (Knötel).

46 Grand Duchy of Würzburg. *The three infantrymen in the foreground are wearing the single-breasted coatee which was often worn to save wear on the more expensive, double-breasted tunic with red lapels. For some reason the artist has omitted the brass, rhombic shako plates bearing an 'F' and the cockade's centre (red disc) has also been forgotten. On the right-hand side is a Chevauléger trooper — rear view. Although mobilised in 1812, this unit, one squadron strong, never went to Russia and was employed on coastguard duties on the Baltic and North Sea coasts* (Augsburger Bilder).

37 *Right* Kingdom of Westfalia, 1st and 2nd Hussars.

38 *Below* Kingdom of Westfalia, Jäger-Carabinier of the Guard.

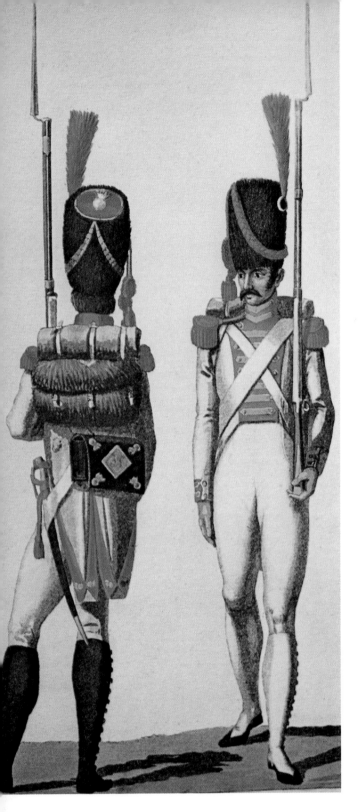

39 *Above* Kingdom of Westfalia, Garde-Jäger.

40 *Left* Kingdom of Westfalia, Garde-Grenadiere, parade dress.

41 *Right* Kingdom of Westfalia, private, Garde du Corps, Gala uniform.

42 *Below* Kingdom of Westfalia.

43 *Far right* Kingdom of Württemberg, officers.

44 *Above* Kingdom of Württemberg, horse artillery.

45 *Below* Kingdom of Württemberg, cavalry.

46 *Right* Grand Duchy of Würzburg.

the front of the leg than at the back, and having a cut-out at the front centre. The top of the boot was often trimmed with a coloured lace and a coloured tassel hanging from the bottom of the front cut-out. Screw-in spurs were worn with this type of boot; **b** (jacked or heavy cavalry) Stiff, heavy leather boots with cuffs to the front and sides of the knee, extending above the knee. Buckle-on spurs were worn with this type of boot.

Breeches: a (Hungarian or hussar) Close-fitting, full-length legwear worn inside hussar boots (qv), usually having decoration to the sides of the fly-flap and along the outer sides of the leg and running from there across the seat; **b** (knee) Close-fitting legwear extending to below the knee (from the waist), fastening below the knee with side buttons and/or buckles. Usually white and worn by dismounted personnel.

Busby: Fur-trimmed headdress with a soft, coloured cloth top (or bag) hanging to one side (also called a colpack qv) worn by some élite hussar companies and Chasseurs à Cheval.

Cartouche (or cartoucheir): Small leather cartridge pouch, often highly decorated, worn by mounted officers on a bandolier (qv) as a sign of office.

Chinscales: Metal scales (brass or tin) fastened on to the chinstrap of a hat in an overlapping style.

Cockade: A round disc of metal, felt, cloth or leather about two inches in diameter, painted in the national colours in concentric rings and worn on the headdress.

Colpack: Traditional Hungarian fur-trimmed cap with soft, coloured cloth top, worn by some hussar élite companies (see also busby).

Combe (or comb): Solid section fixed to the top and back of a helmet, usually of leather or metal and designed to increase the height, appearance and protective property of the helmet. Often surmounted by a crest (qv).

Cords: Decorative, coloured cords, terminating in 'racquets' or 'flounders' (flat, oval discs of plaited cords) and tassels, draped around a bearskin (qv), busby (qv), colpack (qv), czapka (qv) or shako (qv) for parades or participation in set-piece battles. Originally a retaining cord worn by cavalrymen to prevent loss of the hat if it fell off during a ride.

Crest: Decoration of hair (long or short) or wool, affixed to the top of a combe (qv).

Cuffs: a (Brandenburg) Plain round cuff in the facing (qv) colour, over which was superimposed a rectangular three-button flap in the coat colour (often piped in some distinctive colour; **b** (French) As for the Brandenburg but the rear edge of the cuff flap was scalloped into three points; **c** (Polish) A pointed cuff in the facing colour, with a button in the point or at the rear edge of the sleeve; **d** (Swedish; also called Saxon) Plain round cuff in the facing

colour with buttons either along the top or the back edge.

Cuirass (see Kürass).

Czapka: Traditional Polish headgear, with or without a peak, square-topped with a point of the top square at front centre. Adopted as the headgear of lancers all over the world since the original lancers came from Poland.

de compatibilité: Field cashier.

Dolman: Traditional jacket of a hussar, having many rows of lace across the chest and three or five rows of spherical buttons down the chest. It had no skirts or buttonholes, the buttons fastening into the lace loops. It always had Polish cuffs (qv) and rank was indicated by varying numbers of chevrons (point up) above each cuff.

Epaulette: Coloured, decorative shoulder strap with a stiffened circular end from which hung fringes. It took the place of a shoulder strap and was often a badge of rank for officers or of status for soldiers (Grenadiers wore red, Voltigeurs green and yellow).

Facings: Colours related to a particular regiment and shown on collar, lapels, cuffs (qv) and turnbacks (qv) of a coat. Originally only shown on the cuffs of a uniform.

Gaiters: Coverings for the lower legs, either long (covering the knee), medium (from just below the knee) or short (calf-length), in all cases covering the instep and front of the foot. In white (summer) or black cloth (winter) and fastened on the outside of the leg with leather, bone, brass or tin buttons.

Kürass: Metal armour to the upper body, consisting either of just the front plate or of breast and back plates (see also cuirass).

Kurtka: Traditional Polish tunic (and lancer costume). Double-breasted with lapels turned back to show the facings (qv); short-skirted and with contrasting piping along the rear sleeve seams and in the seams of the back of the garment.

Litewka: Traditional Lithuanian coat, often long-skirted and closed either with buttons or with hooks and eyes; usually double-breasted.

Overalls: Long trousers, relatively loose-fitting and made of heavy cloth, frequently reinforced on the insides of the legs and around the bottoms with leather. Along the outer leg seams were buttons of leather or metal. The garment was made to be worn over the cavalryman's parade breeches (qv) when on campaign.

Pelisse (Pelz): Traditional winter coat of a hussar. Lined and edged with fur (*pelz* = fur) and laced and buttoned in the manner of a dolman (qv) but showing no facings. It had no skirts and was worn slung over the left shoulder on parades or in summer.

Pickers: Large needles on chains, worn on the front of a bandolier. Originally functional tools for cleaning out the touch holes of muzzle-loading firearms, these later became extremely ornate and were worn by officers as a badge of office.

Plume: Vertical column of feather, hair or worsted, worn on a shako (qv) and usually inserted into a pompon (qv) for parades. Frequently a badge of rank or of office by virtue of its colour scheme.

Pockets: Usually false in this period and consisting of stylised flaps in the rear skirts of a tunic. They could be either vertical or horizontal.

Pompon: Spherical or lenticular-shaped woollen decoration worn on a busby (qv), colpack (qv), czapka (qv) or shako (qv) as an inter-company distinction or as a badge of office.

Portmanteau: Rolled cylindrical or rectangular valise strapped to the back of a saddle and containing the rider's blanket; his cloak was frequently strapped to the top. Usually in the same colour as the shabraque (qv), with or without a regimental number or device on its ends.

Sabretache: Flat, square pouch carried at knee height on three straps hanging from the waistbelt by hussars and some Chasseurs à Cheval. Often highly decorated and thus a badge of office or rank.

Sash: a (barrel) Traditional Hungarian item worn by hussars, fastening at the small of the back and having a long 'whip' which tucked into the front of the waist. This item was made up of multiple cords bound together by four or five rows of knots. Its colours made it a distinctive item of regimental wear; **b** (officer's) Often a badge of office and in silver/gold and the national colours (like the cockade). Originally used to carry the wearer from the field of battle if he was wounded. Terminated in two heavy tassels. Worn around the waist (or over the shoulder if the wearer was an adjutant).

Shabraque (or shabrack): Saddle cloth, in a distinctive regimental or 'type' colour, usually with lace edging and often with a regimental number or national monogram in its rear corners; also applied to the sheepskin saddle furniture (black or white) worn by many hussar and chasseur horses in particular.

Shako (Czako): Cylindrical hat, with or without peaks to front and rear, which replaced the old cocked hat. Usually decorated with a front plate, cockade (qv), cords (qv), plume (qv) and pompon (qv).

Spencer: French coat of simplified cut and with short tails introduced in 1811 to replace the older long-tailed coat (which was, however, retained by the Old Guard).

Surtout (Überrock): Lightly waisted, double-breasted, long-skirted coat, usually of simple appearance and worn on campaign or in undress.

Turnbacks: That part of the skirt of a garment which is turned over (originally to facilitate mobility) and is often in the facing (qv) colour and bearing a badge indicating the company or regiment of the wearer.

Section 3

Orders of battle, maps and casualty graphs

Author's note

The figures in this section have been taken verbatim from G. Fabry's *Campagne de Russie 1812* (Paris, 1903). In a large number of instances the columns of figures do not add up to the totals given. These anomalies have been left since there is now no way of checking whether the fault lies in simple arithmetic, or whether the totals are correct but some of the individual numbers are wrong. In a couple of places where independent sources have, however, validated the individual figures, the totals have been corrected. Furthermore, as stated in the Foreword, the figures cited are only correct for the precise dates shown. Blank spaces indicate a blank in the original regardless of whether this makes any sense or not!

The Imperial Guard July 4
(The Duke of Treviso)

	Officers	Men	Officers' horses	Men's horses	Train horses
The Young Guard					
1st Infantry Division (General Delaborde)					
5th Regiment of Voltigeurs (Colonel Sicard): 1st and 2nd Battalions	28	917	18		
6th Regiment of Voltigeurs (Colonel Rousseau): 1st and 2nd Battalions	25	621	19		
5th Regiment of Tirailleurs (Colonel Hennequin): 1st and 2nd Battalions	28	1,011	18		
6th Regiment of Tirailleurs (Colonel Carré): 1st and 2nd Battalions	22	548	18		
Canonniers conscrits: 4th Company	3	81	8		
Artillery Train: 5th Company	1	143	2		
5th Sapper Battalion: 2nd Company	2	90			
Total	**109**	**3,411**	**83**		
2nd Infantry Division (General Roguet)					
Flanquers (Colonel Pompejac): 1st and 2nd Battalions	25	1,134	14		
1st Regiment of Voltigeurs (Colonel Mallet): 1st and 2nd Battalions	25	788	20		
1st Regiment of Tirailleurs (Colonel Lenoir): 1st and 2nd Battalions	22	928	18		
Fusiliers Chasseurs (Colonel Vrigny): 1st and 2nd Battalions	33	1,322	22		
Fusiliers Grenadiers (Colonel Bodelin): 1st and 2nd Battalions	30	1,391	20		
8th Artillery Regiment: 13th and 14th Companies	8	178	25		
4th Train Battalion: 6th Company	1	97	2	16	128
7th Train Battalion: 2nd Company		41		7	51

2nd Infantry Division (continued)	**Officers**	**Men**	**Officers' horses**	**Men's horses**	**Train horses**
Sappers	5	102	9		4
Train of Equipages		44		77	77
Administration	2	44	4		
Total	**151**	**5,979**	**134**	**100**	**260**

The Legion of the Vistula (General Claparede)
June 25

1st Regiment (Colonel Kasinowski): 1st and 2nd Battalions and artillery	19	1,319	8		50
2nd Regiment (Colonel Michalowski): 1st and 2nd Battalions and artillery	28	1,256	9		50
3rd Regiment (Colonel Fondzieski): 1st and 2nd Battalions and artillery	27	1,245	13		50
Total	**74**	**3,820**	**30**		**150**

The Old Guard

3rd Division (Duke of Danzig)

1st Regiment of Chasseurs (General Gros): 1st and 2nd Battalions and artillery	34	1,452	40		
2nd Regiment of Chasseurs (Major Rosey): 1st and 2nd Battalion and artillery	41	1,245	36		
1st Regiment of Grenadiers (Lieutenant-Colonel Lorede): 1st and 2nd Battalions and artillery	31	1,294	35		
2nd Regiment of Grenadiers (Major Harlet): 1st and 2nd Battalions and artillery	33	1,079	36		
3rd Regiment of Grenadiers: 1st and 2nd Battalions	41	1,165	27		
Total	**180**	**6,235**	**174**		

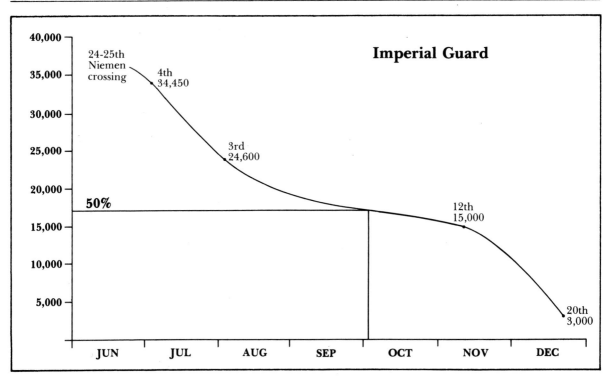

Artillery	Officers	Men	Horses
Foot Artillery of the Young Guard (Major Mabru): 3rd Company	4	77	10
Foot Artillery of the Old Guard (Major Boulard): 1st and 2nd Companies	8	182	18
Ouvriers		6	
? 3rd and 4th Companies (Cottin)	9	199	24
Total	**21**	**464**	**52**
2nd Train Battalion: 3rd Company	1	108	182
1st Train Battalion: 1st Company	2	125	200
1st Train Battalion: 4th Company	1	152	271
Total	**4**	**385**	**653**
Train of Equipages		23	43
Ambulances	1	39	41
Total	**1**	**62**	**84**
Ouvriers of the 3rd Division	2	62	4
Ouvriers of the Reserve	2	89	4
Total	**4**	**151**	**8**
Ambulances	10		10
Total (Old Guard)	**220**	**7,297**	**981**

Cavalry of the Imperial Guard

(General Walther) July 1	Officers	Men	Horses
Chasseurs à Cheval: 1st-5th Squadrons	70	1,107	1,366
Mamelukes: 1st Company	8	67	100
Dragoons: 1st-5th Squadrons	64	1,015	1,217
Grenadiers à Cheval: 1st-5th Squadrons	70	1,096	1,307
1st Chevau-légèrs (Polish): 1st-4th Squadrons	69	887	1,085
2nd Chevau-légèrs (Dutch): 1st-4th Squadrons	57	1,095	1,264
Gendarmerie d'Élite: 1st and 2nd Squadrons	28	363	476
1st Horse Artillery: 1st and 2nd Companies	5	124	113
7th Train Battalion: 2nd and 3rd Companies	2	146	291
Total	**373**	**5,900**	**7,219**

Grand Artillery Park of the Imperial Guard (July 1)

Horse Artillery of the Young Guard	Officers	Men	Horses
2nd, 3rd and 4th Companies	7	173	182
1st Train Battalion: 1st Company	1	125	177
1st and 3rd Companies	6	157	165
2nd Train Battalion: 6th Company	1	152	242
1st Horse Artillery Battery (Line): 5th and 6th Companies	5	134	113
7th Train Battalion (Line): 4th Detachment	1	110	181
Foot Artillery of the Young Guard			
3rd and 4th Companies	6	195	15
2nd Train Battalion: 3rd and 4th Companies	2	267	391
5th and 6th Companies	7	214	17
2nd Train Battalion: 1st and 5th Companies	2	226	428
8th Foot Artillery (Line): 15th and 16th Companies	5	174	12
7th Train Battalion (Line): 5th Company	1	150	272
Total	**44**	**2,077**	**2,195**

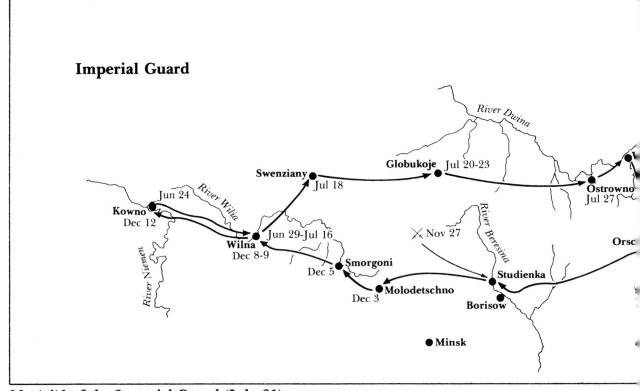

Matériel of the Imperial Guard (July 31)

Batteries	Pieces						Affûts de rechange				
	Cannon			Howitzers			Cannon			Howitzers	
	12 pdr	6 pdr	4 pdr	6 pdr 4 oz	5 pdr 6 oz	Total	12 pdr	6 pdr	4 pdr	6 pdr 4 oz	5 pdr 6 oz
Young Guard 4th Foot Company			8			**8**			9		
Young Guard 3rd Foot Company			8			**8**			9		
Young Guard 1st Foot Company		6			2	**8**		7			2
Reserve HA 1st Division		8			4	**12**		9			5
Reserve HA 2nd Division		8			4	**12**		9			5
Reserve Foot Artillery 1st Division		12			6	**18**		13			7
Reserve Foot Artillery 2nd Division	8			4		**12**	9			5	
Total	**8**	**34**	**16**	**4**	**16**	**78**	**9**	**38**	**18**	**5**	**19**
Coming to join the divisions from Wilna:	4	12			2	**18**	4	13			2
Grand Park 1st Division								2			
Grand Park 2nd Division											
Grand Park 3rd Division											
Grand Park 4th Division								3			
Division coming from Spain:											
1st Foot Battery			8			**8**			9		
2nd Foot Battery			8			**8**			9		
In Kowno	2	4		2	4	**12**	3	4	1	2	4
In Wilna	10	30		2	10	**52**	12	33	1	3	14
Total	**16**	**46**	**16**	**4**	**16**	**98**	**19**	**55**	**20**	**5**	**20**
Grand total	**24**	**80**	**32**	**8**	**32**	**176**	**28**	**93**	**38**	**10**	**39**

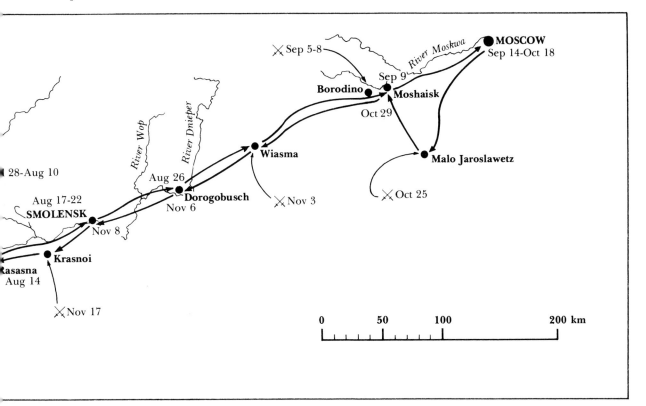

		Cannon		Howitzers	Infan-	Park	Ammuni-	Supply	Field	Total	Ammunition	
				Caissons								
12pdr	6 pdr	4 pdr	6 pdr 4 oz	5 pdr 6 oz	try		tion	vehicles	forges	vehicles	Artillery	Infantry
		12			10		1	1	1	34	1,944	170,000
		12			8		1	1	1	32	1,944	136,000
	9			4	12		1	2	1	38	1,478	204,000
	12		8	2			5	2	2	46	2,176	34,000
	12		8	2			4	2	2	44	2,176	34,000
	18		12				4	1	2	57	3,264	
24			12		7		5	1	2	65	2,436	119,000
24	**51**	**24**	**12**	**32**	**41**		**21**	**10**	**11**	**315**	**15,418**	**697,000**
12	18			4			3		2	58	3,552	
36	22		12	18	16	3	15	2	5	131	7,206	272,000
21	4			31			3		1	60	4,375	
11	16	5	2	11		1	2	1	1	50	4,359	
2	34		12		9		2		1	61	4,744	153,000
		14					1	2	1	27	2,224	
		13					1	1	1	25	2,094	
6	10		6	5	11		1		1	54	2,419	102,000
32	61		6	23	3		18		14	220	11,418	
120	**165**	**32**	**36**	**92**	**39**	**4**	**46**	**6**	**27**	**686**	**42,411**	**527,000**
144	**216**	**56**	**48**	**124**	**80**	**4**	**67**	**16**	**38**	**1,002**	**57,829**	**1,224,000**

Reserve Artillery Park of the Imperial Guard (July 1)

	Officers	Men	Horses
Canonniers conscrits detachment	1	42	2
Artillery Ouvriers of the Guard	2	236	7
Pontonnier Ouvriers of the Guard			
1st Train Battalion of the Guard: (3rd and 6th Companies	2	287	429
Canonniers conscrits detachment	1	53	3
Train of the Guard: 1st Battalion, 2nd Company and detachment of 2nd Battalion, 1st, 2nd, 3rd and 6th Companies	3	285	458
Canonniers conscrits detachment	1	45	2
Ouvriers of artillery: 16th detachment	2	41	5
7th Train Battalion: 6th Company	2	150	304
4th Train Battalion: 1st Company, 6th Detachment	2	210	347
1st Pontonnier Battalion: 3rd Company	2	115	4
4th Train Battalion: 2nd and 3rd Companies	4	267	467
13th (bis) Train Battalions: 1st, 2nd, 3rd, 5th and 6th Companies	5	682	798
Total	**27**	**2,413**	**2,826**

Engineer Park of the Imperial Guard (July 1)

	Officers	Men	Horses
5th Sapper Battalion: 6th Company	3	117	10
Sappers of the Grand Duchy of Berg: 1st Company	3	118	26
Naval Ouvriers: 1st Battalion of the Escaut	16	824	71
Marines of the Guard: 1st and 7th Companies	8	211	
Equipages of the Guard: 3rd Company	8	516	750
7th Battalion of Equipages: 1st-6th Companies	15	705	1,207
Total	**53**	**2,491**	**2,064**

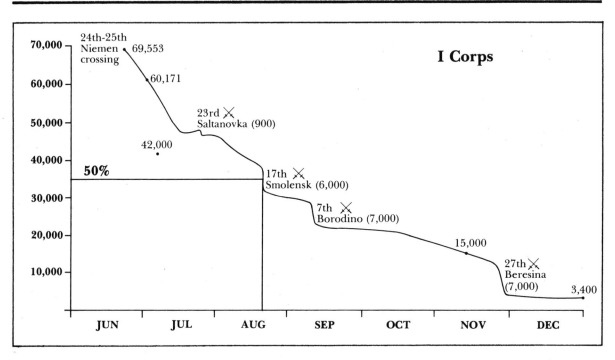

I Corps June 25
(Marshal Davout)

	Officers	Men	Officers' horses	Men's horses	Train horses
1st Infantry Division (General Morand)					
13th French Light Infantry Regiment (Colonel Dargence): 1st, 2nd, 3rd, 4th and 6th Battalions and artillery company	102	3,406	39		108
17th French Line Infantry Regiment (Colonel Vasserot): 1st, 2nd, 3rd and 4th and 6th Battalions and artillery company	96	3,498	28		108
30th French Line Infantry Regiment (Colonel Buquet): 1st, 2nd, 3rd, 4th and 6th Battalions and artillery company	93	3,715	34		107
2nd Line Infantry Regiment of Baden (Colonel Bocklin): 1st and 2nd Battalions and artillery	45	1,343	21		44
7th French Foot Artillery: 1st Company	3	103	7		
1st French Horse Artillery: 7th Company	3	88	7	90	
French Ouvriers of artillery: 7th Company		4		1	
Artillery guard		1		7	
1st Train Battalion: 1st and 2nd Companies	1	156	2	22	256
3rd French Sapper Battalion: 6th Company	3	98	1		9
12th Battalion of Equipages Militaire: 1st Company	1	75	2	13	117
Total	**347**	**12,487**	**141**	**126**	**749**
2nd Division (General Friant)					
15th French (Dutch) Light Infantry Regiment (Colonel Noos): 1st, 2nd, 3rd, 4th and 6th Battalions and artillery company	113	3,671	33		108
33rd French Line Infantry Regiment (Colonel Pouchelon): 1st, 2nd, 3rd, 4th and 6th Battalions artillery company	110	3,359	36		104
48th French Line Infantry Regiment (Colonel Groisne): 1st, 2nd, 3rd, 4th and 6th Battalions and artillery company	98	3,270	34		99
Regiment *Joseph Napoleon* (Spanish) (Colonel De Tschudy): 2nd and 3rd Battalions and artillery company	47	1,678	22	10	40
7th French Foot Artillery: 2nd Company	3	100	7		
3rd French Horse Artillery: 5th Company	3	79	7	94	
Ouvriers of artillery		4			
Artillery guard		1		1	
1st Train Battalion: 4th and 6th Companies	1	154	2		284
5th French Sapper Battalion: 5th Company	2	110	5		6
12th French Battalion of Equipages Militaire: 4th Company	2	120	4	16	171
Total	**379**	**12,546**	**150**	**121**	**812**
3rd Division (General Gudin)					
7th French Light Infantry Regiment (Colonel Rome): 1st, 2nd, 3rd, 4th and 6th Battalions and artillery companies	107	3,600	42		107
12th French Line Infantry Regiment (Colonel Toulouze): 1st, 2nd, 3rd, 4th and 6th Battalions and artillery companies	115	3,760	47		103
21st French Line Infantry Regiment (Colonel Teullé): 1st, 2nd, 3rd, 4th and 6th Battalions and artillery companies	113	3,629	36		106

3rd Division (continued)	**Officers**	**Men**	**Officers' horses**	**Men's horses**	**Train horses**
127th French (Hamburg) Line Infantry Regiment (Colonel Schaeffer): 1st and 2nd Battalions and artillery company	46	1,366	17		64
Mecklenburg-Strelitz Infantry Battalion (Colonel Bonning)	18	399	12		16
7th French Foot Artillery: 3rd Company	3	104	7		
3rd French Horse Artillery: 4th Company	4	89	8	90	
Ouvriers of artillery		4			
Artillery guard		1		1	
1st French Train Battalion: 1st and 4th Companies	1	174	2	24	265
5th French Sapper Battalion: 9th Company	3	117			6
12th French Battalion of Equipages Militaire: 1st and 3rd Companies	2	83	4		140
Total	**289**	**10,644**	**134**	**98**	**728**

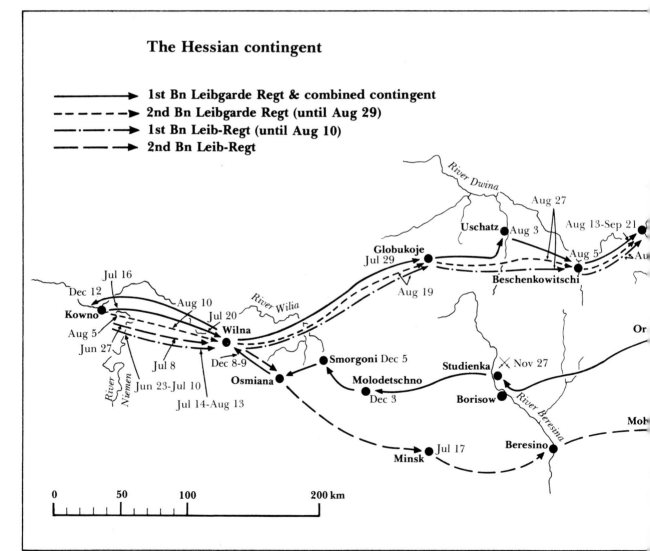

The Hessian contingent

→ 1st Bn Leibgarde Regt & combined contingent
--→ 2nd Bn Leibgarde Regt (until Aug 29)
-·-·→ 1st Bn Leib-Regt (until Aug 10)
— — → 2nd Bn Leib-Regt

4th Division (General Desaix)	Officers	Men	Officers' horses	Men's horses	Train horses
33rd French Light Infantry Regiment (Colonel Marquerie): 1st, 2nd, 3rd and 4th Battalions and artillery company	66	2,470	46		92
85th French Line Infantry Regiment (Colonel Piat): 1st, 2nd, 3rd, 4th and 6th battalions and artillery company	109	3,930	35		100
108th French Line Infantry Regiment (Colonel Achard): 1st, 2nd, 3rd, 4th and 6th Battalions and artillery company	103	3,647	33		93
Leib-Regiment (Hessen-Darmstadt) (Oberst Gall): 2nd Battalion (1st Battalion was retained in Kowno on June 24 as garrison)	9	260	5		
7th French Foot Artillery: 9th Company	3	109	7		

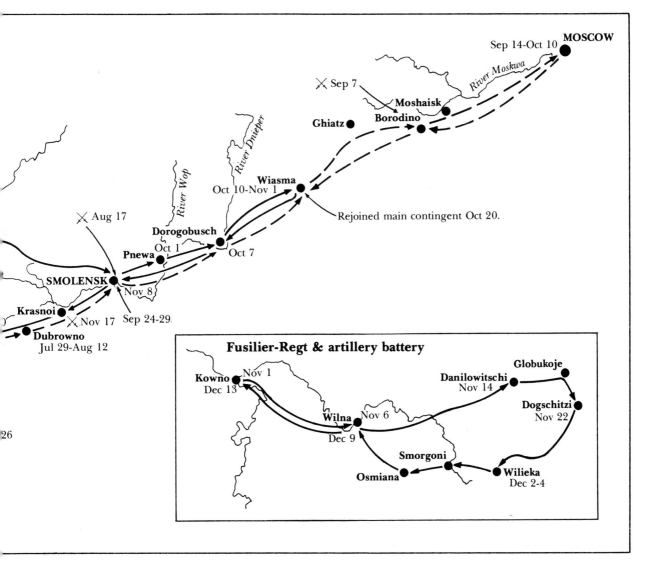

4th Division (continued)	Officers	Men	Officers' horses	Men's horses	Train horses
5th French Horse Artillery: 2nd Company	3	95	7	97	
Ouvriers of artillery		4			
Artillery guard		1			
1st French Train Battalion: 3rd and 6th Companies	1	191	2	1	297
2nd French Sapper Battalion: 3rd Company	2	114			6
12th French Battalion of Equipages Militaire: 4th Company	2	83	4		140
Total	**289**	**10,644**	**134**	**98**	**728**

5th Division (General Compans)

	Officers	Men	Officers' horses	Men's horses	Train horses
25th French Line Infantry Regiment (Colonel Dunesme): 1st, 2nd, 3rd, 4th and 6th Battalions and artillery company	68	2,004	22	12	106
57th French Line Infantry Regiment (Colonel Charrière): 1st, 2nd, 3rd, 4th and 6th Battalions and artillery company	97	3,575	42	8	98
61st French Line Infantry Regiment (Colonel					

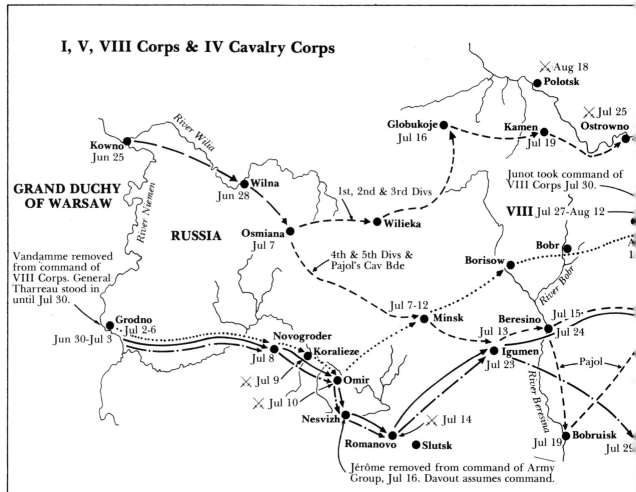

I, V, VIII Corps & IV Cavalry Corps

×Aug 18
Polotsk

Globukoje
Jul 16

Kamen
Jul 19

×Jul 25
Ostrowno

Kowno
Jun 25

River Wilha

Wilna
Jun 28

1st, 2nd & 3rd Divs

Wilieka

Junot took command of
VIII Corps Jul 30.

**GRAND DUCHY
OF WARSAW**

River Niemen

RUSSIA

Osmiana
Jul 7

VIII Jul 27-Aug 12

Bobr

4th & 5th Divs &
Pajol's Cav Bde

Borisow

Vandamme removed
from command of
VIII Corps. General
Tharreau stood in
until Jul 30.

Jul 7-12

Minsk

Beresino
Jul 13

Jul 15

Grodno
Jul 2-6

Jun 30-Jul 3

Novogroder
Jul 8

Koralieze

Igumen
Jul 23

Jul 24

Pajol

×Jul 9

Omir

River Beresina

×Jul 10

Bobruisk

Nesvizh

×Jul 14

Jul 19

Jul 29

Romanovo

Slutsk

Jérôme removed from command of Army
Group, Jul 16. Davout assumes command.

5th Division (continued)	Officers	Men	Officers' horses	Men's horses	Train horses
Bouge): 1st, 2nd, 3rd, 4th and 6th Battalions and artillery company	101	3,570	34		108
111th French Line Infantry Regiment (Colonel Juillet): 1st, 2nd, 3rd, 4th and 6th Battalions and artillery company	85	3,762	46		120
7th French Foot Artillery: 16th Company	2	105	5		
6th French Horse Artillery: 2nd Company	3	92	7	96	
Ouvriers of artillerie		4			
Artillery guard		1		1	
9th French Train Battalion: 2nd and 4th Companies	2	156	4	28	269
3rd French Sapper Battalion: 5th Company	2	117	1		6
12th French Battalion of Equipages Militaire: 3rd and 5th Companies	2	89	4	12	141
Total	**362**	**13,475**	**165**	**157**	**848**

Mecklenburg-Schwerin Infantry Regiment: 1st and
2nd Battalions transferred to IX Corps from
September 3 and to III Corps on November 4 1812

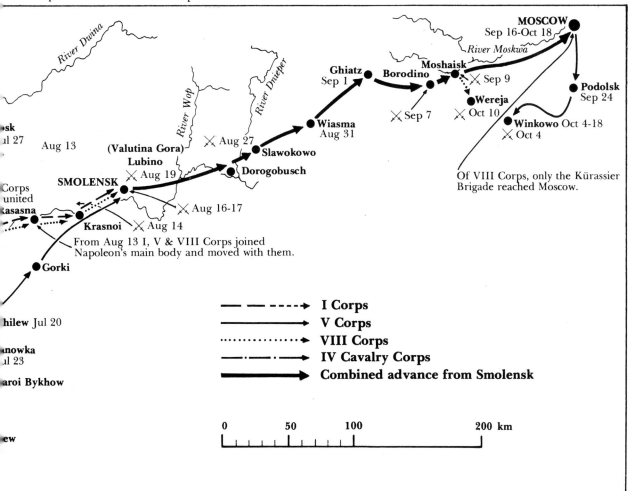

	Officers	Men	Officers' horses	Men's horses	Train horses
1st Light Cavalry Brigade (General Girardin)					
2nd French Chasseurs à Cheval (Colonel Mathis): four squadrons	40	816	103	807	7
9th Polish Lancers (Colonel Pzizichowski): four squadrons	32	645	80	634	17
2nd Light Cavalry Brigade (General Bourdesoulle)					
1st French Chasseurs à Cheval (Colonel Meda): four squadrons	35	824	79	824	8
3rd French Chasseurs à Cheval (Colonel St Mars): four squadrons	34	821	78	810	8
Total	**141**	**3,106**	**340**	**3,075**	**40**
Reserve Artillery					
1st French Foot Artillery Regiment: 3rd and 17th Companies	5	226	12		
Ouvriers of artillery: 7th Company	3	32	7		
1st French Train Battalion: 1st, 5th and 6th Companies	2	223	4	31	372
7th French Foot Artillery: 6th Company	3	99	7		
9th French Foot Artillery: 11th and 14th Companies	6	192	14		

Artillery of I Corps July 1

Equipment	1st Division		2nd Division		3rd Division	
	Divisional	Regimental	Divisional	Regimental	Divisional	Regimental
Cannons						
12 pdr						
6 pdr	10		10		10	
3 pdr		14		12		14
Howitzers						
6 pdr 4 oz						
5 pdr 6 oz	4		4		4	
Total	**14**	**14**	**14**	**12**	**14**	**14**
Caissons						
12 pdr						
6 pdr	15		15		15	
3 pdr		20		18		21
6 pdr 4 oz						
5 pdr 6 oz	8		8		8	
Infantry	16	15	16	15	16	18
Cartridges						
12 pdr						
6 pdr	1,845		1,899		1,905	
3 pdr		3,792		3,841		4,281
6 pdr 4 oz						
5 pdr 6 oz	600		595		600	
Ball						
12 pdr						
6 pdr	435		405		391	
3 pdr		686		625		648
6 pdr 4 oz						
5 pdr 6 oz	30		28		24	
Infantry	291,303	845,042	284,655	820,195	263,817	955,085

	Officers	Men	Officers' horses	Men's horses	Train horses
Artillery Park					
1st French Train Battalion: 1st, 5th and 6th Companies	2	76	5	21	101
3rd French Train Battalion: 6th Company		30		6	44
9th French Train Battalion: 1st, 2nd, 3rd, 4th and 5th Companies	6	431	14	71	786
Engineer Park					
5th French Sapper Battalions: 8th Company	2	100	4		6
Engineer Train: 1st Company	3	115	6	13	195
12th Battalion Train of Equipages: 1st, 3rd, 4th, 5th and 6th Companies	6	200	11	18	285
Ambulance soldiers: 3rd Company	2	106	2		
Gendarmes à Cheval	6	92	23	92	
Total I Corps	**1,977**	**67,576**	**1,217**	**3,952**	**5,733**

Parade states I Corps (present under arms)

Formation	Officers	Men	Men in rear	Officers' horses	Men's horses	Train horses
4th Division	293	9,560	1,155	134	97	728
5th Division	368	12,606	682	180	134	827
Light cavalry	140	3,104		345	3,059	40

	4th Division		5th Division		Artillery Reserve	Artillery Park
Divisional	Regimental	Divisional	Regimental			
					12	
10		10				
	12		12			
					4	
4		4				
14	**12**	**14**	**12**		**16**	
					36	18
15		15				38
	18		18			8
					12	8
8		8				30
16	14	16	15			40
					2,383	1,061
1,932		1,886				4,394
	3,955		4,067			1,782
					612	386
600		584				2,160
					516	246
375		400				949
	636		660			240
					56	30
24		48				87
275,060	700,626	275,760	753,756			715,176

Formation	Officers	Men	Men in rear	Officers' horses	Men's horses	Train horses
Equipages Militaire	5	200		11	18	254
Ambulances	2	112		2		
Artillery	29	1,408		70	131	1,206
Engineers	6	214		12	13	195
Total July 1	**843**	**27,194**	**1,837**	**754**	**3,452**	**3,250**
4th Division	281	8,234	2,110	133	96	718
5th Division	372	11,256	1,933	175	154	760
Light cavalry	136	2,541	580	328	2,525	40
Reserve and Grand Park	31	1,458	24	72	131	1,215
Engineer Train and park	5	219	34	10	13	187
Train	6	205	1	11	18	253
Ambulance	2	102	9	2		
Gendarmerie	4	78	2	13	80	
Total July 10	**837**	**24,093**	**4,693**	**744**	**3,017**	**3,173**
4th Division	278	8,543	1,096	133	95	717
5th Division	374	11,976	798	173	134	776
Light cavalry	130	2,533	181	317	2,522	40
Equipages Militaire	5	168	2	11	20	209
Ambulances	2	61		2		
Artillery	28	1,330	48	61	127	1,103
Engineers	6	206	2	12	13	195
Hessian Regiment and battalion on artillery guard duties	9	260	9	5		
Total July 15	**832**	**25,077**	**2,136**	**714**	**2,911**	**3,040**

II Corps June 1
(Marshal Oudinot)

	Officers	Men	Officers' horses	Men's horses	Train horses
6th Division (General Legrand)					
Divisional staff	22		151		
26th French Light Infantry Regiment (Colonel Gueheneuc): 1st, 2nd, 3rd and 4th Battalions and artillery companies	81	2,931	24		65
56th French Line Infantry Regiment (Colonel Lejeune): 1st, 2nd, 3rd and 4th Battalions and artillery companies	82	2,678	29		67
19th French Line Infantry Regiment (Colonel Aubry): 1st, 2nd, 3rd and 4th Battalions and artillery companies	85	2,791	29		74
128th French (German) Line Infantry Regiment (Colonel Metzinger): 1st and 2nd Battalions and artillery company	34	1,318	17		59
3rd Portuguese Legion Infantry Regiment (Colonel Montigny): 1st and 2nd Battalions and artillery companies	37	1,264	11		
5th French Foot Artillery: 11th Company	3	100	8		
3rd French Horse Artillery: 6th Company	3	92	7	93	
Ouvriers: 17th Company		4			
3rd Train Battalion: 3rd Company and part of 1st Company	1	161	2	22	271
3rd Sapper Battalion: 4th Company	2	96	5		6
Gendarmerie	1	10	2	10	
Total	**351**	**11,445**	**285**	**125**	**542**

	Officers	Men	Officers' horses	Men's horses	Train horses
8th Division (General Verdier)					
Divisional Staff	18		93		16
11th French Light Infantry Regiment (Colonel Casabianca): 1st, 2nd, 3rd and 4th Battalions and artillery companies	82	3,118	28		94
2nd French Line Infantry Regiment (Colonel De Wimpfen): 1st, 2nd, 3rd, 4th and 6th Battalions and artillery companies	104	3,127	31		108
37th French Line Infantry Regiment (Colonel Mayot): 1st, 2nd, 3rd and 4th Battalions and artillery companies	79	2,540	31		100
124th French (Dutch) Line Infantry Regiment (Colonel Hardyau): 1st, 2nd and 3rd Battalions and artillery companies	66	1,447	25		64
5th French Foot Artillery: 15th Company	3	112	7		
3rd French Horse Artillery: 1st Company	1	95	3	77	
Ouvriers: 17th Company		4			
3rd Train Battalion: 1st and 5th Companies	2	170	3		300
3rd Sapper Battalion: 3rd Company	2	123	4		
Gendarmerie	1	13	2	12	
Total	**358**	**10,748**	**227**	**89**	**682**
9th Infantry Division (General Merle)					
Divisional Staff	19		121		
3rd Croatian Infantry Regiment (Colonel Joly): 1st and 2nd Battalions and artillery company	41	1,582	17		33
1st Swiss Infantry Regiment (Colonel Raquetly): 1st and 2nd Battalions and artillery company	57	1,314	20		48
2nd Swiss Infantry Regiment (Colonel Castella de Berlens): 1st, 2nd and 3rd Battalions and artillery company	80	1,707	26	3	49
3rd Swiss Infantry Regiment (Colonel Thomasset): 1st, 2nd and 3rd Battalions and artillery company	67	1,266	19		49
4th Swiss Infantry Regiment (Colonel D'Affry): 1st, 2nd and 3rd Battalions and artillery company	59	1,513	11		41

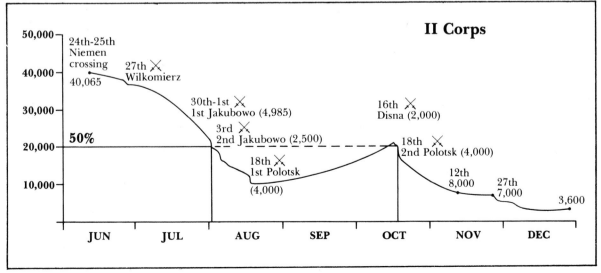

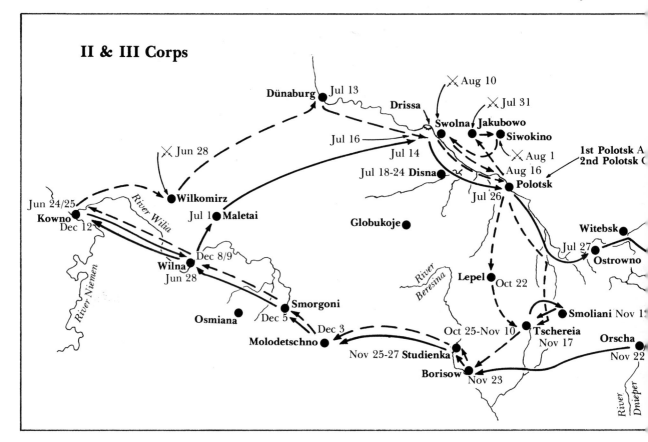

II & III Corps

9th Infantry Division (continued)	Officers	Men	Officers' horses	Men's horses	Train horses
123rd French (Dutch) Line Infantry Regiment (Colonel Avizard): 1st, 2nd and 4th Battalions and artillery company	68	1,660	14		32
7th French Foot Artillery: 4th Company	3	103	7		
2nd French Horse Artillery: 5th Company	3	73	7	77	
Ouvriers: 17th Company		2			
8th French Train Battalion: 3rd and 5th Companies	1	165	2	25	275
1st French Sapper Battalion: 5th Company	2	103			
Gendarmerie	1	11	2	11	
Total	**401**	**9,499**	**146**	**116**	**527**
3rd Cuirassier Division (General Doumerc)					
Divisional Staff	15		73		20
Chevau-légèrs: 1st Company	4	121	9	120	
4th French Cuirassiers (Colonel Dujon)	35	821	87	814	
7th French Cuirassiers (Colonel Dubios)	34	735	84	745	8
14th French Cuirassiers (Colonel Trip)	33	688	85	697	
6th French Horse Artillery: 1st and 3rd Companies	6	186	14	187	
8th French Train Battalion: 1st Company		9		1	16
11th French Train Battalion: 2nd and 6th Companies	2	164	4	27	250
Total	**129**	**2,724**	**356**	**2,591**	**294**

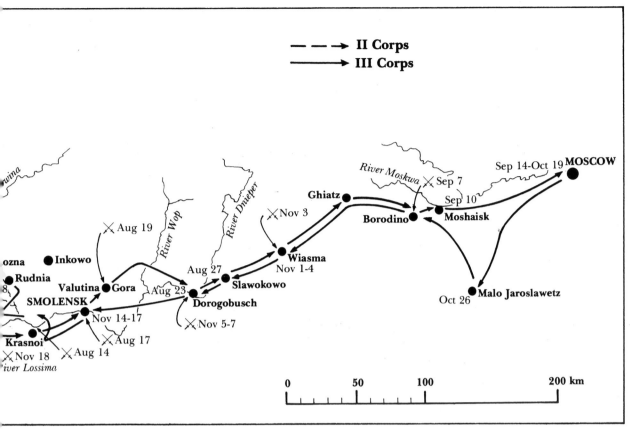

	Officers	Men	Officers' horses	Men's horses	Train horses
5th Light Cavalry Brigade (General Castex)					
Brigade Staff	7		46		
23rd French Chasseurs à Cheval (Colonel Lanougarède): 1st and 2nd Squadrons	30	803	77	811	8
24th French Chasseurs à Cheval (Colonel Amiel): 1st, 2nd and 3rd Squadrons	29	781	66	783	8
Total	**59**	**1,584**	**143**	**1,594**	**16**
6th Light Cavalry Brigade (General Corbineau)					
7th French Chasseurs à Cheval (Colonel De St Chamans): 1st and 2nd Squadrons	26	405	64	412	8
20th French Chasseurs à Cheval (Colonel Idoux): 1st and 2nd Squadrons	18	219	42	221	
8th French Chevau-Légèrs (Colonel Lubienski): 1st, 2nd, 3rd and 4th Squadrons	26	589	57	582	
Total	**70**	**1,213**	**163**	**1,215**	**8**
Artillery Park					
General Staff	18	10	81		20
1st French Foot Artillery: 1st and 15th Companies	6	205	14		
Ouvriers		4			
8th French Train Battalion: 1st and 5th Companies	2	197	4	32	330
Total	**26**	**416**	**99**	**32**	**350**

Artillery Matériel

Formation	| Pieces |					| Affûts de rechange |					
	Cannon			Howitzers			Cannon		Howitzers		
	3 pdr	6 pdr	12 pdr	6 pdr 4 oz	24 pdr	3 pdr	6 pdr	12 pdr	6 pdr 4 oz	24 pdr	3 pdr
6th Division	8	10			4		1				12
8th Division	14	10			4	1	1				16
9th Division	12	10			4	1	1				18
3rd Cuirassier Division		8			4		1		1	1	
Reserve			12	4				1	1		
Park							2	2	1	4	5
Totals	**34**	**38**	**12**	**4**	**16**	**2**	**6**	**3**	**3**	**5**	**51**

	Officers	Men	Officers' horses	Men's horses	Train horses
Artillery Reserve					
9th French Foot Artillery: 21st and 22nd Companies	5	185	12		
1st French Pontonniers: 11th Company	2	83	5		
Ouvriers: 17th Company	4	63	10		
3rd French Train Battalion: Staff 1st, 3rd and 3rd (sic) Companies	1	39		5	69
8th French Train Battalion: 1st-6th Companies	9	405	15	66	644
11th French Train Battalion: 2nd and 6th Companies		8		2	11
3rd French Sapper Battalion: 4th Company (with the Emperor)	1	99	179		
Ambulance troops	2	55	2		
Gendarmerie		34		36	
Total II Corps	**1,465**	**38,600**	**1,860**	**5,871**	**3,143**

Parade states II Corps

	Officers	Men	Officers' horses	Men's horses	Train horses
August 31					
General Staff	22		120		10
6th Infantry Division	258	5,368	253	98	455
8th Infantry Division	198	4,636	170	56	508
9th Infantry Division	333	5,688	233	95	360
3rd Cuirassier Division	147	2,456	416	1,981	255
5th and 6th Light Cavalry Brigades	132	1,648	338	1,452	16
Artillery Reserve	15	364	60	30	298
Artillery Park	26	808	61	55	607
Sappers	5	107	12		21
Equipages Militaire	8	333	15		474
Ambulance troops	2	86	2		
Gendarmerie	11	20		20	
Total	**1,146**	**21,504**	**1,680**	**3,787**	**3,004**

III Corps July 1
(Marshal Ney)

	Officers	Men	Officers' horses	Men's horses	Train horses
10th Infantry Division (General Ledru)					
24th French Light Infantry Regiment (Colonel Belair or Dubelais): 1st, 2nd, 3rd and 4th Battalions and artillery companies	84	3,020	24		66
46th French Line Infantry Regiment (Colonel Baudinot): 1st, 2nd, 3rd and 4th Battalions and artillery companies	82	2,624	29		63

	Caissons								Train Vehicles			
	Cannon		Howitzers		With the	In the	Ammuni-	Field	Rations	Ambu-	de compta-	Totals
6 pdr	12 pdr	6 pdr 4 oz	24 pdr	infantry	Park	tion waggons	forges		lances	bilité	
15			8	30		4	6	10	3	3	**114**
15			8	32		4	6	10	2	2	**125**
15			8	32		4	7	9	4		**125**
18		8	12	2		4	2				**61**
	24	8				4	2				**56**
26	24	16	16	32	5	21	6				**160**
89	**48**	**32**	**52**	**128**	**5**	**41**	**29**	**29**	**9**	**5**	**641**

	Officers	Men	Officers' horses	Men's horses	Train horses
10th Infantry Division (continued)					
72nd French Line Infantry Regiment (Colonel Laffitte): 1st, 2nd, 3rd and 4th Battalions and artillery company	88	2,484	30		56
129th French (German) Line Infantry Regiment (Colonel Freytag): 1st and 2nd Battalions and artillery company	45	984	17		58
1st Infantry Regiment of the Portuguese Legion (Colonel Pego): 1st and 2nd Battalions	51	500	31		6
Total	**350**	**9,612**	**131**		**249**
11th Infantry Division (General Razout)					
4th French Line Infantry Regiment (Colonel Massy): 1st, 2nd, 3rd and 4th Battalions and artillery company	94	2,209	29		43
18th French Line Infantry Regiment (Colonel Pelleport): 1st, 2nd, 3rd and 4th Battalions and artillery company	88	2,657	30		58
93rd French Line Infantry Regiment (Colonel Bauduin): 1st, 2nd, 3rd and 4th Battalions and artillery company	87	2,748	31		67
2nd Infantry Regiment of the Portuguese Legion (Colonel Xavier): 1st and 2nd Battalions	49	1,432	12		
Total	**318**	**9,046**	**102**		**168**
On July 24 this division was joined by 2nd Illyrian Infantry Regiment (Colonel Schmitza): ? Battalions	65	2,505	21		
25th (Württemberg) Infantry Division (General Scheeler)					
1st Jäger Battalion (Major Seeger)	15	688			8
2nd Jäger Battalion (Major Scheidemantel)	14	670			7
1st Light Infantry Battalion (Major Cornotte)	15	675			8
2nd Light Infantry Battalion (Major Stockmeyer)	15	674			8
1st Line Infantry Regiment (Colonel Dernbach): 1st and 2nd Battalions	27	1,173			16
2nd Line Infantry Regiment (Colonel Bauer): 1st and 2nd Battalions	29	1,309			16
4th Line Infantry Regiment (Colonel von Röder): 1st and 2nd Battalions	28	1,235			16
6th Line Infantry Regiment (Colonel Pollnitz): 1st and 2nd Battalions	27	1,220			16
Total	**170**	**7,624**			**95**

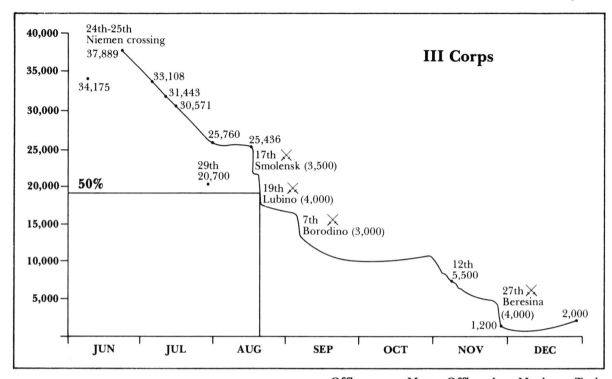

	Officers	Men	Officers' horses	Men's horses	Train horses
9th Light Cavalry Brigade (General Mourier)					
11th French Hussars (Colonel Collaert): 1st-4th Squadrons	29	607	72	602	4
6th French Chevau-légèrs (Colonel Marboeuf): 1st-3rd Squadrons	26	530	60	531	4
4th Württemberg Jäger zu Pferde (Colonel Salm): 1st-4th Squadrons	21	464	92	461	11
Total	**76**	**1,601**	**224**	**1,594**	**19**
14th Light Cavalry Regiment (General Beurmann)					
4th French Chasseurs à Cheval (Colonel Boulnois): 1st-4th Squadrons	32	708	73	656	4
28th French Chasseurs à Cheval (Colonel La Roche): 2nd Squadron plus a detachment	10	191	23	214	
1st Württemberg Chevau-légèrs (Colonel von Brockfeld): 1st-4th Squadrons	23	509	123	497	7
2nd Württemberg Chevau-légèrs (Colonel von Normann): 1st-4th Squadrons	22	496	22	478	12
Total	**87**	**1,904**	**241**	**1,845**	**23**
Train of Artillery					
6th Battalion: 1st-5th Companies	5	567	10	96	683
14th Battalion: 2nd, 3rd and 6th Companies	2	194	4	25	213
Total	**7**	**761**	**14**	**121**	**896**
Engineer Train: 6th Company					17
2nd Battalion Train of Equipages Militaire: 1st and 2nd Companies	3	220	6	29	256
Ambulance troops: 10th Company	2	99	2		4

	Officers	Men	Officers' horses	Men's horses	Train horses
Artillery					
1st French Foot Artillery: 16th, 18th and 21st Companies	7	279	17		
5th French Foot Artillery: 12th and 18th Companies	6	214	14		
9th French Foot Artillery: 2nd and 7th Companies	4	182	10		
6th French Horse Artillery: 5th and 6th Companies	6	121	14	118	
Württemberg Foot Artillery: 1st and 2nd Companies	4	160	12	4	90
Württemberg Horse Artillery: 1st and 2nd Companies	6	250	22	102	143
1st French Pontonnier Battalion: 8th Company	2	92	5		
Ouvriers: 5th Company	3	36	7		
12th Reserve Artillery Company: 1st Detachment	2	171	4	1	86
2nd Detachment	4	294	10	4	208
Total	**44**	**1,809**	**115**	**229**	**527**
Engineers					
1st French Engineer Battalion: 3rd Company	3	104			5
3rd French Engineer Battalion: 7th and 9th Companies	5	248			12
Total	**8**	**352**			**17**
Gendarmerie	3	72			
Total III Corps	**1,066**	**33,109**	**842**	**3,890**	**2,265**

Parade states III Corps (present under Arms)
June 25

	Officers	Men	Officers' horses	Men's horses	Train horses
10th Division	346	10,437	130		233
11th Division	372	11,605	118		256
25th Division	170	7,821			95
9th Brigade	79	1,644	222	1,604	19
14th Brigade	89	2,022	242	1,963	23
Artillery	43	1,811	113	227	582
Engineers	8	333			17
Artillery Train	7	749	14	112	1,113
Engineer Train		9		1	25
Train of Equipages	3	221	6	30	327
Ambulance troops	2	99	2		4
Gendarmerie	3	72	7	72	
Total	**1,022**	**36,817**	**854**	**4,009**	**2,694**

July 5

	Officers	Men	Officers' horses	Men's horses	Train horses
10th Division	350	9,038	136	6	228
11th Division	320	8,935	101		178
25th Division	170	7,624			95
9th Brigade	77	1,568	217	1,512	8
14th Brigade	87	1,899	221	1,802	23
Artillery	44	1,809	115	229	509
Engineers	8	352			17
Artillery Train	7	770	14	121	860
Train of Equipages	1	242			285
Ambulance troops	2	99	2		4
Gendarmerie	3	40	4		
Total	**1,069**	**32,439**	**810**	**3,670**	**2,207**

	Officers	Men	Officers' horses	Men's horses	Train horses
July 10					
10th Division	307	8,381	119		172
11th Division	321	8,414	109		157
25th Division	163	6,814			89
9th Brigade	80	1,681	223	1,569	15
14th Brigade	83	1,836	203	1,742	19
Artillery	69	1,797	210	223	496
Engineers	8	352			17
Artillery Train	6	755	12	120	849
Engineer Train		9			17
Train of Equipages	3	220	6	29	256
Ambulance troops	2	99	2		4
Gendarmerie	3	40	4	40	
Total	**1,045**	**30,398**	**888**	**3,723**	**2,091**
July 15					
10th Division	306	8,150	119		163
11th Division	319	8,119	102		154
25th Division	158	6,654			89
9th Brigade	79	1,700	222	1,547	15
14th Brigade	78	1,712	198	1,617	19
Artillery	42	1,784	111	222	492
Engineers	9	333			16
Artillery Train	6	744	12	120	859
Engineer Train		7			11
Train of Equipages	3	213	6	29	223
Ambulance troops	2	99	2		4
Gendarmerie	3	40	7	40	
Total	**1,005**	**29,566**	**779**	**3,575**	**2,045**
August 1					
10th Division	303	7,314	117		184
11th Division	317	6,964	102		149
25th Division	147	4,320			85
9th Brigade	79	1,483	222	1,326	15
14th Brigade	85	1,689	220	1,565	19
Artillery	41	1,753	109	204	492
Engineers	10	286	16		
Artillery Train	6	664	12	31	701
Engineer Train		7			10
Train Equipages	3	156	6	22	149
Ambulance troops	2	89	2		4
Gendarmerie	3	39	7	39	
Total	**996**	**24,764**	**813**	**3,187**	**1,808**
August 15					
10th Division	299	7,569	117		183
11th Division	317	7,144	102		146
25th Division	146	3,462			75
9th Brigade	74	1,652	214	1,321	6
14th Brigade	73	1,619	196	1,480	17
Artillery and Train	47	2,417	121	243	1,193
Engineers and Train	9	302	16		11
Train of Equipages	3	170	6	19	137
Ambulance troops	2	88	2		4
Gendarmerie	3	40	7	40	
Total	**973**	**24,463**	**781**	**3,103**	**1,772**

Artillery Matérièl

Equipment	10th Division	11th Division	25th Division	Park	Reserve	Total
Cannon						
French 12 pdr					12	**12**
French 6 pdr	10	10				**20**
Foreign 12 pdr			6			**6**
Foreign 6 pdr		14				**14**
Howitzers						
French 5 pdr 6 oz	4	4				**8**
Foreign 6 pdr 4 oz					4	**4**
Foreign 5 pdr 6 oz			8			**8**
Affûts de rechange						
Cannon 12 pdr				1	2	**3**
Cannon 6 pdr	1	1		4		**6**
Howitzers 6 pdr 4 oz					1	**1**
Howitzers 5 pdr 6 oz			1	3		**4**
Ammunition caissons						
Cannon 12 pdr			18	8	36	**62**
Cannon 6 pdr	15	15	26	20		**76**
Howitzers 6 pdr 4 oz				6	12	**18**
Howitzers 5 pdr 6 oz	8	8	16	10		**42**
Infantry	16	16	16	21		**69**
Park			7	1		**8**
Ammunition carts	4	4	5	7	4	**24**
Pontonnier tool caissons				1		**1**
Pontoon vehicles				1		**1**
Field forges	2	2	2	5	2	**13**
Regimental artillery						
3 pdr	8	6				**14**
3 pdr (sic)	8	8				**16**
Infantry	11	11				**22**
Forges	4	3				**7**
Total	**91**	**88**	**119**	**88**	**73**	**459**

IV Corps June 25

(Prince Eugene)

	Officers	Men	Officers' horses	Men's horses	Train horses
13th Infantry Division (General Delzons)					
8th French Light Infantry Regiment (Colonel Serrant): 1st and 2nd Battalions and artillery company	44	1,414	4		47
84th French Line Infantry Regiment (Colonel Pégot): 1st, 2nd, 3rd and 4th Battalions and artillery company	84	2,708	4		69
92nd French Line Infantry Regiment (Colonel Lanier): 1st, 2nd, 3rd and 4th Battalions and artillery company	83	2,591	4		69
106th French Line Infantry Regiment (Colonel Bertrand): 1st, 2nd, 3rd and 4th Battalions and artillery company	80	2,704	4		72
1st Croatian Infantry Regiment (Colonel Slivarich): 1st and 2nd Battalions	45	1,462			8

13th Infantry Division (continued)	Officers	Men	Officers' horses	Men's horses	Train horses
2nd French Foot Artillery: 9th Company; 4th French Horse Artillery: 2nd Company; 7th French Train Battalion: 2nd and 3rd Companies; and Ouvriers: 7th Company	8	350	11	63	314
1st French Sapper Battalion: 7th Company	2	128			6
9th French Battalion of Equipages Militaires: 1st Company	2	116	4		187
Total	**348**	**11,473**	**31**	**63**	**772**

14th Infantry Division (General Broussiere)

	Officers	Men	Officers' horses	Men's horses	Train horses
18th French (German) Light Infantry Regiment (Colonel Gaussard): 1st and 2nd Battalions and artillery company	36	1,401	2		48
9th French Line Infantry Regiment (Colonel De Vautré): 1st, 2nd, 3rd and 4th Battalions and artillery company	86	2,561	4		73
35th French Line Infantry Regiment (Colonel Penant): 1st, 2nd, 3rd and 4th Battalions and artillery company	76	2,456	4		70
53rd French Line Infantry Regiment (Colonel Grobon): 1st, 2nd, 3rd and 4th Battalions and artillery company	78	2,442	2		70
Regiment *Joseph Napoleon* (Spanish) (Major Doreille): 1st and 4th Battalions and artillery company	35	1,294			16
2nd French Foot Artillery: 7th Company; 4th French Horse Artillery: 3rd Company; 7th French Train Battalion: 1st and 6th Companies; and Ouvriers	8	357	11	62	315
1st French Sapper Battalion: 2nd Company	2	135			6
9th French Battalion of Equipages Militaire: 3rd Company	2	111	4		174
Total	**323**	**10,757**	**27**	**62**	**772**

15th (Italian) Infantry Division (General Pino)

	Officers	Men	Officers' horses	Men's horses	Train horses
1st Italian Light Infantry Regiment (Colonel Della Forre): 4th Battalion	22	741			8
3rd Italian Light Infantry Regiment (Colonel D'Arèse): 1st, 2nd, 3rd and 4th Battalions and artillery company	87	3,039	3		61
2nd Italian Line Infantry Regiment (Colonel Dubois): 1st, 2nd, 3rd and 4th Battalions and artillery company	86	2,690	4		61
3rd Italian Line Infantry Regiment (Colonel Lévié): 1st, 2nd, 3rd and 4th Battalions and artillery company	89	2,892	3		62
Dalmatian Infantry Regiment (Colonel Lorot): 1st, 2nd and 3rd Battalions and artillery company	65	1,681	3		53
1st Italian Foot Artillery: 14th Company; 1st Italian Horse Artillery: 2nd Company; Train of Artillery: 3rd and 4th Companies; and Ouvriers: 2nd Company	13	406	20	87	290
1st Sappers: 6th Company	3	101			6
1st Battalion of Equipages Militaire: 2nd Company	2	152	6		286
Total	**367**	**11,702**	**39**	**87**	**827**

Parade states IV Corps (present under arms)	Officers	Men	Officers' horses	Men's horses	Train horses
July 1					
13th Division	346	11,389	31	63	774
14th Division	323	10,753	29	62	764
15th Division	362	11,500	39	89	823
Italian Royal Guard	219	5,394	200	1,308	879
Cavalry	123	2,229	286	2,185	25
Artillery Reserve	19	763	10		616
Artillery Park	49	1,658	54	23	1,859
Total	**1,441**	**43,659**	**649**	**3,730**	**5,740**
July 5					
13th Division	345	11,189	31	63	764
14th Division	322	10,540	29	62	750
15th Division	344	10,574	40	89	818
Italian Royal Guard	219	5,394	200	1,308	879
Cavalry	121	2,206	284	2,157	21
Artillery Reserve	12	534	4		363
Artillery Park	43	1,405	50	24	1,579
Total	**1,406**	**41,842**	**638**	**3,703**	**5,174**
July 10					
13th Division	345	11,189	31	63	764
14th Division	322	10,539	29	62	750
15th Division	344	10,574	40	89	818
Italian Royal Guard	219	5,392	200	1,308	867
Cavalry	121	2,067	284	2,014	17
Artillery Reserve	12	534	4		363
Artillery Park	43	1,405	50	24	1,579
Total	**1,406**	**41,839**	**638**	**3,703**	**5,166**
July 15					
13th Division	341	11,134	29	62	637
14th Division	320	10,324	29	62	732
15th Division	323	9,413	37	89	758
Italian Royal Guard	220	5,373	200	1,308	867
Cavalry	121	2,067	284	2,014	17
Artillery Reserve	12	536	4		313
Artillery Park	46	1,413	50	26	1,578
Total	**1,383**	**40,262**	**633**	**3,561**	**4,952**
July 25					
13th Division	324	10,257	130	69	582
14th Division	321	9,505	145	71	595
15th Division	322	6,325	146	6	686
Italian Royal Guard	220	5,294	252	1,264	836
Cavalry	121	2,067	284	1,984	17
Artillery Reserve	12	536			313
Artillery Park	46	1,415	40	26	1,578
Total	**1,366**	**35,299**	**1,011**	**3,420**	**4,607**
August 1					
13th Division	286	8,858	27	44	609
14th Division	301	9,197	25	55	653
15th Division	306	5,352	26	80	382
Italian Royal Guard	224	5,063	210	1,238	689
Cavalry	71	1,027	165	908	3
Artillery Reserve	44	1,318	50	26	1,355
Artillery Park	12	522	4		339
Total	**1,253**	**31,337**	**507**	**2,351**	**4,040**

Artillery Matériel

Equipment	13th Division	14th Division	15th Division	Italian Guard	Light Cavalry	Artillery Reserve	Park	Total
Pieces								
3 pdr	8	8	8					24
6 pdr	10	10	10	16				46
12 pdr						24		24
Howitzers 5 pdr 6 oz	4	4	4	4		6		22
Affûts de rechange								
Cannon	3	3	3	4		4	6 (a)	23
Howitzers	2	1	1	1		2		7
Caissons								
3 pdr	12	8	8					32
6 pdr	15	15	15	24			58 (b)	137
12 pdr						72	42 (c)	114
Howitzer	8	8	8	8		12	64 (d)	108
Infantry	30	32	32	32			67 (e)	183
Park							8 (f)	8
Field forges	7	7	6	6	4	4	10 (g)	45
Ammunition carts	4	4	4	4		8	32 (h)	56
Regimental Equipages								
Caissons								
Rations	16	16	16	10	2			60
de comptabilité	4	4	4	5	2			19
Ambulances	4	4	8	9	4			29
Author's total	**127**	**124**	**127**	**123**	**12**	**132**	**287**	**937**

Remarks   (a) Remainder in Glogau, (b) About 40 in Glogau, (c) About 24 in Glogau, (d) About 44 in Glogau, (e) About 34 in Glogau, (f) About 3 in Glogau, (g) About 4 in Glogau, (h) About 11 in Glogau

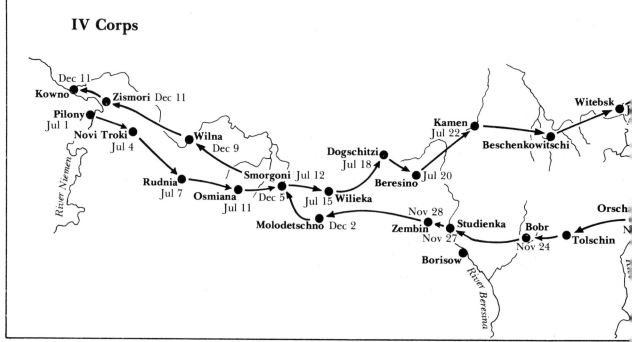

IV Corps

	Officers	Men	Officers' horses	Men's horses	Train horses
Italian Royal Guard Division (General Lecchi)					
Gardes d'Honneur (Colonel Bataglia): five companies	17	274	40	269	16
Vélites (Colonel Moroni): 1st and 2nd Battalions and artillery company	43	1,105	3		52
Infantry Regiment (Major Crovi): 1st and 2nd Battalions and artillery company	45	1,137	3		54
Conscripts Infantry Regiment (Colonel Peraldi): 1st and 2nd Battalions and artillery company	40	1,084	3		49
Cavalry of the Italian Guard (General Villata)					
Dragoons of the Guard (Colonel Jacquet): 1st and 2nd Squadrons	19	392	49	371	8
Dragoons *Regina* (Colonel Narboni): 1st-4th Squadrons	37	616	86	595	8
Italian Foot Artillery and Italian Horse Artillery: 1st and 2nd Companies; Italian Artillery Train	10	373	11	70	327
Ouvriers: 2nd Company					
1st Italian Sapper Battalion: 4th Company	3	81			6
1st Italian Battalion of Equipages Militaire: 1st and 3rd Companies	3	239	4		352
Italian Marines: one company	3	99			
Total	**220**	**5,400**	**199**	**1,305**	**872**
12th Light Cavalry Brigade (General Ornano)					
9th French Chasseurs à Cheval (Colonel De St Suzanne): 1st-3rd Squadrons	28	513	67	503	6
19th French Chasseurs à Cheval (Colonel Vincent): 1st-3rd Squadrons	23	506	54	505	3
7th Polish Lancers (Colonel Klicki): joined later					
Total	**51**	**1,019**	**121**	**1,008**	**9**

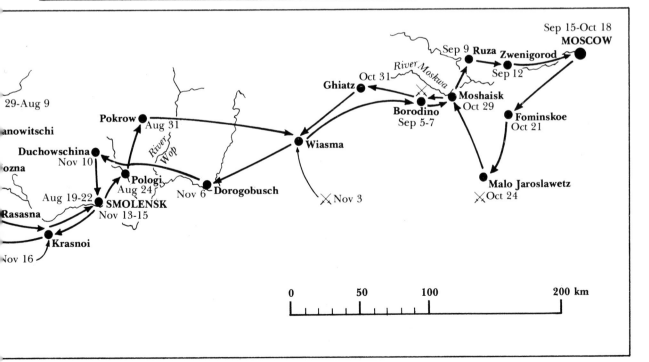

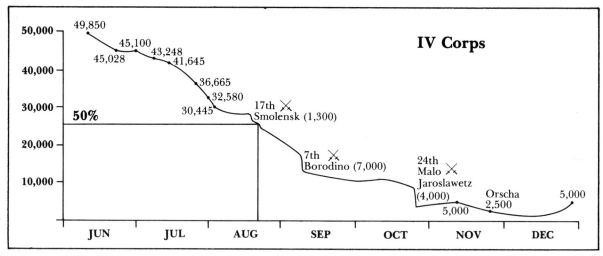

	Officers	Men	Officers' horses	Men's horses	Train horses
13th (Italian) Light Cavalry Brigade					
2nd Chasseurs à Cheval (Colonel Banco): 1st-4th Squadrons	39	608	89	587	8
3rd Chasseurs à Cheval (Colonel Rambourg): 1st-4th Squadrons	33	601	76	590	8
Total	**72**	**1,209**	**165**	**1,177**	**16**
Artillery Reserve					
2nd French Foot Artillery: 5th and 12th Companies	6	191			
7th French Train Battalion: 5th and parts of the 1st, 2nd and 6th Companies	1	166	2		306
French Ouvriers detachment		5			
Italian Foot Artillery: 2nd and 7th Companies	8	172			
Italian Artillery Train: 5th and 6th Companies and a detachment of the 9th Company	4	197	8		310
Italian Ouvriers: detachment of the 2nd Company		5			
Total	**19**	**736**	**10**		**616**
Artillery Park					
French units					
2nd Foot Artillery: 8th, 10th and 20th Companies	6	250			
7th Train Battalion: part of 6th Company		176			323
2nd Pontonnier Battalion: 1st Company	2	83			
Ouvriers: 10th Company	4	53			
9th Battalion of Equipages: 2nd Company	2	121	4		193
Italian units					
Pontonniers: 2nd Company	5	72			
Artillery Train: 7th, 8th and 9th Companies	5	211	10		340
Artillery Ouvriers: 2nd Company	1	14			
1st Sapper Battalion: 2nd Company	2	39			6
2nd Transport Battalion: 4th and 5th Companies	4	137	8		238
2nd Transport (*Attele de boeufs*) Battalion: 1st-6th Companies	14	334	30	23	572
Engineer Train Company	2	95	2		130
Total	**47**	**1,585**	**54**	**23**	**1,802**
Total IV Corps	**1,147**	**43,881**	**646**	**3,725**	**5,686**

V Corps June 25
(Prince Poniatowski)

	Officers	Men	Officer's horses	Men's horses	Train horses
16th Infantry Division (General Zayonchek)					
3rd Infantry Regiment (Colonel Zakrzewski): 1st, 2nd and 3rd Battalions and artillery company	63	2,558	13	6	90
13th Infantry Regiment (Colonel Zymirski): 1st, 2nd and 3rd Battalions and artillery company	67	2,612	16	6	87
15th Infantry Regiment (Colonel Miaskowski): 1st, 2nd and 3rd Battalions and artillery company	59	2,616	13	6	82
16th Infantry Regiment (Colonel Czartoryski): 1st, 2nd and 3rd Battalions and artillery company	58	2,313	19	6	84
4th Chasseurs à Cheval (Colonel Dulfus): 1st-4th Squadrons	38	748	81	730	18
Artillery					
Foot Artillery: 3rd Company	5	139	12	10	128
Foot Artillery: 12th Company	4	153	9	10	130
Supplementary Battalion: 3rd Company	1	56	2	6	102
Sapper Battalion	1	71	2		17
Ouvriers of artillery		7			
Total	**296**	**11,273**	**167**	**780**	**738**
17th Infantry Division (General Dombrowski)					
1st Infantry Regiment (Colonel Malachowski): 1st, 2nd and 3rd Battalions and artillery company	60	2,336	12	6	88
6th Infantry Regiment (Colonel Siorawski): 1st-4th Battalions and artillery company	54	2,633	12	6	89
14th Infantry Regiment (Colonel Siemianowski): 1st-4th Battalions and artillery company	55	2,489	14	6	84
17th Infantry Regiment (Colonel Hornowski): 1st-4th Battalions and artillery company	60	2,606	14	6	86
19th Cavalry Brigade					
1st Chasseurs à Cheval (Colonel Przebendowski): 1st-4th Squadrons and artillery company	28	624	79	613	18
12th Lancers (Colonel Rzyszczewski): 1st-4th Squadrons and artillery company	30	647	67	651	19
Artillery					
Foot Artillery: 10th Company	5	162	12	10	130
Foot Artillery: 11th Company	5	170	12	10	129
Supplementary Battalion: 1st Company	1	55	2		110
Sapper Battalion	2	69	3		14
Ouvriers of artillery		7			
Total	**300**	**11,798**	**222**	**1,308**	**767**
18th Infantry Division (General Kamienicki)					
2nd Infantry Regiment (Colonel Krukowiecki): 1st-3rd Battalions and artillery company	56	2,364	14	6	89
8th Infantry Regiment (Colonel Stuart): 1st-3rd Battalions and artillery company	60	2,362	16	6	92
12th Infantry Regiment (Colonel Wierzbinski): 1st-3rd Battalions and artillery company	57	2,173	13	5	91
20th Light Cavalry Brigade					
5th Chasseurs à Cheval (Colonel Kurnatowski): 1st-4th Squadrons and artillery company	32	759	82	756	18
13th Hussars (Colonel Tolinski): 1st-4th Squadrons and artillery company	33	722	83	717	32

	Officers	Men	Officers' horses	Men's horses	Train horses
Artillery					
Foot Artillery: 4th Company	5	158	10	10	130
Foot Artillery: 5th Company	5	148	10	10	127
Supplementary Battalion: 2nd Company	1	56	2	7	104
Sapper Battalion	2	59	4		14
Ouvriers of artillery		7			
Total	251	8,808	234	1,517	697
Artillery Reserve					
Horse Artillery: 2nd Company	5	147	12	96	130
Foot Artillery: 14th Company	3	152	6	10	128
Supplementary Battalion: 4th Company	2	119	4	10	210
Ouvriers of artillery		7			
Total	10	425	22	116	468
Bridging Train					
Pontonniers	3	118	6		30
Supplementary Battalion	1	47	2		87
Total	4	165	8		117
Artillery Park					
Foot Artillery: 7th Company	5	164	10	10	130
Foot Artillery: 8th Company	1	80	2	10	127
Foot Artillery: 9th Company	1	85	2	10	130
Foot Artillery: 13th Company	1	74	2	10	130
Foot Artillery: 15th Company	2	87	4	10	130
Ouvriers of artillery	2	27	4		
Total	12	517	24	50	647
Engineer Park					
Sapper Battalion	6	84	8	90	
Battalion of Equipages Militaire	8	640			936

Parade states V Corps (present under arms)

July 1	Officers	Men	Officers' horses	Men's horses	Train horses
16th Division	296	11,273	167	780	738
17th Division	300	11,798	222	1,308	767
18th Division	251	8,808	234	1,517	697
Artillery Reserve	10	425	22	116	468
Artillery Park	12	517	24	50	647
Bridging Train	4	165	8		117
Engineer Park	6	84	8		90
Equipages Militaire	8	640			936
Total	887	33,710	685	3,771	4,460

July 16	Officers	Men	Officers' horses	Men's horses	Train horses
16th Division	296	11,133	166	811	740
17th Division	301	11,018	226	1,306	762
18th Division	252	8,509	233	1,503	695
Artillery Reserve	10	425	22	116	468
Artillery Park	12	517	24	50	647
Bridging Train	4	165	8		117
Engineer Park	5	116	10		47
Equipages Militaire	8	640			936
Total	888	32,523	689	3,786	4,412

Artillery matériel

Equipment	16th Division	17th Division	18th Division	Reserve	Park	Bridging Train	Total
Line artillery							
Pieces with carriages and armament							
Cannon 12 pdr				6			6
Cannon 6 pdr	8	8	8	6			30
Howitzer 7 pdr	4	4	4				12
Total pieces	**12**	**12**	**12**	**12**			**48**
Affûts de rechange							
12 pdr				1			1
6 pdr	1	1	1	1	2		6
3 pdr	1	1	1	1			4
Howitzers 7 pdr	1	1	1		1		4
Caissons							
Cannon 12 pdr				12	6		18
Cannon 6 pdr	16	16	16	14	6		68
Cannon 3 pdr	4	4	4	4	3		19
Howitzers 7 pdr	8	8	8	4	14		42
Infantry	8	8	8	12	32		68
Cavalry	1	1	1	2	2		7
Artificers					2		2
Locally purchased carts					2		2
Carts and Waggons (of ammunition?)	5	5	5	5	19	14	53
Field forges	2	2	2	2	3	1	12
Total vehicles	**47**	**47**	**47**	**58**	**92**	**15**	**306**

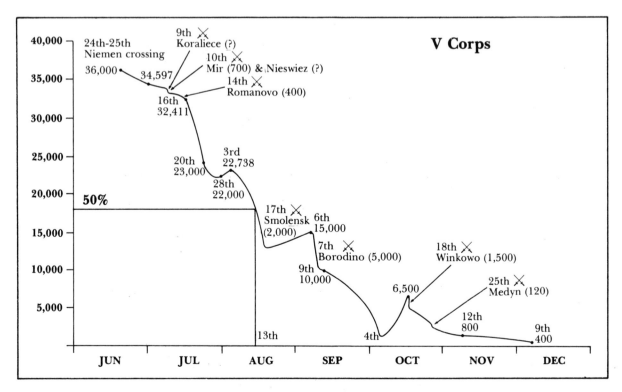

V Corps Regimental artillery and ammunition supply

Equipment	16th Division	17th Division	18th Division	Reserve	Park	Total
Cannon on carriages						
3 pdr	8	8	6			**22**
Caissons						
3 pdr	12	12	9			**33**
Infantry	12	12	9			**33**
Cartridges in the caissons and in the chests						
Canister 12 pdr				720	360	**1,080**
Canister 6 pdr	1,440	1,440	1,440	1,260	540	**6,120**
Canister 3 pdr	1,920	1,920	1,520	480	360	**6,200**
Howitzer shell 7 pdr	460	460	460	240	840	**2,460**
Ball 12 pdr				240	120	**360**
Ball 6 pdr	400	400	400	350	150	**1,700**
Ball 3 pdr	320	320	260	80	60	**1,040**
Howitzer ball 7 pdr	96	96	96	48	168	**504**
Infantry	340,000	340,000	289,000	216,000	544,000	**1,729,000**
Cavalry	18,000	18,000	18,000	36,000	36,000	**126,000**
Flints	25,000	25,000	20,000	18,000	45,000	**133,000**

VI Corps
(Marshal St Cyr)

	Officers	Men	Officers' horses
19th Division (I Bavarian Corps) (General Deroy — killed at Polozk August 20) **1st Brigade** (General-Major von Siebein)			
1st Light Battalion (Major Gedoni)	16	581	8
1st Line Infantry Regiment *König* (Colonel von Strohl): 1st and 2nd Battalions	38	1,514	14
9th Line Infantry Regiment *Ysenburg* (Colonel de la Motte): 1st and 2nd Battalions	41	1,507	14
Total	**95**	**3,602**	**36**
2nd Brigade (General-Major von Raglovich)			
3rd Light Battalion (Major Bernklau)	19	745	8
4th Line Infantry Regiment *Sachsen-Hildburghausen* (Colonel von Ziller): 1st and 2nd Battalions	39	1,444	14
10th Line Infantry Regiment *Junker* (Colonel Preysing): 1st and 2nd Battalions	37	1,473	12
Total	**95**	**3,662**	**34**
3rd Brigade (General-Major Graf Rechberg)			
6th Light Battalion (Major La Roche)	20	1,009	12
8th Line Infantry Regiment *Herzog Pius* (Colonel von Wreden): 1st and 2nd Battalions	37	1,272	11
Total	**57**	**2,281**	**23**
Total 19th Division	**247**	**9,545**	**93**
20th Division (II Bavarian Corps) (General Wrede) **1st Brigade** (General-Major von Vincenti — later General-Major Minucci)			
2nd Light Battalion (Major Treuberg)	21	710	9
2nd Line Infantry Regiment *Kronprinz* (Colonel Spauer): 1st and 2nd Battalions	41	1,513	15

	Officers	Men	Officers' horses	Men's horses	Train horses
1st Brigade (continued)					
6th Line Infantry Regiment *Herzog Wilhelm* (Colonel Deroy): 1st and 2nd Battalions	36	1,528	17		
Total	**98**	**3,751**	**41**		
2nd Brigade (General-Major Graf Beckers — later General-Major von Vincenti)					
4th Light Battalion (Major Theobald)	19	732	9		
3rd Line Infantry Regiment *Prinz Carl* (Colonel Waldkirch): 1st and 2nd Battalions	37	1,508	19		
7th Line Infantry Regiment *Löwenstein* (Colonel Maillot): 1st and 2nd Battalions	37	1,481	8		
Total	**93**	**3,721**	**36**		
3rd Brigade (Oberst von Habermann [or Dalwigk] — later General-Major Graf Beckers)					
5th Light Battalion (Major Buttler)	13	460	10		2
5th Line Infantry Regiment *Preysing* (Colonel Habermann): 1st and 2nd Battalions	39	1,504	11		16
11th Line Infantry Regiment *Kinkel* (Colonel Dallwig): 1st and 2nd Battalions	39	1,528	7		12
Total	**91**	**3,492**	**28**		**30**
Total 20th Division	**282**	**10,964**	**105**		**30**
20th Light Cavalry Brigade (General-Major von Seidewitz)					
3rd Chevau-Légers Regiment (Colonel Ellbracht): 1st, 2nd, 4th and 5th Squadrons	19	481	65	478	
6th Chevau-Légers Regiment *Bubenhofen* (Colonel Dietz): 1st, 2nd, 4th and 5th Squadrons	20	494	53	489	
Total	**39**	**975**	**118**	**967**	
21st Light Cavalry Brigade (General-Major von Preysing)					
4th Chevau-Légers Regiment *König* (Colonel Seyssel): 1st-4th Squadrons	19	442	51	432	
5th Chevau-Légers Regiment *Leiningen* (Colonel Gaddum): 1st-4th Squadrons	19	461	47	456	
Total	**38**	**903**	**98**	**888**	
Artillery with the 19th Division					
1st Light 6 pdr Battery (Widemann)					
3rd Light 6 pdr Battery (Halder)	6	155	14		
11th 6 pdr Foot Battery (Brack)	2	74	3		
6th 12 pdr Foot Battery (Rois)	3	84	3		
Total	**11**	**313**	**20**		
Train					
Attached to 1st Battery	1	52	2	14	79
Attached to 3rd Battery	1	49		14	82
Attached to 11th Battery	1	36	1	2	58
Attached to 6th Battery	1	39	1	3	64
Park	1	196	1	6	326
Total	**5**	**372**	**5**	**39**	**609**
Artillery with the 20th Division					
2nd Light 6 pdr Battery (Gotthard)	4	78	4	15	
4th Light 6 pdr Battery (Gravenreuth)	4	76	5	17	
4th 12 pdr Foot Battery (Berchem)	3	86		4	
5th 6 pdr Foot Battery (Hoffstetten)	3	80		4	
8th 6 pdr Foot Battery (Ulmer)	4	77		4	
Total	**18**	**397**	**9**	**44**	

VI Corps (July 1—October 21) & Preysing's Cavalry Division (July 2—October 15)

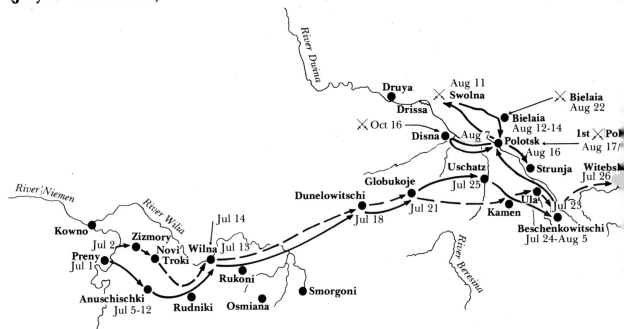

VI Corps (October 18—December 12) & Preysing's Cavalry Division (October 15—December 12)

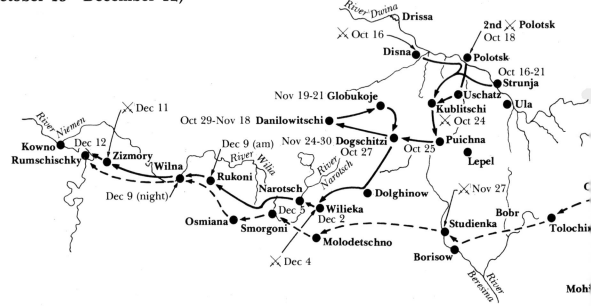

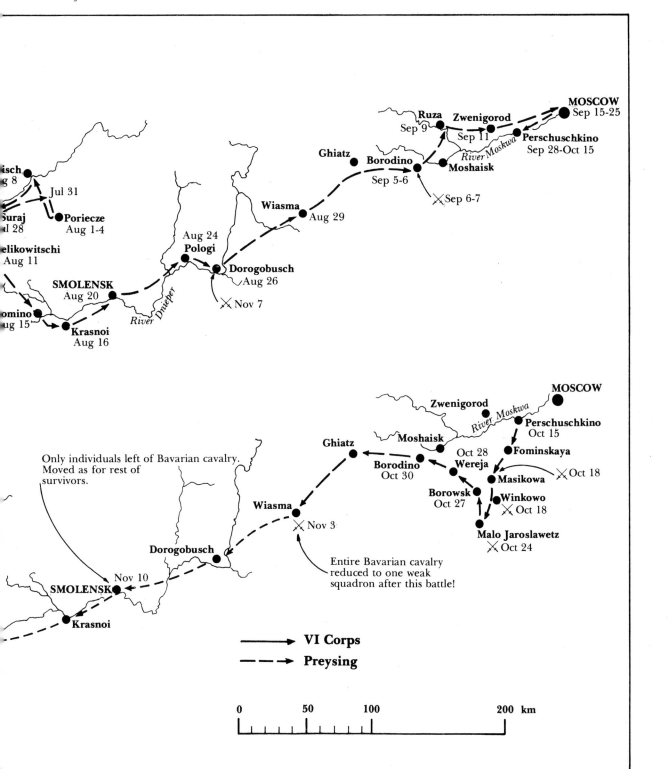

isch
g 8

Jul 31

Poriecze
Aug 1-4

Suraj
l 28

elikowitschi
Aug 11

SMOLENSK
Aug 20

omino
ug 15

Krasnoi
Aug 16

River Dnieper

Pologi
Aug 24

Dorogobusch
Aug 26

✕ Nov 7

Wiasma
Aug 29

Ghiatz

Borodino
Sep 5-6

✕ Sep 6-7

Ruza
Sep 9

Zwenigorod
Sep 11

Moshaisk

River Moskwa

Perschuschkino
Sep 28-Oct 15

MOSCOW
Sep 15-25

MOSCOW

Zwenigorod

Moshaisk

River Moskwa

Perschuschkino
Oct 15

Fominskaya

Oct 28

Ghiatz

Borodino
Oct 30

Wereja

✕ Oct 18

Masikowa

Borowsk
Oct 27

Winkowo
✕ Oct 18

Malo Jaroslawetz
✕ Oct 24

Only individuals left of Bavarian cavalry.
Moved as for rest of
survivors.

Wiasma
✕ Nov 3

Entire Bavarian cavalry
reduced to one weak
squadron after this battle!

Dorogobusch

Nov 10

SMOLENSK

Krasnoi

→ **VI Corps**

--→ **Preysing**

0   50   100   200 km

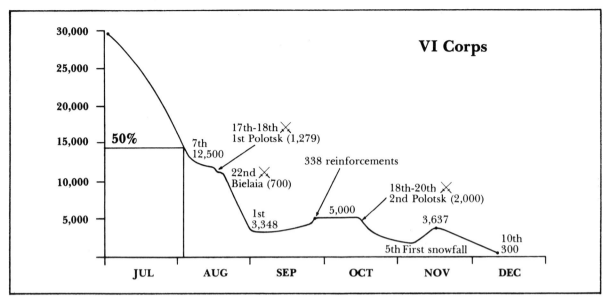

	Officers	Men	Officers' horses	Men's horses	Train horses
Train					
Attached to the 2nd Battery	1	79	2	5	82
Attached to the 4th Battery		47		4	83
Attached to the 4th Battery	1	37	2	3	68
Attached to the 5th Battery	1	32	1	3	68
Attached to the 8th Battery	1	32	2	1	55
Park	1	238	2	11	357
Total	**5**	**465**	**9**	**27**	**713**
Engineers	4	22	9	1	4
Total VI Corps	**629**	**22,947**	**454**	**1,966**	**1,356**

Artillery Matériel

Cannon 12 pdr	8
Cannon 6 pdr	30
Howitzers	20
Caissons	
12 pdr	20
6 pdr	42
Howitzer	46
6 pdr *Würst*	16
Howitzer *Würst*	8
Infantry	90
Cavalry	8
Affûts de rechange	12
Field forges	12
Charcoal waggons	12
Baggage waggons	4
Ambulances	2
Tool waggons	4
Harness waggons	4
Waggons for cash	16
Artificers caissons	6

Ammunition

Cartridges		
Canister 12 pdr	1,184	
Canister 6 pdr	5,060	of which 200 in Danzig
Ball 12 pdr	312	
Ball 6 pdr	1,480	of which 60 in Danzig
'Boites' ball 12 pdr	68	
'Boites' howitzer	632	
Obuls	3,052	

Cartridges		
Infantry	1,285,000	of which 28,560 in Danzig
Cavalry pistols	48,384	
Cavalry carbines	96,768	

Flints		
Musket	180,000	
Pistols	16,000	

VII Corps June 30

(General Reynier)

	Officers	Men	Officers' horses	Men's horses	Train horses
21st Infantry Division					
(General Lecoq)					
1st Brigade (General von Steindel)					
General staff	7	15	78		15
Grenadier Battalion *von Liebenau* (formed of the Grenadiers of the regiments *Prinz Friedrich* and *Prinz Clemens*)	17	688	12		15
Regiment *Prinz Friedrich* (Colonel von Brochewski):					
1st Battalion	16	684	19		30
2nd Battalion	15	659	10		
Regiment *Prinz Clemens* (Colonel von Mellentin):					
1st Battalion	18	698	16		30
2nd Battalion	20	694	8		
2nd Brigade					
(General von Nostitz)					
Regiment *Prinz Anton* (Colonel von Ryssel):					
1st Battalion	20	670	21		23
2nd Battalion	18	703	10		8
1st Light Infantry Regiment (Colonel von Egidy):					
1st Battalion	16	694	14		19
2nd Battalion	18	690	13		11
Total	**158**	**6,180**	**123**		**136**
Artillery					
General staff (Colonel von Grossman)	2		8		
Regimental artillery					
Prinz Friedrich	1	62	1		34
Prinz Clemens	1	62	1		34
Prinz Anton	1	62	1		34
4th Foot Artillery Battery (Captain von Brause)	4	115	4		80
Divisional Park	3	110	3		128
Total	**12**	**411**	**18**		**310**
Sapper Company (Captain Plödterl)	2	66	2		17
Total 21st Division	**179**	**6,672**	**221**		**478**

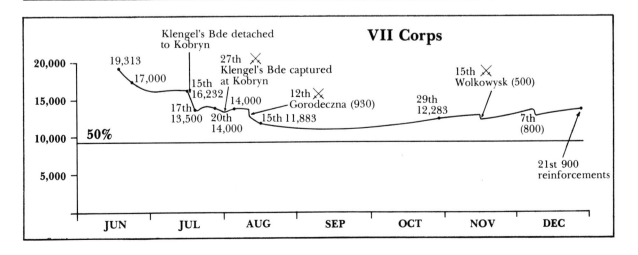

VII Corps

Klengel's Bde detached to Kobryn

27th ✕
Klengel's Bde captured at Kobryn

15th ✕
Wolkowysk (500)

20,000 — 19,313
17,000

15th
16,232
14,000

12th ✕
Gorodeczna (930)

29th
12,283

15,000 —

17th
13,500   20th
14,000

15th 11,883

7th
(800)

50%
10,000 —

21st 900
reinforcements

5,000 —

JUN   JUL   AUG   SEP   OCT   NOV   DEC

	Officers	Men	Officers' horses	Men's horses	Train horses
22nd Infantry Division (General Funck)					
1st Brigade* (General von Klengel)					
General staff	8	8	77		10
Grenadier Battalion (Colonel von Brause): (formed of the Grenadiers of the regiments *König* and *Niesemeuschel*)	17	692	14		15
Regiment *König* (Colonel von Göphardt):					
1st Battalion	15	691	15		30
2nd Battalion	16	618	11		
Regiment *von Niesemeuschel* (Colonel von Vogel):					
1st Battalion	17	713	17		29
2nd Battalion	16	687	15		
2nd Brigade (General von Sahr)					
Grenadier Battalion (Colonel Anger): (formed of the Grenadiers of the regiments *Prinz Anton* and *von Low*	18	673	8		15
Grenadier Battalion (Colonel von Spiegel): formed of the Grenadiers of the *Prinz Max* and *Rechten*	17	647	9		15
2nd Light Infantry Regiment (Colonel von Tettenborn):					
1st Battalion	20	685	14		31
2nd Battalion	17	661	13		
Total	**153**	**6,067**	**116**		**135**
Artillery					
General staff (Colonel Auenmuller)	2		6		
Regimental artillery					
Regiment *König*	1	62	1		34
Regiment *Niesemeuschel*	1	62	1		34
3rd Foot Artillery Battery (Captain Bonniot)	4	115	4		80
Divisional Park	3	110	3		128
Total	**11**	**349**	**15**		**276**
Total 22nd Division	**172**	**6,424**	**208**		**421**
23rd Light Cavalry Brigade (General von Gablenz)					
General staff	1		12		
Prinz Clemens Ulans (Colonel von Gablenz):					
Staff	5	14	19	2	28
1st Squadron	7	149	14	141	6
2nd Squadron	6	147	14	139	5
3rd Squadron	6	137	14	141	5
4th Squadron	7	145	10	142	6
von Polenz Chevau-légèrs (Colonel von Hann):					
Staff	6	15	16	2	30
1st Squadron	7	141	16	135	6
2nd Squadron	6	127	16	141	5
3rd Squadron	7	138	15	138	6
4th Squadron	7	136	15	143	3
Husaren-Regiment (Colonel von Engel):					
Staff	7	12	30	1	26
1st Squadron	4	101	9	99	3
2nd Squadron	4	99	9	101	4
3rd Squadron	4	94	9	98	4
4th Squadron	3	96	7	100	4
5th Squadron	2	97	5	100	4

*This brigade was captured at the battle of Kobryn, July 30.

23rd Light Cavalry Brigade (continued)	Officers	Men	Officers' horses	Men's horses	Train horses
6th Squadron	3	96	7	100	3
7th Squadron	4	87	9	99	4
8th Squadron	4	98	9	97	3
Total	**99**	**1,929**	**243**	**1,919**	**155**
1st Horse Artillery Battery (Major von Roth)	4	156	8	86	124
Total	**104**	**2,085**	**263**	**2,005**	**279**
Cavalry Division (General von Thielmann)					
General staff	7		19		
Garde du Corps (Colonel Leysser): 1st-4th Squadrons	36	639	93	628	27
Kürassier-Regiment *Zastrow* (Colonel von Trützschler): 1st-4th Squadrons	36	639	95	628	27
Chevau-légèrs Regiment (Colonel von Lessing): 1st-4th Squadrons	36	639	93	628	27
2nd Horse Artillery Battery (Major von Hiller)	7	169	8	84	157
Total	**122**	**2,086**	**308**	**1,968**	**238**

Corps artillery

	Officers	Men	Officers' horses	Men's horses	Train horses
General staff	3		10		
21st Division	2		8		
1st Horse Artillery Battery (Major von Roth)	3	91	7	86	
Artillery Train	1	65	1		24
1st Foot Artillery Battery (Major von Brause)	3	73	3		
Artillery Train	1	42	1		80
Regimental artillery					
Prinz Friedrich	1	44	1		
Artillery Train		18			34
Prinz Clemens	1	44	1		
Artillery Train		18			34
Prinz Anton	1	44	1		
Artillery Train		18			34
Divisional Park	3	42	3		
Train		68			128
22nd Division	2		6		
2nd Horse Artillery Battery (Major von Hiller)	3	87	7	84	
Artillery Train	1	82	1		157
3rd Foot Artillery Battery (Major Bonniot)	3	73	3		
Artillery Train	1	42	1		80
Regimental Artillery					
König	1	44	1		
Artillery Train		18			34
Niesemeuschel	1	[no other figures appear]			
Artillery Train		18			34
Divisional Park	3	42	3		
Train		68			128
Artillery Reserve					
(Major von Hoyer)	2		6		
2nd Foot Artillery Battery (Major Sontag)	3	73	3		
Artillery Train	1	42	1		80
4th Foot Artillery Battery (Major Rouvroy)	3	73	3		
Artillery Train	1	42	1		80
Grand Reserve Park	2		6		
Artillery	8	156	8		
Train	4	237	7		440
Total	**58**	**1,708**	**94**	**170**	**1,367**

Parade states VII Corps (present under arms)
July 15

	Officers	Men	Officers' horses	Men's horses	Train horses
General staff	19	13	95		26
21st Division	179	6,560	220		477
22nd Division	172	6,427	208		422
1st Cavalry Brigade (sic)	104	2,105	249	1,985	279
2nd Cavalry Brigade (sic)					
Reserve and Grand Artillery Park	24	629	35		594
Total	**498**	**15,734**	**807**	**1,985**	**1,798**
July 31					
General staff	17	13	19		26
21st Division	176	6,418	222		473
22nd Division	113	4,220	156		350
1st Cavalry Brigade (sic)	81	1,729	216	1,627	264
2nd Cavalry Brigade (sic)					
Reserve and Grand Artillery Park	24	603	35		616
Total	**411**	**12,983**	**724**	**1,627**	**1,729**
August 15					
General staff	17	13	95		26
21st Division	174	6,046	224	18	444
22nd Division	98	3,668	125	12	336
1st Cavalry Brigade (sic)	72	1,569	181	1,362	251
2nd Cavalry Brigade (sic)					
Reserve and Grand Artillery Park	24	587	35	30	564
Total	**385**	**11,883**	**660**	**1,412**	**1,621**

Artillery Matérièl

		21st Division			22nd Division	
Equipment	1st Foot Battery	Divisional Park	Regimental Artillery	3rd Foot Battery	Divisional Park	Regimental Artillery
Pieces with carriages and armaments						
Cannon 6 pdr	4			4		
Cannon 4 pdr			12			8
Howitzers	2			2		
Total	**6**		**12**	**6**		**8**
Affûts de rechange						
Cannon 6 pdr		1			1	
Cannon 4 pdr						
Howitzers 8 pdr		1			1	
Caissons						
Cannon 6 pdr	4	4		4	4	
Cannon 4 pdr			12			8
Howitzers 8 pdr	4	2		4	2	
Infantry		15			15	
Cavalry		2			2	
Spare tools	1	1		1	1	
Artificers tools						
Waggons						
Equipment	1			1	1	
Ambulances		1			1	
Administrative		1			1	
Train						
Charcoal carts						
Field forges	1			1	1	
Total	**11**	**28**	**12**	**11**	**28**	**8**

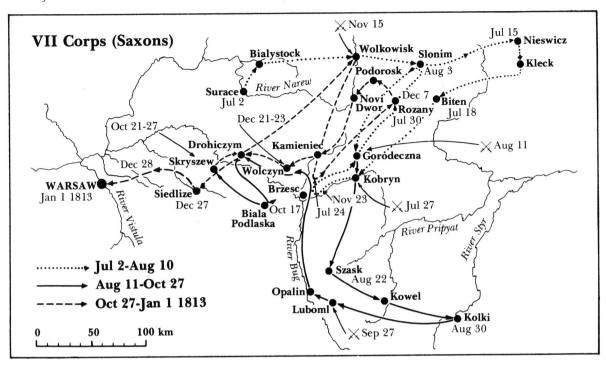

VII Corps (Saxons)

Cavalry Brigade	2nd Foot Battery	Reserve 4th Foot Battery	Park	Total	Remarks
4	4	4		**20**	**Ammunition** (rounds)
				20	Ball:
2	2	2		**10**	6 pdr 6,000
6	**6**	**6**		**50**	4 pdr 4,200
1			1	**4**	Howitzer 2,004
					Canister:
			1	**3**	6 pdr 1,632
					4 pdr 1,160
6	4	4	11	**41**	Howitzer 630
			5	**25**	Infantry 1,235,520
			11	**35**	Cavalry 180,000
			48	**78**	Balles à feu 126,000
			4	**8**	Flints 126,000
1	1	1	8	**15**	Cartridges:
			1	**1**	Infantry 187,200
					Cavalry 45,000
1	1	1	1	**6**	
			1	**3**	
			6	**8**	
			1	**1**	
			2	**2**	
1	1	1	2	**7**	
14	**11**	**11**	**103**	**227**	

VIII Corps June 25

(King Jérôme, General Vandamme, finally Junot)	Officers	Men	Officers' horses	Men's horses	Train horses
23rd Infantry Division					
(General Tharreau)					
1st Brigade (General-Major Damas)					
3rd Light Battalion (Major von Hessberg)	23	733	6		12
2nd Line Infantry Regiment (Colonel von Fullgraf):					
1st-4th Battalions and artillery company	67	2,400	22		63
6th Line Infantry Regiment (Colonel Ruelle): 1st					
and 2nd Battalions and artillery company	44	1,522	20		54
2nd Brigade (General-Major Wickenberg)					
2nd Light Battalion (Major von Bödicker)	23	737	6		12
3rd Line Infantry Regiment (Colonel Bernard): 1st					
and 2nd Battalions and artillery company	43	1,634	19		55
7th Line Infantry Regiment (Colonel Smallian): 1st-					
3rd Battalions and artillery company	67	2,252	24		67
Artillery					
1st Foot Battery (Major Fröde)	4	184	15		119
24th Infantry Division					
(General von Ochs)					
1st Brigade (General-Major Legras)					
Chasseurs Carabiniers Battalion (Major von Hessberg)	28	641	6		22
Jäger-Garde Battalion (Major Picot)	26	810	11	12	
Grenadier-Garde Battalion (plus artillery) (Major Muldner)	27	805	10		8
Artillery of the Guard (Captain Brunig)	1	38	3		28
1st Light Battalion (Major von Rauschenplatt)	19	795	6		12
5th Line Infantry Regiment (Colonel Gissot): 1st and					
2nd Battalions and artillery company	47	1,716	19		57

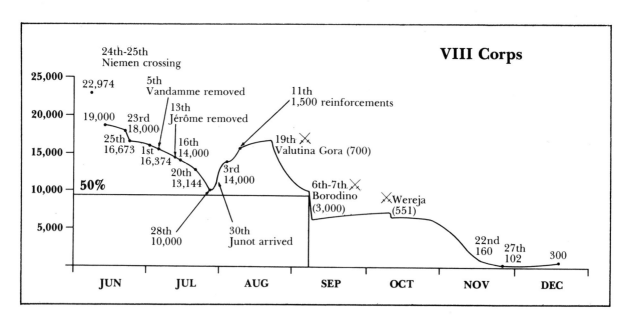

	Officers	Men	Officers' horses	Men's horses	Train horses
2nd Brigade					
1st Line Infantry Regiment (Colonel Plessmann)	[No data given]				
8th Line Infantry Regiment (Colonel Bergeron)	[No data given]				
Divisional artillery (Captain Volmar)					
2nd Foot Battery	4	188	9	11	110
Horse Battery	4	161	7	57	161
Cavalry					
1st Hussars (Colonel Zandt)	38	579	94	566	18
2nd Hussars (Colonel Hessberg)	39	585	89	573	22
Reserve Park (Major Schulz)					
Artillery	3	76	5		
Sappers	2	99	5		
Ouvriers	1	22	2		
Train	1	132	2	19	184
Gendarmerie	3	50	6	50	
Total	**514**	**16,159**	**386**	**1,276**	**1,000**

Parade States VIII Corps

July 1

	Officers	Men	Officers' horses	Men's horses	Train horses
23rd Division	258	9,160	94		255
24th Division	145	4,789	55		137
Light Cavalry	72	1,093	173	1,079	30
Artillery and Sappers	18	839	42	109	510
Total	**493**	**1,588**	**364**	**1,188**	**932**

July 20

	Officers	Men	Officers' horses	Men's horses	Train horses
23rd Division	213	7,353	93	17	335
24th Division	115	3,930	49	14	218
Light Cavalry	69	1,081	166	1,042	29
Artillery and Sappers	7	345	17	22	200
Gendarmerie	2	29	5	30	
Total	**406**	**12,738**	**330**	**1,125**	**782**

Artillery Matériel

24 pdr howitzers	8
6 pdr cannon	26
Affûts de rechange	4

Caissons	
Howitzer	25
6 pdr cannon	41
Infantry	23
Charges d'effets de rechange	2

Waggons	
Howitzer ammunition	1
6 pdr ammunition	2
Infantry ammunition	13
Coal	1
Engineer tools	9
Bridging equipment	5
Divisional vehicles	11
Field forges	11

Ammunition quantities	
Howitzer charges	1,472
Canister for howitzer	48
Spare cartridges	1,050
6 pdr ball	4,375
6 pdr canister	1,020
Powder (lbs)	928½
Priming wads	10,657
Matches	1,855
Packets of wadding	1,118
Infantry cartridges	980,743
Cavalry cartridges	17,940
Lead (lbs)	135¾
6 pdr ball with sabot	11
Flints	85,935

IX Corps August 31
(Marshal Victor)

	Officers	Men	Officers' horses	Men's horses	Train horses
12th Infantry Division (General Partouneaux) **1st Brigade** (General Camus)					
10th French Light Infantry Regiment (Colonel Florquin): 4th Battalion	22	929	8		
29th French Light Infantry Regiment (Colonel St Suzanne): 1st-4th Battalions and artillery company	78	2,663	29		55
2nd Brigade (General Blanmont)					
Provisional Regiment (Major Wable): 36th French Line, 4th Battalion; 51st French Line, 4th Battalion; and 55th French Line, 4th Battalion	52	1,911	17		24
125th French (Dutch) Line Infantry Regiment: 1st, 2nd and 3rd Battalions and artillery company	59	1,417	24		61
3rd Brigade (General Billard)					
44th French Line Infantry Regiment (Major Teulle): 3rd and 4th Battalions and artillery	39	1,749,	16		49
126th French (Dutch) Line Infantry Regiment (Colonel Demoulin) 1st-4th Battalions and artillery	84	1,937	20		28
5th Artillery Regiment (Major Levasseur): 20th Company	3	113	7		
7th Artillery Regiment (Major Gresset): 5th Company	3	98	7		
14th Train Battalion: 1st Company		23		3	27
14th Train Battalion: 5th Company	1	84	2	16	303
Ouvriers		4			
Total 12th Division	**341**	**10,928**	**130**	**19**	**547**

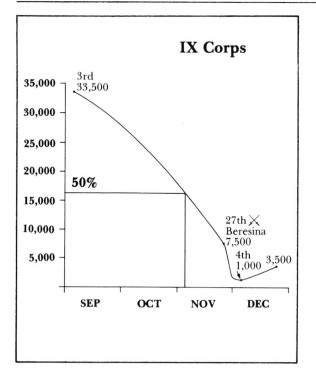

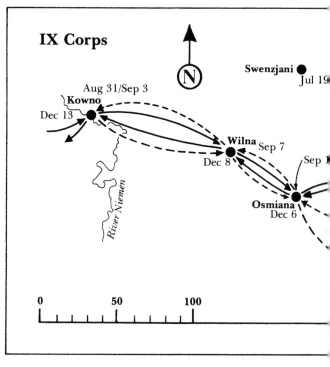

26th Infantry Division (General Daendels)	Officers	Men	Officers' horses	Men's horses	Train horses
1st Brigade (General Damas)					
General Staff	2		17		
1st Line Infantry Regiment (Colonel Genty): 1st and 2nd Battalions	41	969	15		18
4th Line Infantry Regiment (Colonel Förch): 1st and 2nd Battalions	48	926	16		17
2nd Brigade (General Lingg)					
2nd Line Infantry Regiment (Colonel Hoffmeyer): 1st and 2nd Battalions	43	1,079	16		16
3rd Line Infantry Regiment (Colonel Boisdavid): 1st Battalion	23	579	6		10
Baden Brigade (General Hochberg)					
1st Line Infantry Regiment (Colonel von Francken): 1st and 2nd Battalions	40	1,494	19	1	28
3rd Line Infantry Regiment (Colonel Brückner): 1st and 2nd Battalions	35	1,416	16		
1st Jäger Battalion (Major Peternel)	19	779	10	1	15
Artillery					
Artillery of Berg (Lt Colonel Bogärt) staff	2		10		
Foot Battery (Captain Vussenberg)	6	102	17	3	
Horse Battery (Captain Heymer)	4	86	10	82	
Train (Captain Klopmann)	3	143	7	18	216
Baden Foot Battery (Captain Fischer)	2	60	12		
Baden Horse Battery (Captain Süsburg)	6	64	8	28	
Baden Train (Captain Petermann)	1	166	3	13	276
Total 26th Division	**275**	**7,863**	**182**	**144**	**624**

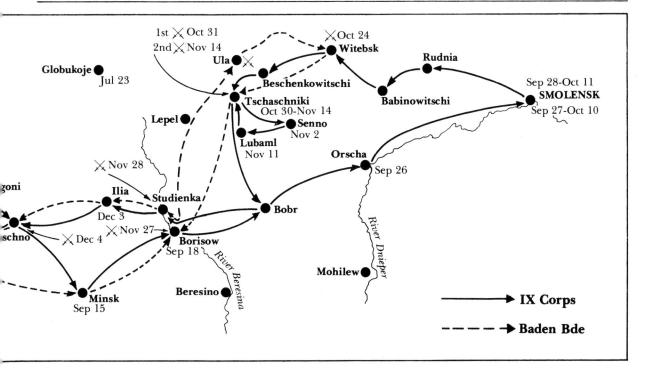

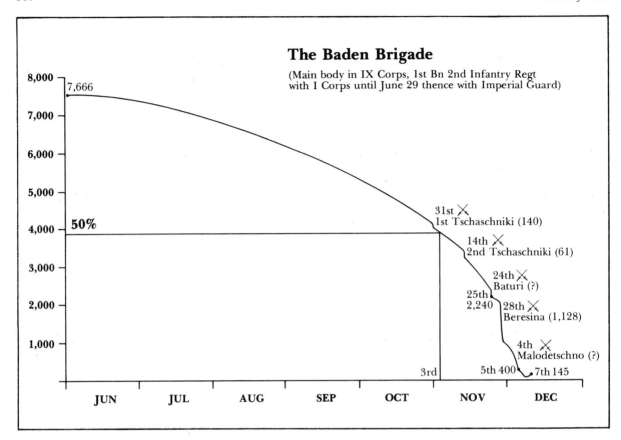

The Baden Brigade

(Main body in IX Corps, 1st Bn 2nd Infantry Regt
with I Corps until June 29 thence with Imperial Guard)

28th (Polish) Infantry Division (General Girard)	Officers	Men	Officers' horses	Men's horses	Train horses
4th Infantry Regiment (Colonel Zdzitowiecki): 1st and 2nd Battalions and artillery company	37	1,294	23		56
7th Infantry Regiment (Colonel Oranowski): 1st and 2nd Battalions and artillery company	39	928	28		48
9th Infantry Regiment (Colonel Cicoski): 1st and 2nd Battalions and artillery company	44	1,237	20		56
Sappers (Major Szweycer)	4	93	9		5
Foot Artillery (Major Camiaski)	4	63	9		
Total 28th Division	**128**	**3,615**	**89**		**165**
30th Light Cavalry Brigade (General Fournier)					
2nd Lancers of Berg (Colonel Nesselrode): 1st-4th Squadrons	29	664	73	664	21
Garde Chevau-légers of Hessen-Darmstadt (Colonel Dalwigk): 1st-4th Squadrons	13	335	33	335	18
31st Light Cavalry Brigade (General Delaitre)					
Saxon Chevau-légers Regiment *Prinz Johann* (Colonel Rayski): 1st-4th Squadrons	32	524	108	524	26
Baden Hussars (Colonel Laroche-Starkenfels): 1st-4th Squadrons	17	382	62	387	22
Total	**91**	**1,905**	**276**	**1,910**	**87**

XI Corps

(Marshal Augereau)

	Officers	Men	Officers' horses	Men's horses	Train horses
30th Infantry Division					
(General Heudelet) August 15					
1st Brigade (General Breissand)					
Staff	1		3		
6th Provisional Infantry Regiment (Major Legros):					
16th French Light Infantry Regiment: 4th Battalion	21	646	7		
21st French Light Infantry Regiment: 4th Battalion	14	721	4		
28th French Light Infantry Regiment: 4th Battalion	16	779	4		
28th French Line Infantry Regiment: 5th Battalion	2	148			
43rd French Line Infantry Regiment: 5th Battalion	3	240	2		
65th French Line Infantry Regiment: 5th Battalion	4	226			
7th Provisional Infantry Regiment (Major Dauger):					
Staff	1		3		
8th French Line Infantry Regiment: 4th Battalion	17	698	4		
14th French Line Infantry Regiment: 4th Battalion	11	743	4		
94th French Line Infantry Regiment: 4th Battalion	18	680	4		
8th Provision Infantry Regiment (Major Treny):					
Staff	1		3		
54th French Line Infantry Regiment: 4th Battalion	15	703	5		
88th French Line Infantry Regiment: 4th Battalion	22	638	3		
95th French Line Infantry Regiment: 4th Battalion	20	692	5		
2nd Brigade (General Husson)					
9th Provisional Infantry Regiment (Major Gleizes):					
Staff	11	5	17		
24th French Line Infantry Regiment: 4th Battalion	15	667			
45th French Line Infantry Regiment: 4th Battalion	15	794			
59th French Line Infantry Regiment: 4th Battalion	17	500			
17th Provisional Infantry Regiment (Major Schneider):					
Staff	1		3		
6th French Light Infantry Regiment: 4th Battalion	17	549	8		
25th French Light Infantry Regiment: 4th Battalion	17	531	4		
39th (sic) French Light Infantry Regiment: 4th Battalion	20	421	5		
1st Provisional Dragoon Regiment					
Staff	4		9		
2nd Dragoons: 4th Squadron	4	215	8	220	
5th Dragoons: 4th Squadron	5	107	10	110	
12th Dragoons: 4th Squadron	5	139	11	143	
13th Dragoons: 4th Squadron	3	108	7	114	
17th Dragoons: 4th Squadron	5	117	10	119	
19th Dragoons: 4th Squadrons	5	118	11	128	
20th Dragoons: 4th Squadron	5	101	11	114	
Artillery					
7th Foot Artillery Regiment: 7th Company	2	103	5		
7th Foot Artillery Regiment: 17th Company	3	96	11	8	
13th Battalion 'bis' Train		64			95
Total 30th Division	**320**	**11,549**	**181**	**956**	**95**

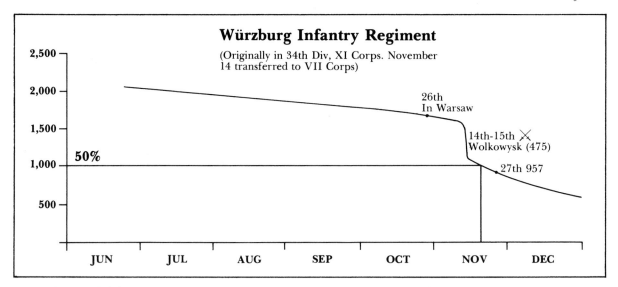

Würzburg Infantry Regiment

(Originally in 34th Div, XI Corps. November 14 transferred to VII Corps)

31st Infantry Division (General Lagrange)	Officers	Men	Officers' horses
10th Provisional Infantry Regiment (Major Suax)			
Staff	1		3
27th French Line Infantry Regiment: 4th Battalion			
63rd French Line Infantry Regiment: 4th Battalion	15	691	5
76th French Line Infantry Regiment: 4th Battalion	20	415	5
96th French Line Infantry Regiment: 4th Battalion	11	646	4
Total	**47**	**1,752**	**17**
13th Provisional Infantry Regiment (Major Tripe)			
Staff	1		3
5th French Line Infantry Regiment: 4th Battalion	15	684	4
11th French Line Infantry Regiment: 4th Battalion	14	636	5
79th French Line Infantry Regiment: 4th Battalion	18	700	4
Total	**48**	**2,020**	**16**
11th Provisional Infantry Regiment (Major Van Ommeren)			
Staff	1		3
50th French Line Infantry Regiment: 4th Battalion	19	549	5
27th French Light Infantry Regiment: 4th Battalion	18	685	5
Total	**38**	**1,234**	**13**
12th Provisional Infantry Regiment (Colonel Desmaroux)			
Staff	1		3
124th French (Dutch) Line Infantry Regiment: 4th Battalion	19	660	5
123rd French (Dutch) Line Infantry Regiment: 3rd Battalion	14	700	4
125th French (Dutch) Line Infantry Regiment: 4th Battalion	19	579	4
129th French (German) Line Infantry Regiment: 3rd Battalion	18	538	4
	71	2,477	20
Total 31st Division	**204**	**7,483**	**66**

32nd Infantry Division (General Durutte)	Officers	Men	Officers' horses	Men's horses	Train horses
Regiment *l'Ile de Ré* (or 132ᵉ de Ligne) (Colonel Tridoulat): 2nd, 3rd and 4th Battalions	52	2,206			
Regiment *Belle-Isle* (Colonel Baum): 2nd, 3rd and 4th Battalions	62	1,757	25		
Regiment *Ile de Walcheren* (Or 131ᵉ de Ligne) (Colonel Maury): 2nd, 3rd and 4th Battalions	60	2,278	23		
1st Regiment *de la Méditerranée* (or 35ᵉ Leger) (Colonel Duche): 1st and 2nd Battalions		1,681			
2nd Regiment *de la Méditerranée* (or 133ᵉ de Ligne) (Colonel ?): 4th Battalion	22	967	2		
Total 32nd Division	**196**	**8,889**	**50**		
33rd (Neapolitan) Infantry Division (General Detres)					
Marines of the Guard	8	176	5		2
5th Neapolitan Line Infantry Regiment (Colonel Lebon)	49	1,594	16		
6th Neapolitan Line Infantry Regiment (Colonel Digennaro)	42	1,564	13		
7th Neapolitan Line Infantry Regiment (Colonel Macdonald)	41	1,475	15		
Horse Artillery	6	75	20	81	4
Gardes d'honneur	31	395	106	405	4
Vélites à Cheval	22	320	78	293	2
Vélites à Pied	46	1,154	25		8
Total 33rd Division	**245**	**6,753**	**278**	**779**	**20**

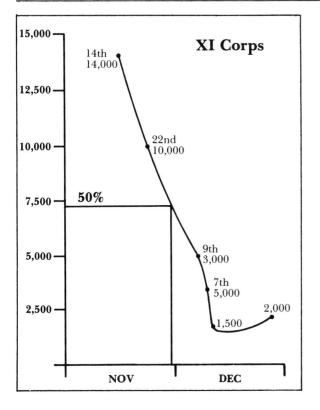

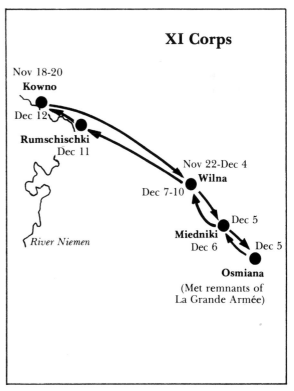

34th Infantry Division (General Morand) September 1	Officers	Men	Officers' horses	Men's horses	Train horses
1st Brigade (General Schram)					
3rd French Line Infantry Regiment: 4th Battalion	7	451	4		
29th French Line Infantry Regiment: 3rd and 4th Battalions	30	1,594	7		
105th French Line Infantry Regiment: 4th Battalion	9	459	4		
113th French Line Infantry Regiment: 3rd and 4th Battalions	38	1,469	13		
2nd Brigade (General Anthing)					
4th Westfalian Line Infantry Regiment (Colonel de Rossy): 1st and 2nd Battalions and artillery company	48	1,638	19		53
4th Rheinbund Regiment (Ducal Saxon) (Colonel von Egloffstein: 1st, 2nd and 3rd Battalions	77	2,524	36		125
1st Light Infantry Regiment of Hessen-Darmstadt (Colonel von Schönberg): 1st and 2nd Battalions and artillery	40	1,549	33		146
8th French Foot Artillery Regiment: 17th Company	4	70	5		
12th Chasseurs à Cheval: detachment	2	79	4	100	
Total 34th Division	**255**	**9,833**	**125**	**100**	**342**

This division later included the 5th and 6th Rheinbund Regiments each with two battalions.

The XI Corps was later joined by the Saxon Infantry Regiment *Prinz Maximilian*; five companies of French Customs Guards and sailors; and a French Foot Artillery Battery.

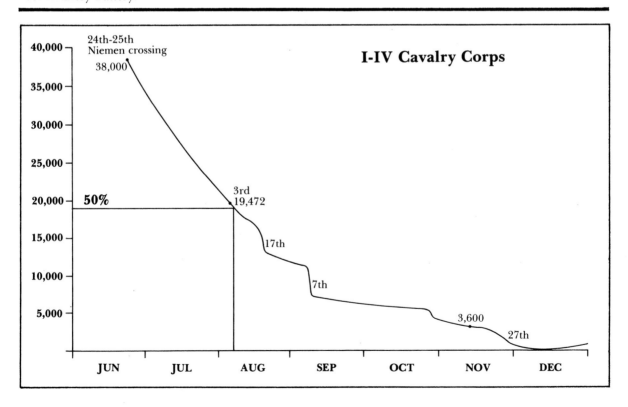

I Cavalry Corps July 1
(General de Division Nansouty)

	Officers	Men	Officers' horses	Men's horses	Train horses
1st Light Cavalry Division					
(General de Division Bruyere)					
3rd (French) Brigade (General Jacquinot)					
9th Chevau légèrs (Colonel Gobrecht): 1st-4th Squadrons	45	665	113	658	4
7th Hussars (Colonel Eulner): 1st-4th Squadrons	39	914	104	935	8
4th French Brigade (General Piré)					
8th Hussars (Colonel Domont): 1st-4th Squadrons	33	902	80	905	4
16th Chasseurs (Colonel Lhaillier): 1st-4th Squadrons	33	804	84	799	8
15th Brigade (General Nienwiewski)					
6th Polish Lancers (Colonel Radziwill): 1st-4th Squadrons	34	636	83	629	27
8th Polish Lancers (Colonel Lagouski): 1st-4th Squadrons	28	739	66	734	15
2nd Prussian Hussars (Colonel Ziethen): 1st-4th Squadrons	20	565	50	553	8
6th French Horse Artillery Regiment: 7th Company	3	76	7	67	
1st Train Battalion: 1st Company		67		7	114
Total	**235**	**5,378**	**587**	**5,287**	**188**
1st (French) Cuirassier Division					
(General de Division St Germain)					
2nd Cuirassiers (Colonel Rolland): 1st-4th Squadrons	33	759	82	742	
3rd Cuirassiers (Colonel D'Audenarde): 1st-4th Squadrons	34	830	82	823	
9th Cuirassiers (Colonel Murat): 1st-4th Squadrons	34	842	88	787	
1st Chevau-légèrs: 1st Company	13	254	29	257	
5th Horse Artillery: 1st Company	3	86	7	77	
5th Horse Artillery: 3rd Company	3	90	7	87	
Ouvriers: 3rd Company		4			
Artillery Guard		1	1		
11th Train Battalion: 1st Company	1	166	2	19	246
Total	**121**	**3,032**	**298**	**2,792**	**246**
5th (French) Cuirassier Division					
(General de Division Valence)					
6th Cuirassiers (Colonel Martin): 1st-4th Squadrons	38	722	92	703	5
11th Cuirassiers (Colonel Duclos): 1st-4th Squadrons	33	653	82	648	8
12th Cuirassiers (Colonel Curnieu): 1st-4th Squadrons	37	812	85	806	8
5th Chevauxlégèrs	7	153	19	156	2
5th Horse Artillery: 4th and 5th Companies	6	169	14	161	
11th Train Battalion: 3rd and 6th Companies	1	131	2	19	207
Total	**122**	**2,645**	**294**	**2,493**	**230**

Parade States June 25

	Officers	Men	Officers' horses	Men's horses	Train horses
1st Light Cavalry Division	239	5,608	586	5,485	192
1st Cuirassier Division	118	2,993	294	2,768	238
5th Cuirassier Division	122	2,645	294	2,493	230
Total	**479**	**11,246**	**1,174**	**10,746**	**660**
July 1					
1st Light Cavalry Division	235	5,378	587	5,287	188
1st Cuirassier Division	121	3,062	298	2,792	246
Total	**356**	**8,440**	**885**	**8,079**	**434**

	Officers	Men	Officers' horses	Men's horses	Train horses
July 15					
1st Light Cavalry Division	242	4,996	594	4,719	161
1st Cuirassier Division	121	2,499	292	2,184	234
Total	**363**	**7,495**	**886**	**6,903**	**395**
July 31					
1st Light Cavalry Division	192	3,770	523	3,439	154
1st Cuirassier Division	111	1,596	267	1,472	
Artillery	7	312	16	155	175
Total	**310**	**5,678**	**806**	**5,066**	**329**

Artillery Matériel	1st Light Cavalry Division	1st Cuirassier Division	5th Cuirassier Division	Total
6 -dr cannon	4	8	8	**20**
24 pdr howitzers	2	4	4	**10**
Affûts de rechange				
6 pdr cannon		1	1	**2**
24 pdr howitzers		1	1	**2**
Caissons				
6 pdr cannon	9	12	12	**33**
24 pdr howitzers	6	8	8	**22**
Infantry		2	2	**4**
Ammunition waggons	2	4	4	**10**
Field forges	1	2	2	**5**
Total	**24**	**42**	**42**	**108**
Cartridges				
Canister 6 pdr cannon	1,095	1,589	1,500	4,193
Canister 24 pdr howitzers	468	586	592	1,646
Ball 6 pdr cannon	618	317	300	1,235
Ball 24 pdr howitzers	520	39	32	591
Ball Infantry		42,600	36,980	79,580
Flints		2,400	3,000	5,400
Signal rockets		15	15	30

II Cavalry Corps July 1
(General Montbrun)

	Officers	Men	Officers' horses	Men's horses	Train horses
2nd Light Cavalry Division					
(General Sebastiani)					
8th (French) Brigade (General St Genies)					
Staff	13		80		
5th Hussars (Colonel Meuziau): 1st-4th Squadrons	34	691	82	675	7
9th Hussars (Colonel Maignet): 1st-4th Squadrons	27	721	52	652	6
7th (French) Brigade (General Burthe)					
11th Chasseurs (Colonel Desirat): 1st-3rd Squadrons	27	682	62	563	
12th Chasseurs (Colonel Ghigny): 1st-3rd Squadrons	30	576	66	569	8
16th Brigade (General Subervie)					
1st Prussian Ulans (Colonel von Werder)	11	228	27	227	
3rd Württemberg Jäger zu Pferde (Colonel Waldburg)	20	432	70	422	
10th Polish Hussars (Colonel Vuinski)	28	653	57	647	
Total	**184**	**3,883**	**496**	**3,755**	**27**

	Officers	Men	Officers' horses	Men's horses	Train horses
2nd (French) Cuirassier Division					
(General Wathier)					
Staff	13		75		
5th Cuirassiers (Colonel Christophe): 1st-4th Squadrons	36	678	78	660	8
8th Cuirassiers (Colonel Grandjean): 1st-4th Squadrons	36	673	85	648	7
10th Cuirassiers (Colonel Franck): 1st-4th Squadrons	37	621	81	597	8
2nd Horse Artillery: 1st and 4th Companies	8	176	16	151	
1st Train Battalion: 1st Company and 11th Train Battalion: 5th Company	2	155	4	17	233
2nd Chevaulégèrs: 1st Company	5	133	13	114	
Total	**137**	**2,416**	**352**	**2,187**	**256**
4th (French) Cuirassier Division					
(General Defrance)					
Staff	17		90		
1st Carabiniers (Colonel Laroche): 1st-4th Squadrons	38	676	90	596	5
2nd Carabiniers (Colonel Blancard): 1st-4th Squadrons	37	650	80	596	6
1st Cuirassiers (Colonel Clerc): 1st-4th Squadrons	37	553	75	475	6
1st Horse Artillery: 3rd and 4th Companies	5	168	12	163	
1st Train Battalion: 3rd Company; and 11th Train Battalion: 5th Company	2	149	2	18	233
4th Chevaulégèrs	4	104	9	104	
Total	**140**	**2,300**	**358**	**1,952**	**250**

Approximate Parade State July 31

	Officers	Men	Officers' horses	Men's horses	Train horses
2nd Cuirassier Division	144	2,323	363	2,024	182
4th Cuirassier Division	144	2,257	377	1,828	150

Artillery Matérièl

Artillery Matérièl	As at July 4	Used on July 5	As at July 6
6 pdr cannon	8		8
24 pdr howitzers	4		4
Caissons 6 pdr	10		10
Caissons 24 pdr	6		6
Field forges	1		
Ammunition waggons	2		2
6 pdr canister cartridges	197	9	188
24 pdr canister cartridges	20		
6 pdr ball	958	126	832
24 pdr ball	298	88	210

	With the Corps	In Bromberg	In Wilna
6 pdr cannon on limbers	8		
24 pdr howitzer on limbers	4		
6 pdr caissons	10	6	2

	With the Corps	In Bromberg	In Wilna
24 pdr caissons	6	4	2
Infantry caissons	1		1
Affûts de rechange 6 pdr			1
Affûts de rechange 24 pdr			1
Ammunition waggons	1		3
Field forges	1		1
6 pdr shot	1,500	690	
6 pdr canister	300	150	
24 pdr canister	20	12	
Infantry cartridges	31,460		
24 pdr cartridges	604	312	
Charges 24 pdr	580	324	
Primers	3,704	1,568	
Matches	405	197	
Matches(kg)	118	50	
Flints	3,000		

III Cavalry Corps*

(General Grouchy)

	Officers	Men	Officers' horses	Men's horses	Train horses
3rd Light Cavalry Division					
(General Chastel)					
10th Light Cavalry Brigade (General Gerard)					
6th (French) Chasseurs (Colonel Ledard): 1st-3rd Squadrons	29	561	65	542	6
25th (French) Chasseurs (Colonel Christophe): 1st-3rd Squadrons	25	583	59	584	4
11th Light Cavalry Brigade (General Gauthren)					
6th (French) Hussars (Colonel Valin): 1st-3rd Squadrons	29	596	69	570	8
8th (French) Chasseurs (Colonel de Perigord): 1st-4th Squadrons	32	524	76	498	8
17th Light Cavalry Brigade (General Dommanget)					
1st (Bavarian) Chevau-Légèrs (Colonel von Wittgenstein)	19	489	73	496	
2nd (Bavarian) Chevau-Légèrs (Colonel Lessing)	22	476	97	474	
(Saxon) Chevau-Légèrs *Prinz Albrecht* (Colonel ?)	30	481	58	460	22
Artillery	3	154	7	73	94
Total	**189**	**3,871**	**489**	**3,803**	**169**
6th (French) Cavalry Division					
(General Lahoussaye)					
7th Dragoons (Colonel Veisier): 1st-3rd Squadrons	28	543	63	523	8
23rd Dragoons (Colonel Briant): 1st-3rd Squadrons	23	554	64	564	7
28th Dragoons (Colonel Montmarie): 1st-3rd Squadrons	24	599	82	571	8
30th Dragoons (Colonel Pinteville): 1st-3rd Squadrons	30	578	70	559	
Artillery	8	300	23	150	225
Total	**123**	**2,574**	**302**	**2,349**	**248**

Parade States

	Officers	Men	Officers' horses	Men's horses	Train horses
July 5					
6th Light Cavalry Division	129	2,074	307	1,978	17
3rd Light Cavalry Division	179	3,539	470	3,321	140
July 10					
6th Light Cavalry Division	131	2,226	314	2,043	140
3rd Light Cavalry Division	179	3,539	470	3,321	140
July 15					
6th Light Cavalry Division	123	2,021	294	1,831	138
3rd Light Cavalry Division	162	3,357	396	3,245	29
July 20					
6th Light Cavalry Division	122	2,022	292	1,816	136
3rd Light Cavalry Division	175	3,354	449	3,158	121
July 25					
6th Light Cavalry Division	111	1,967	281	1,766	136
3rd Light Cavalry Division	176	3,339	455	3,133	121

*3rd Cuirassier Division attached to II Corps.

	Officers	Men	Officers' horses	Men's horses	Train horses
August 5					
6th Light Cavalry Division	120	1,945	288	1,744	133
3rd Light Cavalry Division	192	3,162	452	2,830	195

Artillery Matériel Equipment	3rd Cuirassier Division	6th Cavalry Division	3rd Light Cavalry Division	Total
Pieces				
6 pdr cannon	8	8	4	20
24 pdr howitzers	4	4	2	10
Affûts de rechange				
6 pdr cannon	1	1	1	3
24 pdr howitzers	1	1		2
Caissons				
6 pdr cannon	18	12	6	36
24 pdr howitzer	12	8	4	24
Infantry	2	2	1	5
Ammunition waggons	4	4	2	10
Caisson waggons		1		1
Field forges	2	2	1	5

IV Cavalry Corps

(General Latour-Mauborg)

	Officers	Men	Officers' horses	Men's horses	Train horses
4th (Polish) Light Cavalry Division					
(General Rozniecki)					
2nd Lancers (Colonel Piasecki): 1st-3rd Squadrons	25	571	70	565	16
7th Lancers (Colonel Zawadzki): 1st-3rd Squadrons	33	639	83	639	21
11th Lancers (Colonel Potocki): 1st-3rd Squadrons	27	524	66	514	24
3rd Lancers (Colonel Radzymin): 1st-3rd Squadrons	26	632	66	606	14
15th Lancers (Colonel Pac): 1st-3rd Squadrons	31	697	78	696	17
16th Lancers (Colonel Tarnowski)	31	657	79	657	19
Total	**173**	**3,720**	**442**	**3,667**	**111**
7th Heavy Cavalry Division					
(General Lorge)					
1st Brigade					
(General Thielmann)					
Saxon Garde du Corps (Colonel Leyser): 1st-4th Squadrons	29	613	79	586	27
Saxon Kürassier Regiment *vacant von Zastrow* (Colonel Trutzchler): 1st-4th Squadrons	31	596	89	596	27
2nd Brigade					
(General Lepel)					
14th (Polish) Kürassier Regiment (Colonel Matadem): 1st and 2nd Squadrons	20	352	53	348	8
1st (Westfalian) Kürassier Regiment (Colonel Gitzeen): 1st-4th Squadrons	34	504	87	495	11
2nd (Westfalian) Kürassier Regiment (Colonel Bartinel): 1st-4th Squadrons	32	503	83	498	12
Total	**146**	**2,568**	**391**	**2,523**	**85**

	Officers	Men	Officers' horses	Men's horses	Train horses
Artillery					
Staff	3		12		6
Westfalian artillery: 2nd Battery	3	66	8	63	
Westfalian Train: 2nd Company	1	77	2	7	119
Saxon artillery (Hauptmann Hiller): 2nd Battery	4	167	8	85	149
Polish artillery: 3rd and 4th Batteries	11	324	29	188	246
Total	**22**	**634**	**59**	**343**	**526**
Total IV Cavalry Corps	**341**	**6,922**	**892**	**6,543**	**716**

Parade States

July 15

4th Light Cavalry Division	139	2,448	404	2,459	95
7th Heavy Cavalry Division	147	2,523	384	2,430	77

August 15

4th Light Cavalry Division	145	2,442	390	2,435	107
7th Heavy Cavalry Division	143	2,223	383	2,103	75

Artillery Matériel

Pieces

6 pdr cannon	16
Howitzers	8

Caissons

6 pdr cannon	26
Howitzers	22
Cavalry	4
Affûts de rechange	3
Train waggons	4
Field forges	4
Howitzer cartridges	1,332

Caissons (continued)

Howitzer canister	189
Sachets remphis	1,150
Shot	2,600
Canister	713
Primers	14,126

Matches

Cannon matches	7,800
Livres	587
Paquets	50
Cavalry cartridges	76,673
Flints	11,000

Section 4

Appendices

French regiments in Russia in 1812

Line infantry: 2, 3, 4, 5, 8, 9, 11, 12, 14, 17, 18, 19, 21, 24, 25, 27, 28, 29, 30, 33, 35, 36, 37, 43, 44, 45, 46, 48, 50, 51, 53, 54, 55, 56, 57, 59, 61, 63, 65, 72, 76, 79, 84, 85, 88, 92, 93, 94, 95, 96, 105, 106, 108, 111, 113, 123, 124, 125, 126, 127, 128, 129, 131 *Ile de Walcheren*, 132 *Ile de Ré*, 133 *2nd de la Mediterranée.*

Light infantry: 4, 6, 7, 8, 10, 11, 13, 15, 16, 18, 21, 24, 25, 26, 29, 33, 35 *1st de la Mediterranée*, 39.

Carabiniers: 1, 2.

Cuirassiers: 1, 2, 3, 4, 5, 6, 7, 8, 9, 10, 11, 12, 14.

Dragoons: 2, 5, 7, 12, 13, 17, 19, 20, 23, 28, 30.

Chasseurs à Cheval: 1, 2, 3, 4, 5, 6, 7, 8, 9, 11, 12, 16, 19, 20, 23, 24, 25, 28.

Hussars: 5, 6, 7, 8, 9, 11.

Chevau-légèrs Lanciers: 1, 2, 4, 5, 6, 8.

A list of the major battles and clashes of the 1812 Campaign

Source: *Militär — historisches Kreigs-Lexikon (1618-1905)*, by Dr Gaston Bodart (Vienna and Leipzig, 1908).

July 19 Clash at Eckau

Prussian victory (General Grawert) over Russians (General-Major von Löwis) 30 kilometres east of Mitau.

Forces	Prussians	Russians
	8 battalions	8 battalions
	6 squadrons and	13 squadrons and
	32 guns	10 guns
	(6,600 men)	(6,000 men)

Losses		
D & W*		300 (5%)
PoW**	100 (1.5%)	300 (5%)
Total	100 (1.5%)	600 (10%)

July 23 Clash at Saltanowka (Mohilew)

French victory (Davout) over Russians (Lieutenant-General Rajewsky).

Forces	French	Russians
	25 battalions,	22 battalions,
	20 squadrons	24 squadrons
	(14,000 infantry	(13,000 infantry
	and 3,000 cavalry)	and 3,000 cavalry)

Losses		
D & W	900 (5.5%)	1,900 (11.8%)
PoW	500 (3%)	600 (3.8%)
Total	1,400 (8.5%)	2,500 (15.6%)

July 25-27 Clash at Ostrowno

French victory (Murat) over Russians (Lieutenant-General Konownitzyn) on the left bank of the Dwina, 20 kilometres west of Witebsk.

Forces	French	Russians
	35 battalions,	24 battalions,
	44 squadrons	64 squadrons
	(21,000 infantry	(12,000 infantry
	and 7,000 cavalry)	and 8,000 cavalry)

Losses		
D & W	3,400 (12.1%)	2,700 (13.5%)
PoW	300 (1.1%)	1,100 (5.5%)
Total	3,700 (13.2%)	3,800 (19%)

July 27 Clash at Kobryn

Russian victory (General Graf Tormassow) over Saxons (General-Major von Klengel) 47 kilometres east of Brest-Litowsk.

*Dead and wounded.
**Prisoners of war.

Forces	Saxons	Russians
	4 battalions,	33,000 (only 12,000
	3 squadrons and	men and 36 guns
	8 guns (2,600 men)	came into action)
Losses		
D & W	300 (11%)	600 (1.8%)
PoW	2,300 (89%)	
Total	2,600 (100%) plus	600 (1.8%)
	8 guns and	
	3 colours	

July 30-31 and August 1
Battle of Jakubovo (Kliastitza Oboiarszina)

Russian victory (Lieutenant-General Graf Wittgenstein) over French (Oudinot) 35 kilometres north of Polosk.

Forces	French	Russians
	36 battalions,	36 battalions,
	28 squadrons and	28 squadrons and
	92 guns	108 guns
	(20,000 men)	(23,000 men)
Losses	3,700 (18.5%)	4,300 (18.7%)
		and 9 guns

August 11 Clash at Swolna

Russian victory (General-Major d'Auvray) over French (Oudinot) on the Swolna River, 90 kilometres east of Dünaburg.

Forces	French	Russians
	10,000 men	8 battalions,
		15 squadrons and
		21 guns (9,000 men)
Losses		
D & W	1,200 (12%)	800 (9%)
PoW	300 (3%)	
Total	1,500 (15%)	800 (9%)

August 12 Battle of Gorodeczna (Podobna)

Austro-Saxon victory (General Fürst Schwarzenberg) over Russians (General Graf Tormassow) 53 kilometres north-east of Brest-Litowsk.

Forces	Austro-Saxons	Russians
Austrians	27,000	24 battalions,
Saxons	13,000	36 squadrons,
Total	40,000 (actually	3 cossack regiments
	engaged were	(18,000 men)
	27 battalions,	
	36 squadrons and	
	36 guns, or	
	24,000 men)	
Losses		
Austrians	1,300 (5.4%)	
Saxons	900 (3.8%)	
Total	2,200 (9.2% of	3,000 (17%)
	those engaged)	

August 14 Clash at Krasnoi

French victory (Ney) over Russians (Lieutenant-General Newjerowsky) 40 kilometres south-west of Smolensk.

Forces	French	Russians
	5,000 infantry and	5,500 infantry,
	artillery,	1,500 cavalry and
	15,000 cavalry	14 guns (7,000 men)
	(20,000 men)	
Losses		
D & W	500 (2.5%)	700 (10%)
PoW		800 (12%)
Total	500 (2.5%)	1,500 (22%)
		and 7 guns

August 16-18 First battle of Polozk

Franco-Bavarian victory (St Cyr) over Russians (Lieutenant-General Graf Wittgenstein) on the Dwina River, 95 kilometres north-west of Witebsk.

Forces	Franco-Bavarians	Russians
Infantry	77 battalions	45 battalions
	(30,000 men)	(18,500 men)
Cavalry	36 squadrons	27 squadrons
	(4,000 men)	(3,500 men)
Total	34,000 men and	22,000 men and
	150 guns	98 guns
Losses	6,000 (18%)	6,000 (27.3%)

August 17-18 Battle of Smolensk

Franco-Polish victory (Napoleon) over Russians (General Barclay de Tolly).

Forces	Franco-Poles	Russians
Infantry	150,000	95,000
Cavalry	30,000	25,000
Total	180,000	120,000
Actually		
engaged	45,000	30,000
Losses	10,000 (22%)	6,000 (20%)

August 19 Battle of Walutina-Gora (Lubino)

Russian victory (Lieutenant-General Tutschkov I) over French (Ney) 8 kilometres north-east of Smolensk.

Forces	French	Russians
Infantry	25,000	19,000
Cavalry	10,000	6,000
Total	35,000	25,000
Losses	8,800 (25%)	6,000 (20%)

August 22 Clash at Dahlenkirchen

Russian victory (General-Major von Löwis) over

Prussians (Oberst von Horn) on the left bank of the Dwina, 14 kilometres south-east of Riga.

Forces	Prussians	Russians
	1,500 men and 8 guns	12 battalions and 6 squadrons (6,000 men)
Losses	800 (54%)	300 (5%)

September 5 Clash at Schewardino

French victory (Napoleon) over Russians (General Bagration) 3 kilometres south-west of Borodino.

Forces	French	Russians
Infantry	53 battalions (26,000 men)	28 battalions (16,000 men)
Cavalry	132 squadrons (10,000 men)	38 squadrons (4,000 men)
Total	36,000	20,000
Losses	3,600 (10%)	6,000 (30%) and 3 guns

September 7 Battle of Borodino (the Moskwa)

French victory (Napoleon) over Russians (General Fürst Kutusow).

Forces	French and allies	Russians
Infantry	214 battalions (82,000 men)	180 battalions (72,000 men)
Cavalry	317 squadrons (27,000 men)	164 squadrons (18,000 men)
Artillery	507 guns (15,000 men)	637 guns (15,000 men)
Militia		10,000 irregulars
Cossacks		7,000 irregulars
Total	124,000	122,000
Losses		
D & W	28,000 (22.6%)	43,000 (35.2%)
PoW		1,000 (0.8%)
Stragglers		8,000 (6.6%)
Total	28,000 (22.6%) and 13 guns	52,000 (42.6%) and 40 guns

September 10 Clash at Moshaisk

French advance guard victory (Murat) over Russian rearguard (Lieutenant-General Mildoradowitsch) 95 kilometres south-west of Moscow.

Losses	French	Russians
D & W	?	2,000
PoW	?	10,000 (all wounded from Borodino)
Total	2,000	

September 26-October 1 Clashes at Mesoten, Bauske, Gräfenthal, Leutschkrug and Garosse

Prussian victory (General York) over Russians (Lieutenant-General Graf Steinheil) 30 kilometres south-east of Mitau.

Forces	Prussians	Russians
Infantry	13,500	20,500
Cavalry	2,500	1,500
Total	16,000	22,000
Losses		
D & W	900 (5.6%)	1,500 (6.8%)
PoW	350 (2.2%)	2,500 (11.4%)
Total	1,250 (7.8%)	4,000 (18.2%)

October 18 Clash at Winkowo

Russian victory (Field Marshal Fürst Kutusow) over French (Murat) 67 kilometres south-west of Moscow.

Forces	French	Russians
Infantry	12,000	30,000
Cavalry	8,000	6,000
Total	20,000	36,000
Losses		
D & W	2,000 (10%)	800 (2.3%)
PoW	1,500 (7.5%)	700 (1.9%)
Total	3,500 (17.5%)	1,500 (4.2%)

October 18-20 Second battle of Polozk

Franco-Bavarian victory (St Cyr) over Russians (Wittgenstein).

Forces	Franco-Bavarian	Russians
Infantry	23,000	27,000
Cavalry	4,000	5,000
Total	27,000	32,000 and 136 guns
Losses		
D & W	6,000 (22.1%)	10,000 (31.3%)
PoW	2,000 (7.4%)	2,000 (6.3%)
Total	8,000 (29.5%)	12,000 (37.6%)

October 24 Battle of Malojaroslawez

French victory (Napoleon) over Russians (Kutuzow) on the Luscha River, 103 kilometres south-west of Moscow.

Forces	French and allies	Russians
	24,000	24,000
Losses	6,000 (25%)	8,000 (33.3%)

October 31 Clash at Tschaschniki

Russian victory (Wittgenstein) over French (Victor) on the Ula River, 70 kilometres south-west of Witebsk.

Forces	French	Russians
	30,000	30,000

Losses		
Losses	400 (1.33%)	400 (1.33%)
PoW	800 (2.66%)	
Total	1,200 (3.99%)	400 (1.33%)

November 3 Clash at Wiasma

Russian victory (General Miloradowitsch) over French (Eugène) on the Dnieper River, 150 kilometres north-east of Smolensk.

Forces	French and Italians	Russians
Infantry	22,000	19,000
Cavalry	3,000	8,000 and 8 guns
Total	25,000	27,000
Losses		
D & W	4,000 (16%)	1,800 (7%)
PoW	3,000 (12%)	
Total	7,000 (28%) and 3 guns	1,880 (7%)

November 9 Clash at Ljachowo

Russian victory (3,500 cossacks under Orlow-Denisow) over French (2,000 under Augerau) 40 kilometres south-east of Smolensk.

Losses	French	Russians
D & W	250 (10.25%)	200 (5.7%)
PoW	1,750 (89.75%)	
Total	2,000 (100%)	200 (5.7%)

November 13 Clash at Nowo-Swerschen

Russian victory (General-Major Graf Lambert) over Poles (Brigadier-General Kosezky) 70 kilometres west of Minsk on the upper Niemen.

Forces	Poles	Russians
	3,500	4,500
Losses		
D & W	500 (14.3%)	50 (1.1%)
PoW	800 (22%)	
Total	1,300 (36.3%)	50 (1.1%)

November 14 Battle of Smoljäntzi

Russian victory (Wittgenstein) over French (Victor) 70 kilometres south-west of Witebsk.

Forces	French and allies	Russians
	25,000	28,000
Losses		
D & W	2,200 (8.8%)	3,000 (10.7%)
PoW	800 (3.2%)	
Total	3,000 (12%)	3,000 (10.7%)

November 14-16 Clash at Wolkowisk (Izabelin)

Allied victory (Austrians, Saxons and French under Schwarzenberg) over Russians (Lieutenant-General Freiherr von Sacken).

Forces	Allies	Russians
Infantry	51 battalions	47 battalions
Cavalry	29 squadrons	32 squadrons and 6 cossack Pulks (regiments)
Total	35,000 men	27,000 men and 92 guns
Losses		
D & W		
Austrians	200 (0.6%)	
Saxons	650 (1.8%)	
French	450 (1.3%)	1,500 (5.6%)
Total	1,300 (3.7%)	1,500 (5.6%)
PoW	500 (1.4%)	2,500 (9.4%)
Total	1,800 (5.2%)	4,000 (15%)

November 15 Clash at Kaidanowo

Russian victory (Graf Lambert) over Poles and French (Brigadier-General Kosezky).

Forces	Poles and French	Russians
	2,000	4,000
Losses	100% (mostly captured) plus 2 flags, 2 guns and 10 ammunition waggons	?

November 15-19 Battle of Krasnoi

Russian victory (Kutuzow) over allies (Napoleon) 40 kilometres south-west of Smolensk (including Kobisewo, Rschawka, Kutkowa, Merlino, Uwarowa and Losmino).

Forces	Allies	Russians
	50,000	90,000
Losses		
D & W	6,000 (12%)	2,000 (2.2%)
PoW	12,000 (24%)	
Stragglers	14,000 (28%)	
Total	32,000 (64%) and 93 guns (a further 112 guns were abandoned on the march from Smolensk to Krasnoi)	2,000 (2.2%)

November 21 First clash at Borisow

Russian victory (Graf Lambert) over Poles and French (General Dombrowsky) on the left bank of the Beresina, 58 kilometres north-east of Minsk.

Forces	Poles and French	Russians
	3,000	3,500
Losses	3,000 (100%) plus 6 guns, 2 colours and 1 Eagle	2,000 (58%)

November 23 Second clash at Borisow

French and allied victory (Oudinot) over Russians (Admiral Graf Tschitschagoff).

Forces	Allies	Russians
Infantry	2,500	2,800
Cavalry	1,100	
	12 guns	
Losses	?	2,000 (70%)

November 26-28 Battle of the Beresina crossing

Russian victory (Kutusow) over allies (Napoleon) at Studienka, Stachow and Stary-Borisow.

Forces	Allies	Russians
Infantry	30,000	173 battalions (64,000 men)
Cavalry	3,000	138 squadrons, including 10,000 cossacks (23,000 men)
Total	33,000 (without stragglers)	87,000 (without 39,000-strong main army at Kobis)
Losses		
D & W	10,000 (30%)	8,000 (9.2%)
PoW	10,000 (30%)	2,000 (2.6%)
Total	20,000 (60%) without stragglers, and 50 guns (20%)	10,000 (11.8%)

French account of the Russian loss

Bulletin	Battles, etc	Date	Men lost
6th		July 11	2,500
7th	Mer	16	1,500
8th	Sebastiani's Action	14	500
10th	Ostronovo	27	7,500
	Mohilo	23	6,400
11th		30, 31	6,500
13th	Krasnoy	August 13	2,500
and	Smolensk	17	14,000
14th	Valentina	19	not stated
16th	Viasma	27	100
18th	Mojaisk	September 7	40,000
	Mittaw		2,000
	Finland		2,000
	Total		**85,000**

From this period we have no further account of the French Successes.

Russian account of the French loss

Date	Battles, etc	Men lost
July 15		150
	Mer. 3 Regiments cut up	200
19	Polotzk	1,000
	Nine Regiments cut up	
25	Ostronovo	8,000
26	Ostronovo	6,000
23	Mohilo	5,000
30 and 31		8,000
	Kobryn	10,000
29	Wittgenstein's Victory	1,000
	Jacobou	3,000
August 13	Krasnoi	

Allied Officers' losses at the Beresina

	Generals	Field officers	Junior officers	Total	Killed	
Poles	5	28	153	186	15	
Badeners	1	5	79	85	63	
Swiss		6	79	85	48	
Berg	2	9	68	79	45	
Italians		4	39	43	41	
Portuguese		2	41	43	39	
Westfalians		1	25	26	11	
Croats		1	24	25	2	
Saxons			9	9	6	
Württembergers		1	5	6	3	
Bavarians		1	5	6	5	
Prussians		2	1	3	3	
Hessians		1		1		
Spaniards			1	1	1	
Total Allies	**8**	**61**	**529**	**598**	**282**	**47% killed**
French	18	80	708	806	469	58% killed
Grand Total	**26**	**141**	**1,237**	**1,404**	**751**	**53.5% killed**

	17	Smolensk	12,000
	19	Valentina	
	6	Wittgenstein's Victory	500
	3	Polotzk	2,000
September	7	Mojaisk	40,000
October		Defeat of Murat's Cavalry	6,000
		Prince Kutusow's Victory	5,000
	18	Loss of Murat's Advanced	
		Guard	17,000
	22	Moscow	15,000
		Polotzk stormed	6,000
November	9	Dorogobouz	15,000
		Wilna	25,000
		Prussian Revolt	30,000
		Total	**215,850**

Statement of the Russian and French loss

From *A view of the French Campaign in Russia in 1812,* by an Officer, Swansea, 1813. 'Statement of the killed, wounded, &c of the Grand French and Russian Armies, taken from the Official Accounts.

'It is next to an impossibility, to give such an account of the Killed and Wounded as can be *relied on* for accuracy. In order to come as near to the truth as possible, we give the Statement published by each Nation of its *adversaries loss,* leaving out entirely *that of their own*; because we are aware that each of them will under-rate their own loss for obvious reasons, and are persuaded at the same time, that in detailing that of the enemy, it may be overcharged. Yet we think *this mode* most likely to come nearest the fact.

'It appears, therefore, by allowing the French the *whole of their account,* that the Russian loss has been eight-five thousand five hundred men, whilst that of the French is two hundred and fifteen thousand eight hundred and fifty men. This loss, great as it is, falls very short of the loss sustained by the French during the whole of this disastrous campaign.

'Since their retreat from Moscow, to their arrival at Beresyna, they were so closely pursued, so incessantly harrassed by the Cossacks, and so cut up in detail, no regular bulletin account has been received in this country since the surrender of Wilna; but by a return made to the Russian government at Petersburgh, from the different armies, and published at the War-office, to the battle of Beresyna, their loss was 235,033 men.

Surrendered at Wilna . . . 25,000
Surrender of the Prussians under Gen D'York . . . 30,000

Making the whole . . . 290,133 men.

In addition to this, the French have lost Sixty Generals, Three thousand one hundred Officers, Seven hundred Cannon, Thirty Stand of Colours, Sixteen Eagles, Twelve hundred Ammunition Waggons, Two thousand Provision Waggons.'

Calculation of Provision, Forage, & c, for the support of a large army one week

From *A view of the French Campaign in Russia in 1812,* by an Officer, Swansea, 1813.

'To such of our readers as are unacquainted with the mode of subsisting an army in the field, we give the following calculation, for the support of an Army for *one week* — supposing it to be composed as follows:

'300,000 Infantry
  50,000 Cavalry
  50,000 Followers
400,000.

'**Bread.** Each Man will require per Day ½ lb. Making per Week 4,200,000 lbs [sic].

'**Meat,** Beef or Mutton. Each Man would require per day ½ lb. Allowing each Bullock to weight 500 lbs, and each Sheep 50 lbs, it would require per week 1,400 Bullocks and 14,000 Sheep, Or 1,400,000 lbs.

'**Drink.** Half a pint of Wine or Spirits per day ½ lb. Per Week 1,400,000 lbs.

'**Horses** For Cavalry, Staff, Regimental Baggage, Artillery, Ammunition and Commissariat, must amount to 150,000.

'**Oats.** Each Horse would require per day 8 lbs. Making per Week 8,400,000 lbs.

'**Hay.** Each Horse would require per day 12 lbs. Making per Week 12,600,000 lbs.

'Now all this requires carriage. Supposing the magazines 50 miles in the rear; and that each horse goes 100 miles per week; it would require for the transport of *food only* for the army 112,000 Horses.

'*This number* must also be fed. It would therefore require 4,659 Horses more, to carry *their* food, and that for themselves; Oats for these per week, at 8 lb per day for each Horse, is 6,532,904 lbs and Hay, at 12 lb per day for each Horse, is per week 9,799,356 lbs, making in the whole, 44,332,264 lbs or 22,180 tons [sic].'

Section 5

The Russian Armies

These orders of battle were valid for the start of the campaign; many changes took place in the subsequent fighting. It is clear that the peacetime organisation of the divisions of the Russian army (see Stein) had been extensively modified before hostilities commenced. All grenadier, infantry and Jaeger regiments had two battalions in the field unless otherwise noted.

The 1st Army of the West

Commander General of Infantry M B Barclay de Tolley

I Corps

Commander Lieutenant-General P X Wittgenstein.

5th Infantry Division. Commander Major-General G M Berg.
1st Brigade. Sievski IR, Kalugski IR.
2nd Brigade. Permski IR, Mogilevski IR.
3rd Brigade. 23rd and 24th Jaeger Regiments.
5th Artillery Brigade. Lieutenant-Colonel Muruzi. 5th Position Battery, 9th and 10th Light Batteries (36 guns).

14th Infantry Division. Commander Major-General I T Sazonoff.
1st Brigade Tulski IR, Navaginski IR.
2nd Brigade Tenginski IR, Estlandski IR.
3rd Brigade 25th and 26th Jaeger Regiments.
14th Artillery Brigade. Lieutenant-Colonel Stadem. 14th Position Battery, 9th and 10th Light Batteries (36 guns).

1st Cavalry Division. Commander Major-General P D Kazoffskoi.
Riaski Dragoons, Yamburg Dragoons (4 squadrons each).
Grodno Hussars (8 squadrons).
Don Cossacks; the Pulks of Platoff IV, Rodianoff and Selivan (5 Sotnia each).
1st HA Battery (12 guns).

9th Reserve Cavalry Division. Commander Major-General N G Repnin-Volkonski.
Guard Kuerassier Regiment, Chevalier Guard Regiment (4 squadrons each).
Combined Depot squadrons, 1st and 3rd Cavalry Divisions (6 squadrons).
Don Cossack Pulk of Grekoff VI (5 Sotnia).
3rd HA Battery (12 guns).
1 engineer company, 2 pontonnier companies.

II Corps
Commander Lieutenant-General K F Baggowut.

4th Infantry Division. Commander Major-General Prince Eugen von Wuerttemberg.
1st Brigade. Tobolski IR, Wolhynski IR.
2nd Brigade. Kremenchugski IR, Minski IR.
3rd Brigade. 4th and 34th Jaeger Regiments.
4th Artillery Brigade. Colonel Woiskoff. 4th Position Battery, 7th and 8th Light Batteries (36 guns).

17th Infantry Division. Commander Lieutenant-General E D Olsuffieff.
1st Brigade. Riasanski IR, Brestski IR.
2nd Brigade. Bieloserski IR, Wilmannstrandski IR.
3rd Brigade. 30th and 48th Jaeger Regiments.
17th Artillery Brigade. Colonel Dietrichs II. 17th Position Battery, 32nd and 33rd Light Batteries (36 guns).

III Corps
Commander Lieutenant-General Tutchkoff I.

3rd Infantry Division. Commander Lieutenant-General P P Konnovnitzin.
1st Brigade. Muromski IR, Revalski IR.
2nd Brigade. Chernigoffski IR, Selenginski IR.
3rd Brigade. 20th and 21st Jaeger Regiments.
3rd Artillery Brigade. Lieutenant-Colonel Dietrichs V. 3rd Position Battery, 5th and 6th Light Batteries (36 guns).

1st (Grenadier) Division. Major-General P A Stroganoff.
1st Brigade. Leib Grenadier Regiment, Grenadier Regiment Count Arakchejeff.
2nd Brigade. Pavloff Grenadier Regiment, Yekaterinoslaff Grenadier Regiment.
3rd Brigade. St Petersburg Grenadier Regiment, Tauride Grenadier Regiment.
1st Artillery Brigade. Colonel Gluchoff. 1st Position Battery, 1st and 2nd Light Batteries.

IV Corps
Commander Lieutenant-General Count P A Schuvaloff.

11th Infantry Division. Commander Major-General N N Bachmetieff II.
1st Brigade. Kexholmski IR, Pernovski IR.
2nd Brigade. Polotski IR, Yeletzki IR.
3rd Brigade. 1st and 33rd Jaeger Regiments.
11th Artillery Brigade. Lieutenant-Colonel Malejeff. 2nd Position Battery, 3rd and 4th Light Batteries (36 guns).

23rd Infantry Division. Commander Major-General A N Bachmetieff I.
1st Brigade. Rialski IR, Yekaterinburgski IR.
2nd Brigade. Kaporski IR, Combined Grenadiers.
3rd Brigade. 18th Jaeger Regiment.
23rd Artillery Brigade. Lieutenant-Colonel Gulevitza. 23rd Position Battery, 43rd and 44th Light Batteries (36 guns).

V Corps

Commander Grand Duke Constantine Pavlovitch.
(As of 26 July Lieutenant-General N I Lavroff)

Imperial Guard Division. Commander Major-General G V Rosen.
1st Brigade. Preobrazhenski Life Guards, Semenovski Life Guards (3 battalions each).
2nd Brigade. Izmailovski Life Guards, Litovski Life Guards (3 battalions each).
3rd Brigade. Life Guard Jaegers, Finlandski Jaeger Regiment (3 battalions each), Marine Equipage
(1 battalion).

Combined Grenadier Division. Major-General Kantakuzen.
Combined Grenadier Battalions of the 1st Grenadier Division (2 battalions).
Combined Grenadier Battalions of the 4th Division (2 battalions).
Combined Grenadier Battalions of the 17th Division (2 battalions).
Combined Grenadier Battalions of the 23rd Division (1 battalion).
Life Guard Artillery Brigade. Colonel Yaeler. Batteries of HRH Count Arackchejeff (48 guns).

VI Corps

Commander General of Infantry D S Dochturoff.

7th Infantry Division. Lieutenant-General P M Kapsevitch.
1st Brigade. Moscow IR, Pskoffski IR.
2nd Brigade. Libauski IR, Sophiiski IR.
3rd Brigade. 11th and 36th Jaeger Regiments.
7th Artillery Brigade. Lieutenant-Colonel Dietrichs III. 7th Position Battery, 12th and 13th Light Batteries
(36 guns).

24th Infantry Division. Major-General P G Lichacheff.
1st Brigade. Ufimski IR, Schirwanski IR.
2nd Brigade. Butyrski IR, Tomski IR.
3rd Brigade. 19th and 40th Jaeger Regiments.
24th Artillery Brigade. Lieutenant-Colonel Yefremoff. 24th Position Battery, 45th and 46th Light Batteries
(36 guns).

I Guards Cavalry Corps

Commander Lieutenant-General Count F P Uvaroff.

Guards Cavalry Division. Major-General I E Schewitsch.
1st Brigade. Life Guard Hussars, Life Guard Ulans (4 squadrons each).
2nd Brigade. Life Guard Dragoons, Life Guard Cossacks (4 squadrons each).
3rd Brigade. Nezhinski Dragoons (4 squadrons), Yelisabethgrad Hussars (8 squadrons), Kazanski Dragoons
(4 squadrons).
Artillery. 2nd HA Battery (12 guns).

1st Kuerassier Division. Major-General N I Deperadovitch.
1st Brigade. Chevalier Guards, Horse Guards (4 squadrons each).
2nd Brigade. His Majesty's Life Kuerassiers, Her Majesty's Life Kuerassiers (4 squadrons each).
Artillery. Colonel Kozen. 1st and 2nd HA Batteries (24 guns).

II Cavalry Corps
Commander Major-General Baron F K Korff.

1st Brigade. Pskoffski Dragoons, Moscow Dragoons (4 squadrons each).
2nd Brigade. Kargopolski Dragoons, Ingermannlandski Dragoons (4 squadrons each).
3rd Brigade. Polish Ulans, Isumski Hussars (8 squadrons each).
Artillery. 6th HA Battery (12 guns).

III Cavalry Corps
Commander Lieutenant-General Count P P Pahlen II.

1st Brigade. Courland Dragoons, Orenburgski Dragoons (4 squadrons each).
2nd Brigade. Sibirski Dragoons, Irkutski Dragoons (4 squadrons each).
3rd Brigade. Mariupolski Hussars, Ssumski Hussars (8 squadrons each).
Artillery. 7th HA Battery (12 guns).

Cossack Corps
Commander General of Cavalry M I Platoff.

Don Cossack Pulks of Andrianoff II (5 Sotnias), of the Ataman (10 Sotnias), Charitnoff VII, Chernozuboff VII, Denisoff VII, Grekoff XVIII, Vlassoff III (5 Sotnias each).
Don Cossack Artillery (12 guns).
Illowaiski V, Melnikoff III (5 Sotnias each).
1st Baschkirs, Perekop Tartars, Simferopol Tartars (5 Sotnias each).
1st and 2nd Cossacks of the Bug (5 Sotnias each).
1st Tjeptjarski Cossacks (5 Sotnias).
1st and 3rd Pontonnier Companies (100 men). 2nd, 3rd and 4th Engineer Companies.
Artillery. 4th, 5th, 10th and 22nd Reserve Artillery Batteries (48 guns).

The 2nd Army of the West
Commander General of Infantry Prince P I Bagration.

VII Corps
Commander Lieutenant-General N N Rajevski.

12th Infantry Division. Commander Major-General I M Koljubakin. As of 4 July 1812 Major-General I V Vassiltchikoff.
1st Brigade. Narvaski IR, Smolenski IR.
2nd Brigade. New Ingermannland IR, Alexopolski IR.
3rd Brigade. 6th and 41st Jaeger Regiments.
12th Artillery Brigade. Lieutenant-Colonel Sablin. 12th Position Battery, 22nd and 23rd Light Batteries (36 guns).

26th Infantry Division. Commander Major-General I F Paskewitsch.
1st Brigade. Ladogaski IR, Poltawaski IR.
2nd Brigade. Nishegorodski IR, Orelski IR.
3rd Brigade. 5th and 42nd Jaeger Regiments.
26th Artillery Brigade. Colonel Schulmann. 26th Position Battery, 47th and 48th Light Batteries (36 guns).

VIII Corps

Commander Lieutenant-General M M Borosdin.

2nd (Grenadier) Division. Commander Major-General Prince Karl von Mecklenburg.
1st Brigade. Kievski Grenadiers, Moscow Grenadiers.
2nd Brigade. Astrakhanski Grenadiers, Fanagorski Grenadiers.
3rd Brigade. Sibirski Grenadiers, Little Russia Grenadiers.
2nd Artillery Brigade. Colonel Boguslavski. 11th Position Battery, 20th and 21st Light Batteries (36 guns).

27th Infantry Division. Commander Major-General D P Neveroffski.
1st Brigade. Wilna IR, Simbirski IR.
2nd Brigade. Odessa IR, Tarnopol IR.
3rd Brigade. 49th and 50th Jaeger Regiments.
27th Artillery Brigade. Commander Lieutenant-Colonel Bellingshausen. 32nd Position Battery, 48th Light Battery (24 guns).

IV Cavalry Corps

Commander Major-General K K Sievers.

4th Cavalry Division. Commander?
1st Brigade. Kievski Dragoons, New Russia Dragoons (4 squadrons each).
2nd Brigade. Charkovski Dragoons, Tchernigoffski Dragoons (4 squadrons each).
3rd Brigade. Achtirski Hussars, Litovski Ulans (8 squadrons each).
8th HA Battery (12 guns).

2nd Cavalry Division. Commander Major-General I F Knorring. As of 8 July Major-General I M Duka.
1st Brigade. Military Order Kuerassiers, Yekaterinoslavski Kuerassiers (4 squadrons each).
2nd Brigade. Gluchovski Kuerassiers, Little Russia Kuerassiers, Novgorodski Kuerassiers (4 squadrons each).
HA Battery (12 guns).

Cossack Corps. Commander Major-General A A Karpoff.
The Don Cossack Pulks of Bichaloff I, Grekoff XXI, Illowaiski X, Illowaiski XI, Karpoff II, Kommissaroff I, Melnikoff IV, Platoff V, Sissojeff III (5 Sotnias each).
1st Don Cossack HA Battery (12 guns).
5th and 6th Engineer Companies, 4th Pontonnier Company.

The 3rd Army of the West

Commander General of Cavalry A P Tormassoff.

Corps of General of Infantry Graf S M Kamienski II

As of 6 August 1812 Lieutenant-General Baron F V Osten-Sacken.

18th Infantry Division. Commander Major-General Prince A G Scherbatoff.
1st Brigade. Tambovski IR, Vladimirski IR.
2nd Brigade. Dnieprovski IR, Kostromski IR.
3rd Brigade. 28th and 32nd Jaeger Regiments.
18th Artillery Brigade. Lieutenant-Colonel ? 18th Position Battery, 34th and 35th Light Batteries (36 guns).
Combined Grenadier Battalions of the 9th, 15th and 18th Divisions (6 battalions).
Pavlogradski Hussars (8 squadrons), Don Cossack Pulk of Diatzkin (5 Sotnias).
11th HA Battery (12 guns).

Corps of General of Cavalry A P Tormassoff

9th Infantry Division. Commander Major-General E E Udom.
1st Brigade. Nascheburgski IR, Apsheronski IR.
2nd Brigade. Riashski IR, Yakutski IR.
3rd Brigade. 10th and 38th Jaeger Regiments.
9th Artillery Brigade. Lieutenant-Colonel ? 9th Position Battery, 16th and 17th Light Batteries (36 guns).

15th Infantry Division. Commander Major-General F V Nazimoff.
1st Brigade. Koslofski IR, Vitebski IR.
2nd Brigade. Kura IR, Koliwanski IR.
3rd Brigade. 13th and 14th Jaeger Regiments.
15th Artillery Brigade. Lieutenant-Colonel ? 15th Position Battery, 28th and 29th Light Batteries (36 guns).
Alexandriaski Hussars (8 squadrons), Don Cossack Pulk of Vlassoff II (5 Sotnias).
12th HA Battery (12 guns).

Corps of Lieutenant-General F V Osten-Sacken

36th Reserve Infantry Division. Commander Major-General M M Sorokin.
Depot battalions of the 12th and 15th Infantry Divisions (12 battalions). *
11th Reserve Cavalry Division. Commander ?
16 Depot squadrons.
Lubno Hussars (8 squadrons).
Artillery Brigade: 33rd Position Battery, 49th Light Battery, 13th HA Battery (36 guns).

* according to Stein and Viskovatov, this division contained the depot battalions of the 12th and 15th Divisions. Other sources give 15th and 18th Divisions.

Cavalry Corps of Major-General Count K O Lambert

5th Cavalry Division.
Starodubski Dragoons, Twerskoi Dragoons, Zhitomirski Dragoons, Arsamaski Dragoons (4 squadrons each).
Tartar Ulan Regiment (8 squadrons).
Vladimirski Dragoons, Taganrogski Dragoons, Serpuchoffski Dragoons (4 squadrons each).
34th Position Battery, 19th HA Battery (24 guns).
5th Pontonnier Company, one Engineer Company, Captain Kutzevitz.
The Don Cossack Pulks of Barabantchikoff II, Tsickileff and Janoff (5 Sotnias each).
1st and 2nd Kalmuks (10 Sotnias).
2nd Baschkirs (5 Sotnias).
Evpatoriaski Tartars (5 Sotnias).

The Army of the Moldau (or of the Don)
Commander Admiral P V Tchitchagoff.

Corps of General of Infantry Count A F Langeron

22nd Infantry Division. Commander ?
1st Brigade. Wiborgski IR, Wiatkaski IR.
2nd Brigade. Staroi-Okolski IR.
3rd Brigade. 29th and 45th Jaeger Regiments.
22nd Artillery Brigade. 22nd Position Battery, 41st and 42nd Light Batteries (36 guns).
St Petersburg Dragoons, Lifland Dragoons (4 squadrons each).
The Don Cossack Pulks of Grekoff IV, Pantelejeff II and the 1st Ural Cossacks (5 Sotnias each).

Corps of Lieutenant-General P K Essen

8th Infantry Division. Commander ?
1st Brigade. Archangegorodski IR, Schlusselburgski IR.
2nd Brigade. Staroi-Ingermannlandski IR, Ukrainski IR.
3rd Brigade. 37th Jaeger Regiment.
8th Artillery Brigade. 8th Position Battery, 14th and 15th Light Batteries (36 guns).
Smolenski Dragoons (4 squadrons), Sieverski Dragoons (2 squadrons).
Don Cossack Pulk of Grekoff VIII, 2nd Uralski Cossacks (5 Sotnias each).
Artillery. 15th HA Battery (12 guns); 8th Pontonnier Company.

Corps of Lieutenant-General A L Voinoff

10th Infantry Division. Commander Major-General I A Lieven.
1st Brigade. Kurski IR.
2nd Brigade. Krimski IR, Bialostokski IR.
3rd Brigade. 8th and 39th Jaeger Regiments.
10th Artillery Brigade. Commander ? 10th Position Battery, 18th and 19th Light Batteries (36 guns).
Kinburnski Dragoons (4 squadrons), Bielorusski Hussars (8 squadrons).
Artillery. 38th Position Battery, 50th Light Battery (24 guns).
Don Cossack Pulks of Melnikoff V, 3rd and 4th Cossack Pulks of the Urals (5 Sotnias each).

Corps of Lieutenant-General Baron A P Zass
As of 8 August 1812 Major-General M L Bulatoff.

16th Infantry Division. Commander ?
1st Brigade. Ochotski IR.
2nd Brigade. Kamchatski IR, Mingrelski IR.
16th Artillery Brigade Commander ? 16th Position Battery, 31st Light Battery (24 guns).

7th Cavalry Division. Commander ?
Dorpatski Dragoons, Pereslavski Dragoons, Tiraspolski Dragoons (4 squadrons each).
Tchugujevski Ulan Regiment (8 squadrons).
Don Cossack Pulks of Melnikoff III and Kutainikoff IV (5 Sotnias each).
Artillery: 3rd Position Battery, 17th HA Battery (24 guns).

Reserve Corps of Lieutenant-General I V Sabanieff

The units in this corps seem to have been drawn from various peace-time divisions.

Olonetski IR, Yaroslavski IR, Galitzki IR, 7th and 12th Jaeger Regiments.
Olviopol Hussars (8 squadrons).
Don Cossack Pulk of Lukovkina II (5 Sotnias).
Artillery. 16th HA Battery (12 guns).
Engineer Battalion Commander Lieutenant-Colonel Gebener and Captain Kanatzikoff.
Sapper Company Captain Tichanoff.
75th Naval Equipage with the pontoon bridging train.

Detachment of Major-General N I Lieders.
Neuschlotski IR, 27th and 43rd Jaeger Regiments (from the 16th Division).
Saratovski IR, 22nd Jaeger Regiment (from the 13th Division).
Volhynski Ulan Regiment (8 squadrons).
Don Cossack Pulks of Kireev II and Turtsaninoff (5 Sotnias each).
Artillery. 24th Light Battery (from the 13th Division), 30th Light Battery (from the 16th Division) 24 guns.

The Finland Corps

Commander Lieutenant-General Count F F Steinheil.

6th Infantry Division. Commander Major-General V S Rachmanoff.
1st Brigade. Azovski IR, Uglitsch IR.
2nd Brigade. Brianski IR, Nizovski IR.
3rd Brigade. 3rd and 35th Jaeger Regiments.
6th Artillery Brigade. 6th Position Battery, 11th Light Battery (24 guns).

21st Infantry Division. Commander Major-General F F Rosen.
1st Brigade. Nevaski IR.
2nd Brigade. Litovski IR, Podolski IR.
3rd Brigade. 2nd and 44th Jaeger Regiments.
21st Artillery Brigade. 21st Position Battery, 40th Light Battery (24 guns).

25th Infantry Division Commander Major-General A J Gamen.
1st Brigade. 1st and 2nd Naval Infantry Regiments.
2nd Brigade. Voroneshski IR. 3rd Naval Infantry Regiment.
3rd Brigade. 31st and 47th Jaeger Regiments.
25th Artillery Brigade. 25th Position Battery, three naval batteries (30 guns).

27th Cavalry Brigade Finland Dragoons, Mittau Dragoons (4 squadrons each).
Don Cossack Pulk of Poschilin (5 Sotnias).

The Garrison of Riga

30th Reserve Infantry Division.
12 depot (2nd) battalions of the 4th and 14th Divisions.

31st Reserve Division.
12 depot (2nd) battalions from the 5th and 17th Divisions.

33rd Reserve Division.
12 depot (2nd) battalions from the 3rd and 7th Divisions.
Composite Cavalry Regiment. (4 combined squadrons of the Riga and Mittau Dragoons)
Courland – Livland Dragoon Regiment (4 squadrons).

Dunaburg Garrison

32nd Reserve Infantry Division.
14 depot (2nd) battalions of the 1st Grenadier Division and the 11th and 23rd Divisions.

Bobruisk Garrison

34th Reserve Infantry Division.
12 depot (2nd) battalions from the 24th and 26th Divisions.

II Reserve Corps of Lieutenant-General F F Ertell

35th Reserve Infantry Division.
12 depot (2nd) battalions from the 2nd Grenadier and 18th Divisions.

36th Reserve Infantry Division.
12 depot (2nd) battalions from the ?th and 18th Divisions.

37th Reserve Infantry Division.
12 depot (2nd) battalions from the 9th and 27th Divisions.

In early 1812 a corps, designated 'The Georgia Corps', was formed to operate in Georgia. There are many mysteries surrounding exactly which regiments served in which divisions here and which generals commanded where and when. The whole Russian army seems to have undergone almost continuous regrouping during the campaign. One solution for the Georgian corps seems to have been as shown below, but the date and the duration of this arrangement are not known. The brigading of regiments is not known.

19th Division. General Rutcheff.
Bielev IR, Kazan IR, Sevastopol IR, Susdal IR, 16th and 17th Jaegers.

20th Division. General Paulucci. Paulucci is shown by some sources as commanding the whole corps.
Causasus IR, Kabardinsk IR, Kherson GR, Tiflis IR, Troitsk IR, 9th, 15th and 46th Jaegers.

24th Cavalry Brigade.
Taganrog and Vladimir DragRs.

25th Cavalry Brigade.
Borissoglebsk and Narva DragRs.

Russian Army Uniforms

The Line Infantry

Grenadiers

In January 1812 the famous Kiwer, with its curved top, was introduced. This meant, of course, that many regiments took the field in this fateful year in the old model shakos. The front of the top was with no peak. The red headband was plain for all three battalions. The initials of the wearer's company were embroidered in yellow thread on the front of the headband.

The tunic was dark green with two rows of six brass buttons to the front. The closed collar, the cuffs and the short turnbacks were red, the dark green cuff flaps bore three buttons and there were two buttons at the rear of the back.

The shoulder straps were in various colours which

	Shoulder Strap Colour	Divisional Number
1st Regiment	red	yellow
2nd Regiment	white	yellow
3rd Regiment	yellow	red
4th Regiment	dark green*	yellow
5th Regiment	sky blue	yellow
6th Regiment	buff	yellow

* piped red

higher than the rear and the sides. The top was of leather and there were leather reinforcing bands to the bottom and 'V-shaped' struts to the sides. The peak was of black leather and the leather chinscales were in the button colour. White cords and flounders were worn for parades as were narrow, black horsehair plumes. On the front of the shako was a three-flamed brass grenade under a pompon in the battalion colour: 1st Battalion – all red; 2nd Battalion – red over green; 3rd Battalion – red over sky blue.

The Pavloff Grenadiers wore their famous, brass-fronted mitre grenadier cap with white headband and piping to the red backing. On the front plate was the imperial double eagle. There were three brass grenades on the white headband. The tassel was red.

The forage cap was a flat-topped, dark green cap reflected the seniority of the regiment within its division and the divisional number was embroidered on the strap.

White linen trouser-gaiters were worn in summer, white woollen trousers with black leather booting with nine brass buttons at the bottom in the winter. The white sabre strap had a coloured tassel which reflected the company of the wearer.

Belts were white; the black cartridge pouch bore the three-flamed cap badge. The brass-hilted sabre had a brown leather sheath with a brass tip as did the bayonet. The musket sling was of red leather. A black, square leather pack was worn on the back with a tin water bottle strapped to the lid. The grey greatcoat was normally worn on the march, rolled bandolier fashion over the left shoulder.

Grenadier Privates' Sabre Tassel Colours

	Crown	Body	Wreath	Fringes
1st Battalion	red	red	red	white
2nd Battalion	green	red	green	white
3rd Battalion	sky blue	red	sky blue	white

Grenadier Non-Commissioned Officers (NCOs)

All details as for privates except as follows.

The shako pompon was quartered in white and black and orange, the plume tip was white with a vertical orange stripe down it. The flounders of the white shako cords were mixed white, orange and black. Yellow / gold lace was worn to the top of the cuff and to top and front of the collar. The wreath of the sabre strap was mixed black, white and orange. No canes were carried.

Grenadier Drummers

Uniform as for privates with the addition of white lace loops across the chest and up the front and back seams of the sleeves. At the top of each sleeve was a swallows nest in the coat colour, edged in white and having white vertical laces on it. There were seven white lace chevrons, point up, on each sleeve. The cuff flap buttons had white lace button hole laces. The top and back of the cuff flap were edged white as were the turnbacks. Drums were brass with white cords and green and white hoops. The drum apron was brown leather; the sticks were black with brass ends. They were carried in a brass holder on the white drum bandolier. The battalion and regimental drummers wore NCO's distinctions.

Grenadier Officers

All details of uniforms as for privates except as follows. Uniforms of better cloth and cut; skirts reached to the back of the knee. Shako cords were mixed orange, black and silver, the pompon was silver with the imperial initials AI embroidered in silver on a black and orange ground. Company officers wore red, unfringed epaulettes, edged gold, with the divisional number in gold. Field officers had gold fringes to their epaulettes. They wore silver waist sashes and sword knots with three black and orange stripes and black and orange internal fringes to the tassels. Straight-topped knee boots were worn.

Officers wore gorgets bearing the crowned double eagle, worn on a black ribbon with orange edges.

The colours of the gorget varied with rank: ensign – all silver; junior lieutenant – silver with a gold edging; senior lieutenant – silver with a gold eagle; staff captain – silver with gold eagle and edging; captain – gold with silver eagle; field officers – all gold. On campaign captains and below wore packs like the men. Senior officers wore bicorns with black cockades edged in white and orange and gold loop and side tassels.

Musketeer Privates

As for grenadier privates except as follows. The brass shako and pouch grenades had only a single

Musketeer Privates' Sabre Tassel Colours

1st Battalion		2nd Battalion		3rd Battalion	
Body	Crown and Wreath	**Body**	Crown and Wreath	**Body**	Crown and Wreath
White	1st white	**Green**	4th white	**Sky blue**	7th white
	2nd sky blue		5th sky blue		8th sky blue
	3rd orange		6th orange		9th orange

flame. Pompon colours were: 1st Battalion – green within white; 2nd – white within green; 3rd – white within sky blue. The headbands of the forage caps also identified the battalion of the wearer: 1st – all red; 2nd – red piped green; 3rd – red piped sky blue. On the front of the headband were the company initials in yellow: 1P (1st company).

The sabre straps were in the company colours; all straps and tassels were white; details of the bodies, crowns and wreaths varied as shown above.

Musketeer NCOs

Uniforms as for musketeer privates, with pompons, plumes, collar and cuff lace and sabre knots as for grenadier NCOs.

Jaegers

All details were as for the line infantry except as follows. Collar, cuff flaps and cuffs were dark green, piped red as were the turnbacks. Black belts; the winter trousers were dark green. The pouch bore the regimental number in brass. Jeagers wore a single flamed grenade on the shako, carabiniers wore a triple-flamed grenade. NCOs carried short rifles with sword bayonets.

Shoulder straps were coloured by regiment: 1st – 13th, 16th, 18th – 20th, 23rd, 25th, 27th – 31st, 49th.

Regiments – yellow with red divisional numbers; all the others of the fifty regiments were light blue with yellow numbers. The grenadiers and skirmishers (one platoon each in the grenadier companies) wore sabres as for the line; the others had only bayonets.

The Jaegers of the guard wore the double eagle on their kiwers and guards' lace to collar and cuffs.

Officers' epaulettes were dark green, edged in gold and backed in the colour of the shoulder straps worn by the men of their regiment. The divisional numbers were in gold.

Jaegers Forage Cap Colours

	1st Battalion		2nd Battalion		3rd Battalion	
	Piping	**Band**	**Piping**	**Band**	**Piping**	**Band**
Grenadiers	red	red	green	red	sky blue	red
Skirmishers	yellow	yellow	green	yellow	sky blue	yellow
Jaegers	white	white	green	green	sky blue	sky blue

The dark green forage caps were decorated with a top piping and a headband in the colours shown above.

NCOs
All details as for NCOs of the line.

The Imperial Guard Infantry
Grenadiers
All details as for the grenadiers of the line except as follows. All buttons, cap and pouch badges and other metalwork was copper. The cap plate was the imperial double eagle. Guards' lace was worn on collar and cuff flaps. The regimental facing colours on the collars, cuffs and forage cap headbands were Preobrazhenski – red, Semenowski – light blue, Izmailovski – white. Sabre straps and tassels were white for privates with company distinctions as follows: 1st Battalion – body, crown and wreath red; 2nd – body red, crown and wreath green; 3rd – body red, crown and wreath sky blue.

Tirailleur Privates
All details as for grenadiers except as follows.
Sabre straps and tassels were white; the body, crown and wreaths of the 1st Battalion were yellow; 2nd – yellow body, green crown and wreath; 3rd – yellow body, sky blue crown and wreath.
The sabre straps of privates of FUSILIERS, MUSKETIERS and JAEGERS were in the company colours; all straps and tassels were white.

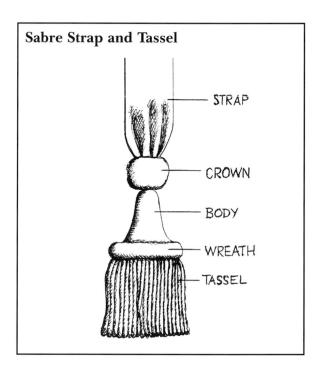

Sabre Strap and Tassel

— STRAP

— CROWN

— BODY

— WREATH

— TASSEL

Imperial Guard Sabre Tassel Colours

1st Battalion		2nd Battalion		3rd Battalion	
Body	**Crown and Wreath**	**Body**	**Crown and Wreath**	**Body**	**Crown and Wreath**
White	1st white 2nd sky blue 3rd orange	Green	4th white 5th sky blue 6th orange	Sky blue	7th white 8th sky blue 9th orange

Officers

All details as for officers of the line except that the gorgets of subalterns of the Preobrazhenski and Semenovski regiments had the inscription '1700 No 19' around the edge of their gorgets in commemoration of the victory over the Swedes at the battle of Narwa. The Marine Equipage of the Guard wore infantry uniform, guards' lace to collar and cuffs and a copper cap plate in the form of the crowned double eagle over crossed anchors.

Infantry Colours

Each battalion carried two colours; the 1st Battalion bore the sovereign's white colour and one regimental colour; the 2nd and 3rd Battalions had two regimental colours each. In 1812 there were three versions of colours still being carried: the M1797, M1800 and the M1803.

M1797

Issued in the reign of Tsar Paul I and thus bearing his imperial cipher in the corners of the colour. In the centre was a round orange disc; within the disc was the crowned, black double eagle under a gold crown. The eagle held an orb and a sceptre, and bore on its chest a red shield with St George and the dragon upon it. It was surrounded by green laurel branches. The brass finial bore the double eagle. Silver, black

and orange cords and tassels depended from the finial and reached almost to the bottom of the cloth. The regimental colours were in the facing colours of the individual regiments. Limitations of space do not allow details to be given here.

M1800

Also issued under Paul I and similar to the older version. In each corner was a gold, crowned wreath enclosing the cipher 'P I' in Cyrillic. The crowned orange central circle held a crowned, black double eagle holding two golden thunderbolts. Above and below the eagle were light blue scrolls with gold inscriptions. The circle was within a gold laurel wreath. Silver, black and orange cords and tassels depended from the finial and reached almost to the bottom of the cloth. The finial bore the double eagle. It seems that the finials of grenadier and guard regiments bore the crossed imperial initials. The layout of the colours was also more complex in that there were eight white sectors instead of the usual four.

M1803

Issued under Alexander, bearing the cipher 'A I' and having no scrolls in the orange central circle. The colours of these flags also varied with regiment. The finial bore the double eagle; cords as before.

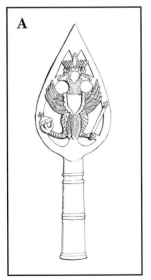

Above *Brass finial M1797 with the double eagle.*

Above *Brass finial M1798 with the cipher of Tsar Paul I.*

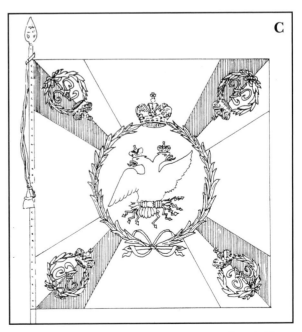

Above *Regimantal colour of the Litovsk Life Guards, M1803 with the cipher of Alexander I. The central disc is orange with a black double eagle and gold painted laurel leaves, crowns, ribbons and laurel leaves. The corner diagonals are black and yellow, corner ciphers are gold.*

St George's Colours

Regiments which had distinguished themselves in battle might be awarded special St George's colours. One such set, given in 1806 to the Kiev Grenadier Regiment was crimson with a white diagonal cross, an orange central, crowned disc enclosed by golden laurel branches and showing the crowned black eagle holding golden thunderbolts and with St George on a red shield on its breast. In the corner wreaths were imperial ciphers ('A I') and the brass finial bore the cross of the Order of St George. The usual cords were replaced by the black and orange ribbon of that order. Along the four sides of the colour were Cyrillic inscriptions recalling the deeds of the regiment.

The militia bore a wild variety of banners.

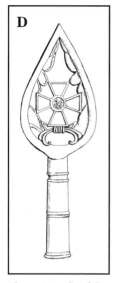

Above *Brass finial for St George's colours and standards. The cross has white arms edged in gold; the centre is red and bears the mounted figure of St George and the dragon.*

Foot Artillery

All details as for the line infantry except as follows. Other ranks wore red pompons and cords to their shakos. Collar and cuffs were black, piped in red; the green cuff flap was also piped red. The turnbacks were black, piped in red. White belts with brass picker equipment. Yellow buttons, the sabre tassels were red with white strap and fringes. Senior NCOs were called 'Fireworkers' as in German. Line regiments wore crossed cannon barrels over a single-flamed grenade on their kiwers; the guard artillery wore the double eagle over crossed barrels.

The artillery of the Guard wore guards' lace on collar and cuffs and their cap plate was the crowned double eagle over crossed cannon barrels and a pile of cannonballs in copper.

Horse Artillery

As for the foot artillery but in dragoon style. Instead of the kiwer, they wore dragoon-style leather helmets with brass plate, chinscales and front to combe. White summer trousers. Red shoulder straps with yellow number. NCOs wore white gauntlets. Horse furniture as for the dragoons, dark green, edged yellow, yellow cypher.

Engineers

This was a small corps of trained engineers who laid out and designed fortifications. All details as for the foot artillery except as follows. White buttons and lace, black facings piped red, red shako cords, white shoulder straps edged red. White sabre tassel with a red wreath.

Pioneers

This was a large corps which actually built field works. All details as for the foot artillery except as follows. White buttons, red shoulder straps with white regimental number and the Cyrillic 'P' (π). Dark green trousers. Officers' epaulettes were red, edged silver on red backing, with the regimental number and 'P' in silver. The men carried tools (spades, axes, picks, hatchets) and a pistol.

They also had a heavy, straight sword in a brown sheath with a brass tip. This sword had saw teeth along the back.

Cavalry

All details of badges of rank were as for the line infantry except that officers wore no gorgets.

Kuerassiers

The black leather helmet had a black leather combe topped with a short, black horsehair crest. The front

Above *Kuerassier standard M1800 with the ciphers of Paul I. The sovereign's standard would be white with small corner shields in the facing colour; regimental standards would be in reversed colours. Fringes and embroidery in the button colour. The eagle was black, the linings of the crowns were red. The Cyrillic inscription means 'Blessings'.*

of the combe was held in a brass stiffener which ran down to the front plate. This bore the imperial double eagle except where otherwise noted. The black front peak was edged in brass; the leather chinstrap was covered on brass chinscales. There was a small peak at the back.

The white tunic was of infantry cut, with facings worn on collar, plain, round cuffs and the wide edging to the white turnbacks; the shoulder straps were in the facing colour, edged white. There were two buttons on each cuff. There was also a narrow piping in the facing colour around the top of the sleeves. White breeches and high, jacked boots. In winter these were worn under grey overalls with regimental buttons. White leather gauntlets.

The black steel kuerass was edged in red leather; the black shoulder scales ended in brass clips. The brass-hilted, straight-bladed sword was carried in a steel sheath on white belts. The sword strap was of red leather with a white tassel.

Trumpeters

Red horsehair crest, special lace in the button colour, embroidered in the facing colour as for infantry drummers, but also to the rear seams of the tunic and to the edges of the turnbacks. In the case of the Military Order Regiment, this lace was that of the Order of St George: orange with three black stripes. Trumpets were brass, cords and tassels were black,

white and orange. NCO trumpeters wore lace in the button colour to collar and cuffs instead of the regimental lace. No kuerass was worn.

Horse Furniture

Square shabraque and pointed holster covers in the facing colour, with broad edging and crowned imperial cipher in the button colour except for the guards' regiments who wore the star of the Order of St Andrew, and the Military Order Regiment who wore the star of the Order of St George.

Grey round portmanteau.

Harness

Black, German style, with white metal fittings Facings were as shown below.

Regiment	Facings	Buttons
Horse Guards	red	yellow
Chevalier Guard	red	white
Tsar's Life Guards	light blue	white
Tsarina's Life Guards	crimson	white
Astrakhan	yellow	white
Military Order	black	yellow
Yekaterinoslav	orange	white
Little Russia	black	yellow
Gluchov	dark blue	white
Novgorod	pink	white
Pskoff	crimson	yellow
Starodub	light blue	yellow

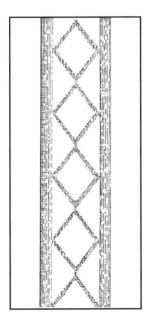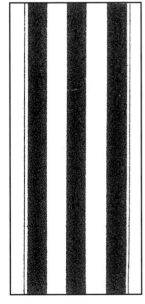

Above *From left to right: The special musicians' lace for kuerassiers and dragoons; the edging and criss-cross pattern are in the facing colour. The black and orange ribbon of the Order of St George.*

Dragoons

All details as for the Kuerassiers except as noted below.

No kuerasses; dark green tunic with red turnbacks. Facings were worn on the collar and plain round cuffs as well as on the shoulder straps. The shabraque was rounded, dark green, with the imperial cipher and a broad edging in the facing colour.

Dragoon swords were carried in brown leather sheaths with brass fittings on white belts. Long carbines and bayonets were also carried.

Facings and buttons were as shown in the column opposite. The Life Guards wore two yellow guards' laces on the collar and the cuffs and the St Andrew's star on helmet plate.

Regiment	Facings	Buttons
Life Guards	red	yellow
Arsamass	light blue*	white
Borisogleb	crimson*	yellow
Vladimir	white*	white
Dorpat	yellow*	white
Zhitomir	red**	white
Ingermannland	dark green	white
Irkutsk	white	yellow
Kasan	crimson	yellow
Kargopol	red	white
Kiev	crimson	white
Kinburn	yellow	white
Courland	light blue	yellow
Livland	red**	yellow
Mittau	white piped red	white
Moscow	pink	white
Narva	pink*	white
Nezhinsk	light blue*	yellow
Nischegorod	white*	white
Novgorod	dark blue	white

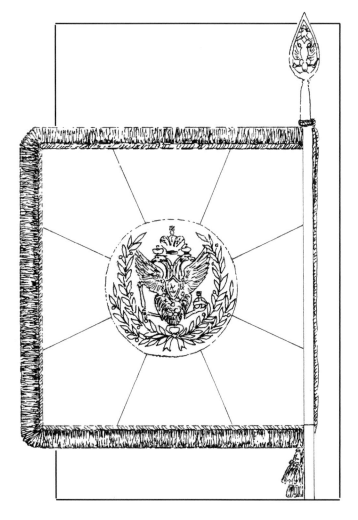

Above *Dragoon standard M1799. The sovereign's standard would be white, with an orange central disc, fringes in the button colour. Regimental standards had the same orange central disc, vertical cross also in orange, with a diagonal cross in the facing*

Above *Russian infantry drawn from life by Georg Adam in Nuremburg, Germany in 1814. This plate throws up some teasing questions, possibly illustrating the differences between the purely theoretical uniform regulations and what was actually worn in the field after a hard campaign and miles away from the regimental depot. The central officer and the private to his right with the brass, double eagle cap plate of the Pavlovski Grenadiers are apparently of the Imperial Guard, as is the private with the black plume. None of them, however, wear guards' lace to collar and cuffs. The figure on the extreme right, with a black fur busby and light blue facings would appear to be from a militia unit.*

Below *Russian hussars in Nuremburg in 1814 by Georg Adam. On the left, in brown costume, is the Achtyrsk Hussar Regiment. With his back to us is a member of the Life Guards Regiment. To his right, in a blue pelisse and grey breeches, possibly the Lubenski Regiment.*

Above *Once again, Georg Adam has given us campaign dress. In the foreground we see a member of the Starodub Kuerassiers. To his right a member of the Lifland Mounted Rifles; to his right a member of the Ulans, but the czapka and lance pennant colours make identification impossible. The Dragoon seems to be from the Kasan Regiment.*

Below *Russian foot and horse artillery on campaign. Drawn from life at Nuremburg by Georg Adam. Note the ammunition chest on the gun trails*

Above *Don Cossacks on the march near Nuremburg in 1814. To the left, in the background, seem to be a pair of Baschkirs.*

Below *A mixed bag of Don Cossacks, Baschkirs and Kalmuks, the latter of obviously Asian stock. Drawn from life by Georg Adam at Nuremburg in 1814.*

Top left *A trooper of dragoons. Note the oak leaf sprig in the chinstrap boss.*

Bottom left *Two officers of Jaegers.*

Above *Fusilier privates of two German regiments.*

Below *Trooper, Hussar Regiment Erzherzog Joseph Nr 2.*

Regiment	Facings	Buttons
Orenburg	black	yellow
Pereseslav	crimson*	white
Pskoff	orange	yellow
Riga	red	yellow
St Petersburg	pink	yellow
Sierwersk	red	white
Serpuchoff	yellow*	yellow
Siberia	white	white
Smolensk	yellow	yellow
Starodub	red	white
Taganrog	pink	yellow
Twer	dark blue	yellow
Tiraspol	red*	yellow
Finland	white piped red	yellow
Tcharkoff	red	yellow
Tchernigoff	dark blue	white
Yamburg	red*	yellow

* collar dark green, piped in the facing colour

** facings piped white

Cavalry Colours

Kuerassiers and dragoon regiments carried standards. Those of the kuerassiers were oblong in shape, dragoon standards were square. The 1st squadron bore a white standard, the others had regimental standards, varying in colour from regiment to regiment. The finial was in the button colour and bore the insignia as for the infantry colours. The sovereign's standard of kuerassier regiments was white with small, crowned corner discs in the facing colour, bearing the imperial cipher. In the bottom, staff corner of the standard was the crowned, black double eagle; towards the upper, fly corner was a cross in a circular sunburst. Embroidery and fringes were in the regimental button colour.

The regimental standards were in the facing colour with white corner discs, otherwise they were the same as the sovereign's standard. Silver, black and orange cords and tassels hung from the finial to about as long again as the standard was high.

Regiments of the Guard had extra embellishments and the Chevalier Guard carried a vexillum, red with an upright white cross, fringed in silver, with the bottom swallow-tailed.

Dragoon standards followed the same colour rules as those of the kuerassiers. The square field bore an upright iron cross. The crowned black double eagle was the central emblem, on a disc and surrounded by green laurel leaves.

St George's standards had the special features as for the corresponding infantry colours.

The Cossacks bore a variety of banners.

Mounted Rifles

All details as for the dragoons except as listed below. On 5 December 1812 the following dragoon regiments were converted to mounted rifles (chasseurs à cheval). The uniform differences were that the helmet was replaced by the kiwer with a large frontal cockade, loop and regimental button. Cords and flounders were white. The dark green tunic bore facings on the collar, shoulder straps, turnback edging and on the pointed cuffs. There was a single button in the point of the cuff and two more above the back of the cuff. The dark green overalls had twin side stripes in the facing colour. Horse furniture was as for the dragoons; harness was black and in hussar style. A hussar style, brass-hilted sabre was carried on white belts in a steel sheath.

All regiments wore white buttons; the facings were as follows.
Arsamass – light blue; Dorpat – pink; Livland – red; Nezhinsk – light grey; Perejeslav – crimson; Sierwersk – red; Tiraspol – orange; Tchernigoff – dark blue.

Hussars

These colourful regiments were dressed as flamboyantly as any other hussar regiments in Europe. They wore the infantry kiwer with a large frontal cockade, loop and regimental button as for the mounted rifles. The Life Guard Hussars wore the usual crowned double eagle cap plate on the kiwer.

The uniform is too complex to describe in great detail; the main points may be seen in the table below.

Harness and saddlery were of the usual hussar style, black with steel fittings. The steel-hilted sabre was carried in a steel sheath with black leather inlay. Belts were white. The shabraques had long, pointed rear corners with the crowned imperial cipher and decorations in the button and facing colours. The sabretasche was in the facing or dolman colour, bore the crowned imperial cipher and was decorated in the facing or button colour.

Regiment	Dolman and Breeches	Facings	Pelisse	Lace and Buttons	Fur	Sabretasche and Shabraque
Life Guards	red dark blue	dark blue	red	yellow	black	red & yellow blue edged red & yellow
Achtyrsk	brown brown	yellow	brown	yellow	white	brown edged yellow brown edged yellow
Alexandria	black black	red	black	white	white	black edged red black edged red
Grodno	black black	light blue	black	white	white	black edged light blue black edged light blue
Issum	red dark blue	blue	dark blue	white	white	red edged white dark blue edged white
Lubenski	blue blue	yellow	blue	white	white	blue edged white blue edged yellow
Mariupol	dark blue dark blue	yellow	dark blue	yellow	black	black edged yellow black edged yellow
Olviupol	dark green red	red	dark green	white	white	dark green edged red dark green edged red
Pavlograd	dark green dark green	light blue	light blue	red; yellow	black	dark green edged red dark green edged red
Ssum	grey red	red	grey	white	black	red edged white grey edged red
White Russian	dark blue dark blue	red	red	white	black	red edged white dark blue edged white
Yelisavetgrad	grey dark green	grey	grey	red; yellow	black	dark green & orange dark green & orange

Ulan Regiments

The costume of these regiments was traditional Polish dress. The square-topped czapka had a top half in the regimental colour with a white plume issuing from a white or yellow pompon. Hat cords varied in colour with the regiment. Only the Life Guard regiment wore a cap badge and this was the double eagle. The tunic was slate blue with red lapels and cuffs. The Life Guards wore two yellow laces on the collar and one on each pointed cuff. There was one button in the point of the cuff and two above the rear of it. Turnbacks were in the coat colour, edged in red, with a button at the junction of the edging.

Around the waist was worn a wide cloth belt in slate blue with two wide red stripes along it. Buttons, chinscales and epaulettes varied according to regiment. Breeches were slate blue with twin, wide red side stripes with a central red piping. The shabraque was in slate blue edged in red, with the crowned imperial cipher in the rounded rear corner.

Belts were white; the cartridge pouch bore a round, brass plate bearing the double eagle. Harness was black with steel fittings and of hussar style as were the sabres. The portmanteau was round and grey. Lance pennants varied with the regiment; where a regiment had two battalions they had different lance pennants. In the table below, the first colour given is that shown in the top half of the pennant. Only the front rank carried lances; the second rank had carbines.

Cossacks

Limits of space restrict the details which may be given here. The Life Guard Cossacks wore red jackets with guards' lace to collar and cuffs, black fur cap with red bag and white plume, baggy blue breeches, white belts. The epaulettes were yellow. The saddle cloth was square cut, edged yellow. Harness was light cavalry style, black with steel fittings. Most other Cossack regiments wore dark blue costumes with much silver ornamentation on the black leatherwork.

Regiment	Czapka Top and Cords	Facings	Buttons	Lance Pennants
Life Guards	blue yellow	red	yellow	red and white
Volhynia	blue yellow	crimson	yellow	1st yellow and red 2nd yellow and white
Litovski	white red	crimson*	white	1st white 2nd white and dark blue
Polish	slate blue white	crimson	white	1st dark blue 2nd crimson and dark blue
Tartar	crimson white	crimson	white	1st crimson 2nd crimson and dark blue
Tchugucheff	red white	red*	white	1st red 2nd red and dark blue
Vladimir	slate blue	crimson**	yellow	yellow and slate blue***
Zhitomir	slate blue white	crimson	white	yellow and slate blue
Orenburg	crimson yellow	crimson	yellow	slate blue and crimson
Serpuchoff	red yellow	red**	yellow	slate blue and red ***
Siberia	white red	red	white	yellow and white
Taganrog	white red	red**	yellow	yellow and red ***
Yamburg	white red	crimson	yellow	white and crimson

* collar slate blue piped crimson   ** collar slate blue   *** pennant quartered with colours reversed

Section 6

The Austrian Army Corps

This corps operated together with the VII Saxon Corps in southern White Russia, just to the north of the Ukraine. Please see the map of VII Corps' operations on page 139 for further details.
Commander General of Cavalry Prince Karl zu Schwarzenberg.
Chief of Staff FML Baron Stutterheim.

1st Division FML Trautenberg.
1st Brigade GM Zechmeister. Warasdiner St Georger Grenz IR Nr 16 (1 bn), 5th Jaeger Bn (4 companies), Hus R Kienmayer Nr 8 (6 squadrons).
2nd Brigade GM Pflacher. IR Beaulieu Nr 58, IR Duka Nr 39 (2 bns each).
Artillery: two light batteries.

2nd Division FML Bianchi.
1st Brigade GM Lilienberg. IR Simbschen Nr 48, IR Alvincy Nr 19 (2 bns each).
2nd Brigade GM Prince Philipp von Hessen-Homburg. IR Colloredo Nr 33, IR Hiller Nr 2 (2 bns each).
3rd Brigade GM Prince Alois von Liechtenstein. Grenadier Bn Kirchbetter (IRs 34,37,60), Grenadier Bn Przeszinsky (IRs 30,41, 58), IR Esterhazy Nr 32, IR Davidovich Nr 34 (2 bns each).
Artillery: two light batteries.

3rd Division FML Siegenthal.
1st Brigade GM Mayer. IR Czartoryski Nr 9 (1st Bn), IR Kottulinsky Nr 41 (2 bns).
2nd Brigade GM Mohr. 7th Jaeger Bn (4 companies), Warasdiner St Georger Grenz IR Nr 16 (1 company).
Hessen-Homburg Hussar-Regiment Nr 9 (6 squadrons).
Artillery: two light batteries.

Cavalry Division FML Frimont.
1st Brigade GM Frelich. Kaiser Franz Hussar Regiment Nr 1, Chevauxlegers Regiment O'Reilly Nr 3, Hohenzollern Chevauxlegers Regiment Nr 2 (6 squadrons each).
2nd Brigade GM Wrede. Dragoon Regiment Riesch Nr 6, Dragoon Regiment Levenehr Nr 4 (4 squadrons each), Hussar Regiment Blankenstein Nr 6 (6 squadrons).

Artillery Brigade GM Wachtenburg.
3 companies of artillery, 2 companies of assistants, 2 three-pounder and 4 six-pounder batteries each of 8 guns; 1 six-pounder and 1 twelve-pounder batteries. Each battery of 4 guns and 2 seven-pounder howitzers.
Two six-pounder cavalry batteries each of six guns and two 7-pounder howitzers.
A total of 76 guns in ten batteries.
The Extra Corps.
Pioniers (3 companies), Pontonniers (1 company with two large & two small infantry bridges & 50 pontoons).
Medical troops – 2 companies with 50 ambulances.
Two companies of staff protection infantry, one squadron of Staff Dragoons; one field bakery.
Totals: 30,904 men, 6,270 horses, 76 guns
On 27 October 1812 reinforcements in the form of IR Kaiser Nr 1, Liechtenstein Nr 12, the 2nd Bn, IR Czartoryski Nr 9 and the Hussar Regiment Liechtenstein Nr 7 arrived.

Uniforms of the Austrian Corps in Russia in 1812

Compared with many other armies of this period, Austrian uniforms were relatively simple and plain, with the exception of the hussars, who were their usual, flamboyant selves.

Infantry
German Fusiliers

In 1806 the old leather infantry helmet began to be replaced by the black, felt shako with a slightly belled-out top. It had leather eye and neck shields and a small, upturned flap over each ear. The chinstrap was of plain black leather. At the front of the shako was a black-within-yellow pompon, extending about an inch above the top; from this a brass 'loop' extended down to the centre of a black-within-yellow cockade, where it was held by a regimental button.

The tunic was pearl grey, single-breasted and closed with ten regimental buttons. The shoulder straps were white, piped in the facing colour, as were the vertical tail pocket flaps of the short skirts. Only the fronts of the skirts were turned back. Facings were also worn on the open collar, the plain, round cuffs, the turnbacks and to the piping from the two seams leading down from the two buttons in the small of the back. The cuffs were closed at the rear edges with two buttons each. Breeches and waistcoats were white, the gaiters reached to below the knee, were black and closed with eight black leather buttons. Regiments often replaced these with regimental buttons.

The pack was made of brown calfskin and was carried on two white straps. In fine weather, the grey greatcoat was carried rolled on top of the pack. The ammunition pouch was of plain, black leather.

Fusiliers carried only the bayonet

Corporals

As for the privates except that they carried a hazelnut stick on a white leather strap, wore buff leather gloves and carried a brass-hilted sabre in a black leather sheath, with a black and yellow woollen fist strap. The sabre grip was topped by a lion's head. Around the top of the shako they wore a yellow woollen band.

Sergeants

As for corporals except that they had gilt-hilted sabres, their sabre fist straps were of black and yellow mohair, the shako had two such bands around the top. They carried 'Spanish canes' on black and gold cords and tassels. The pompon of the sergeant major bore the imperial cipher FI in yellow silk in the black centre.

Pioneers

As for privates, but with a white leather apron with a small black pouch at the front centre of the waist belt. They had corporal's sabre straps, wore moustaches like the grenadiers and carried axes and saws.

Drummers and Musicians

As for privates except that they wore swallows nests at each shoulder in the facing colour. They, and the cuffs, were decorated in white lace. Drums were of brass, all leatherwork was white. The drum hoops were striped black and yellow on the outside and red on the inside. The drumsticks were black with brass ends and were borne in two leather loops on the drum bandolier. Some regiments seem to have added chevrons to their drummers' sleeves as well.

Officers

The items of clothing were basically as those of the men but of much better quality. The shako had gilt fittings and rank was shown by gold bands around the top. Junior officers wore one or two narrow bands, field officers a wide band. The black centre of the pompon bore the imperial cipher FI in gold.

The coat skirts were so long as to reach to the back of the knee. Their pocket flaps were horizontal.

Officers had no shoulder straps and wore no facing colours on their turnbacks. In the field they wore dark grey, single-breasted, full skirted tunics with regimental buttons and facings on the collar. The gilt-hilted sword was worn on a white belt, in a black and gilt sheath and with a black and gold sword strap with heavy, gold-embroidered tassel, silk for junior officers, bullion for field officers. A yellow and black worsted waist sash was worn over the coat by junior officers. For field officers it was of silk.

Officers wore knee boots. Off duty officers wore a gold-edged bicorn with cockade and pompon. They carried 'Spanish canes' with gilt tips on gold and black cords.

Saddle furniture for mounted officers was a red shabraque with yellow-black-yellow edging and the crowned imperial cipher in the pointed rear corners. Harness was black

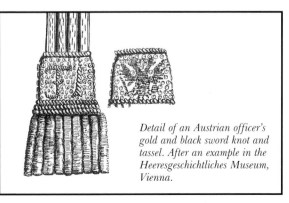

Detail of an Austrian officer's gold and black sword knot and tassel. After an example in the Heeresgeschichtliches Museum, Vienna.

German Grenadiers

All details as for the German fusiliers except as noted below. The shako was replaced by the bearskin, with peak, brass front plate and a backing in the facing colour, decorated with lace in the button colour.

The cockade was worn on the right-hand side of the bearskin. A brass-hilted sabre in a black sheath and having a white leather fist strap was carried. Cartridge pouches and the bandoliers bore a brass grenade badge. Officers carried sabres.

Hungarian Fusiliers

All details as for German fusiliers except as noted below. The cuffs were pointed. From a button in the peak of the point was a vertical lace in the button colour, with a fringe to the rear. Instead of the breeches and gaiters, Hungarian regiments wore long, light blue pantaloons with black and yellow braid decoration to side seams and thighs. Officers' cuff and pantaloon lace was in the button colour.

Junior officers had narrow lace decoration to their trousers, senior officers wore wide lace. All officers wore gold-trimmed, hussar-style boots.

Hungarian Grenadiers

As for Hungarian fusiliers but with grenadier distinctions for all ranks.

Jaegers

All details as for German fusiliers except as noted below. The shako was replaced by the black Corsican hat, with the left-hand brim extended and turned up. The usual black and yellow pompon was worn at the front centre of the top of the crown. On the upturned brim of the hat was a brass hunting horn badge enclosing the battalion number. A green plume was worn for parades.

The coat and trousers were pike grey, with green facings and yellow buttons, embossed with the battalion number. Belts were black and boots were worn. NCOs carried no canes. Officers had Hungarian style gold braid to their breeches and wore golden epaulettes and aiguillettes although these were unofficial. The usual weapon was a smoothbore carbine with the normal bayonet. Sharpshooters carried rifles and sword bayonets and a powder horn was carried on a green cord with heavy tassels.

Instead of drums, signals were sounded on hunting horns which had green cords and tassels.

The facings and buttons of the line infantry regiments that fought in Russia are shown on page 187.

Hungarian regiments are distinguished with an asterisk.

Above *Officers of a German regiment (left; Hoch- und Deutschmeister Nr 4) and a Hungarian regiment (right; Hiller Nr 2).*

Above *Cap plate of a grenadier, M1806. After an example in the Heeresgeschichtliches Museum, Vienna.*

Regiment	Facings	Buttons
Kaiser Nr 1	pompadour	yellow
Hiller Nr 2*	yellow	yellow
Czartorysky Nr 9	apple green	yellow
Liechtenstein Nr 12	dark blue	yellow
Alvintzy Nr 19*	light blue	white
De Ligne Nr 30	pike grey	yellow
Esterhazy Nr 32*	light blue	yellow
Colloredo Nr 33*	dark blue	white
Davidovich Nr 34*	madder red	white
Duka Nr 39*	light red	white
Kottulinsky Nr 41	sulphur yellow	white
Simbschen Nr 48*	steel green	yellow
Beaulieu Nr 58	black	white

The grenadier companies and their facings were as follows.

Kirchenbetter	**Przsezinsky**	
Davidovich Nr 34*	madder red	white
De Ligne Nr 30	pike grey	yellow
Wiedenfeld Nr 37*	light red	yellow
Kottulinsky Nr 41	sulphur yellow	white
Gyulai Nr 60*	steel green	white
Beaulieu Nr 58	black	white

Border Infantry Regiments

All details as for Hungarian fusiliers. Regimental distinctions were as shown below. Regiments 1 – 4, 10 and 11 were in French service at this point.

Warasdiner St Georger Nr 6* tobacco brown coats, lobster red facings, white buttons.

Staff Infantry

As for German fusiliers with red facings and yellow buttons.

Staff Dragoons

Dragoon uniform, pike grey coat, madder red facings, yellow buttons, white belts.

Artillery

All details of the gunners' uniforms were as for German fusiliers except as follows. Instead of the shako they wore the black Corsican hat as for the Jaegers but with black over yellow plume. The coat was roe deer brown with red facings and yellow buttons. Belts were white. Short boots, to below the knee were worn. Senior NCOs wore long-skirted coats.

Above *An Austrian 'Wurst Batterie' ('Sausage Battery') on the march. This battery was designed to provide rapidly mobile artillery support in the field and not only to cavalry formations. The equipments are painted yellow; the drivers wear yellow facings and buttons.*

Artillery Train

As for German fusiliers but with riding boots, yellow facings and buttons.

Pioneers

As for the artillery, but with the rear brim of the Corsican hat turned up. Pike grey coat, grass green facings, white buttons and belts.

Pontonniers

As for the Pioneers, but with pike grey coats and breeches, red facings, white buttons and belts.

Engineers

As for the Pioneers but with the left-hand brim of the hat turned up; purple facings, white buttons and belts.

Above *The standard guard of a Kuerassier regiment. The standard bearer's bandolier is in the regimental facing colour with chain link decoration in the button colour. Note the sprig of oak leaves on the finial. The trumpeter (far right) has a red helmet crest.*

Sappers and Miners

As for the Engineers but with crimson facings, white buttons and belts.

Dragoons

All details as for the German infantry unless noted here as being otherwise.

Black leather helmet with peaks to front and back, the front peak edged in brass. Brass front plate bearing the uncrowned imperial cipher FI, brass covering to the combe, black over yellow caterpillar crest – red for trumpeters. Two brass struts to each side of the helmet, running down from the centre of the crown to the sides of the round, brass chinstrap bosses; plain black chinstrap.

Coat as for the infantry with facings shown on the collar, cuffs and on the braid which edged the white turnbacks. White breeches and belts, below-knee boots. They carried straight, heavy swords in steel sheaths on white slings. It had a plain, white leather fist strap for privates. NCOs carried rifled carbines.

Harness was black with brass fittings. The saddle cover was of white sheepskin with a red edging. The

red shabraque had a slight rear peak in which was the crowned imperial cipher in yellow. The shabraque was edged in black and yellow cord; inside this was a wide yellow lace with a black central stripe. A grey, round portmanteau was carried.

The Levenehr Dragoons Nr 4 had dark green coats, emperor yellow facings and yellow buttons.

Dragoon Regiment Riesch Nr 6 had white coats, light blue facings and yellow buttons

Chevauxlegers

All details as for the dragoons. Regiment Hohenzollern Nr 2 had dark green coats, scarlet facings and white buttons; Regiment O'Reilly Nr 3 had white coats, sky blue facings and yellow buttons.

Hussars

All details as for the German fusiliers except as noted below. The shakos had black and yellow cords and flounders and these regiments wore the traditional Hungarian costume. The fur trim to the pelisses was black. Officers had black bandoliers with gilt picker equipment. Their shakos were decorated with elaborate gold lace. The barrel sash was black and yellow; the red sabretasche was edged in black and yellow and decorated with the crowned imperial cipher. Belts were white. Weapons were a curved sabre with a steel hilt in a steel sheath on red leather slings. The saddle cover was black sheepskin edged red. The red shabraque had long rear corners; it was edged and decorated as for the dragoons.

The portmanteau was round and red.

All regiments wore light blue dolmans, breeches and pelisses with black and yellow lace and yellow buttons. The were distinguished by the colour of their shakos. Regiment Kaiser Nr 1 had purple shakos, Blankenstein Nr 6 had violet and Liechtenstein Nr 7 had dark green.

Colours and Standards

As with other armies of the period, there were various versions of colours and standards carried at this time. The design of these items had been standardised in 1743 by the Empress Maria Theresia; there were two types carried by each regiment; the *'Leib'*, or sovereign's colour/standard and the *'Ordinair'* or regimental colour/standard. The designs were painted onto the silk.

The sovereign's colour was white; on the obverse was the Virgin in clouds, on the reverse the imperial double eagle. The three free sides of the colour/standard was edged in triangles, red and white for the kingdom of Austria, black and yellow for the empire. The flat brass finial had the double eagle engraved on one side and the imperial cipher (FII or FI) according to date of presentation, on the other. The cloth was nailed to the staff with three rows of dome-headed golden nails. Colours and standards were often decorated with cravats as are those of the modern American army. These were often in the regimental facing colour, embroidered in the button colour.

The regimental colour was of the same design as the sovereign's, but had a yellow field with the double eagle on both sides. There were several versions, each differing from its predecessor as the imperial coat of arms reflected the changing crests of the crown lands.

Above *Regimental colour M1792. Heeresgeschichtliches Museum, Vienna. The lining of the crown is red, the ribbons are blue between gold.*

M1792

The heads of the eagles were surrounded by golden haloes; on the wings was the imperial cipher FII in gold. On the central shield were the crests of the imperial possessions. Slung around this shield were the collars of the following orders (from the inside to the outside): Saint Stephen, Maria Theresia and the Golden Fleece.

M1805

Above the heads of the eagles appeared the crown of the Holy Roman Empire; the large, complex central shield was replaced by a smaller one bearing just the double headed eagle. The eagles' heads were surmounted by crowns. The same orders were worn around the shield and the crests of the ten major crown possessions were arranged around the central

shield, each on their own shields. Very few of these were presented, before they were replaced at the end of the disastrous Ulm–Austerlitz campaign.

M1806

The imperial cipher now became FI, the crowns were Austrian, the eagles lost their haloes and the states' shields reflected the losses of territory following that campaign.

It was customary to stitch small white or yellow patches onto the upper corners of the colours carrying the regimental designation. For example; 'Gz.Inf.Reg.' (in the left-hand corner) and 'Nr.6' (in the right) would indicate 'Grenz-Infanterie-Regiment Nummer 6'. This pattern of colour remained unchanged until 1816.

Cavalry Standards were of the same basic design as infantry colours but smaller in size. They were carried on staffs resembling a small jousting lance, fitted with a steel bar and ring. They did not show all the provincial crests that filled the infantry colours. They followed the changes to the colours in 1805 and 1806. They were not supposed to be fringed, but many regiments ignored this rule. The edging triangles showed gold and silver instead of yellow and white.

Above *Sovereign's colour M1805. Heeresgeschichtliches Museum, Vienna. The Virgin's robes are white and blue. The double eagle on the reverse bears eleven shields of imperial states on its wings.*

Below Regimental standard M1806. Heeresgeschichtliches Museum, Vienna. The three central shields (right to left) three silver eagles on red on a yellow ground; the red-white-red shield of Austria and the Habsburg crest of a red rampant lion on a golden ground. The cross behind the central shield is that of the Teutonic Order; Kaiser Franz I was its Grand Master.

Section 7

The Prussian Army Contingent (28th Division)

The Prussians formed part of Marshal Macdonald's X Corps, together with the 7th Division. This corps was not included in my original book; the 7th Division is thus included after the Prussian section. The uniforms, colours and standards of the units in the 7th Division may be found in their national sections.

All Prussian regiments which took part in this campaign were combined from two existing regiments, except for the Leib-Infanterie-Regiment, which was mobilised as a whole. The commander at the outset was General of Infantry von Grawert, but he fell sick and was replaced by Lieutenant-General von Yorck.

Chief of Staff Lieutenant-General von Massenbach.
Deputy Chief of Staff Major-General von Kleist.

	Officers	Men	Horses Officers' & men's	Train
1st Brigade. Colonel von Below.				
1st Combined Infantry Regiment. Major von Soeholm I.	61	2006	49	55
2nd and Fusilier Bns, 1st East Prussian IR Nr 1;				
1st Bn, 2nd East Prussian IR Nr 3.				
2nd Combined Infantry Regiment. Major von Soeholm II.	65	2091	49	55
1st Bn 3rd East Prussian IR Nr 4; 1st and				
Fusilier Bns, 4th East Prussian IR Nr 5.				
2nd Brigade. Lieutenant-Colonel von Horn.				
3rd Combined Infantry Regiment. Major von Steinmetz.	58	1910	49	55
2nd and Fusilier Bns 1st Pommeranian IR Nr 2;				
1st Bn Colberg IR.				
4th Combined Infantry Regiment. Major von Zielinsky.	60	1971	49	55
1st, 2nd and Fusilier Bns, Leib-Infanterie-				
Regiment Nr 9.				
3rd Brigade. Colonel von Raumer.				
5th Combined Infantry Regiment. Major von Schmalensee.	60	2019	49	55
1st Bn 1st West Prussian IR Nr 6; 1st and				
Fusilier Bns, 2nd West Prussian IR Nr 7.				
6th Combined Infantry Regiment. Major von Carnall.	61	2047	49	55
2nd Bn, 1st Silesian IR Nr 11, 2nd and Fusilier Bns,				
2nd Silesian IR Nr 12.				
East Prussian Feld-Jaeger Bn. (1 bn).	19	464	19	17
Total infantry	**384**	**12,508**	**313**	**347**

| | Officers | Men | Horses | |
			Officers' & men's	Train
1st Cavalry Brigade. Colonel von Huenerbein.				
1st Combined Dragoon Regiment. Major von Treskow.	23	574	659	23
2nd and 4th Squadrons, Lithuanian Dragoons Nr 3;				
1st and 2nd Squadrons, 2nd West Prussian Dragoons Nr 4.				
2nd Combined Dragoon Regiment.	24	586	668	24
Lieutenant-Colonel von Juergas.				
1st and 3rd Squadrons, 1st West Prussian Dragoons Nr 2;				
1st and 3rd Squadrons, Brandenburg Dragoons Nr 5.				
Combined Ulan Regiment. Major von St Paul. 3rd				
and 4th Squadrons, Silesian Ulans; 3rd and 4th				
Squadrons, Brandenburg Ulans.				
This regiment was detached in June to the 2nd				
Light Cavalry Brigade, II Cavalry Corps; (see in II Cavalry Corps).				

| | Officers | Men | Horses | |
			Officers' & men's	Train
2nd Cavalry Brigade. Colonel von Jeanneret.				
1st Combined Hussar Regiment. Major von Cosel.	26	614	697	23
(Attached to Grandjean's 7th Infantry Division of the X Corps.)				
3rd and 4th Squadrons, 1st Leib-Hussars; 3rd and				
4th Squadrons, 2nd Leib-Hussars.				
2nd Combined Hussar Regiment Colonel von Gzarnowski.				
3rd and 4th Squadrons, Brandenburg Hussars;				
1st and 2nd Squadrons, Pommeranian Hussars.				
This regiment was detached in June to the				
1st Light Cavalry Division, I Cavalry Corps; (see in I Cavalry Corps).				
3rd Combined Hussar Regiment.				
Major von Eicke. 1st and 3rd	21	504	582	23
Squadrons, 1st Silesian Hussars; 1st and 2nd Squadrons,				
2nd Silesian Hussars.				
Total infantry	**94**	**2,278**	**2,605**	**93**

| | Officers | Men | Horses | |
			Officers' & men's	Train
Artillery.				
Horse Artillery				
1st, 2nd and 3rd East Prussian Horse Artillery Companies	13	439	377	282
1st – 3rd Artillery Train Companies.	?	?	?	?
Foot Artillery				
3rd Silesian 12 pounder Foot Artillery Battery(half a battery),	3	106	7	8
1st, 2nd and 3rd East Prussian 6-pounder Batteries, 6th	16	564	32	349
Brandenburg 6-pounder Foot Battery.				
1st – 5th Artillery Park Companies.	6	452	30	563
1st and 2nd Bridging Companies	–	26	2	48
East Prussian Pionier Company	6	248	–	–
Total Artillery etc.	**44**	**1835**	**448**	**1310**

| | Officers | Men | Horses | |
			Officers' & men's	Train
The 7th Division GdD Grandjean. 1 July 1812.				
13th Bavarian Infantry Regiment. Colonel Schlossberg.	48	1275	20	66
1st and 2nd Battalions and artillery company.				
5th Polish Infantry Regiment. Colonel Oskierka.	85	2553	24	70
1st – 4th Battalions and artillery company.				
10th Polish Infantry Regiment. Colonel Kaminski.	87	2442	28	71
1st – 4th Battalions and artillery company.				
11th Polish Infantry Regiment. Colonel Clebowski.	80	2324	27	71
1st – 4th Battalions and artillery company.				

1st Westfalian Infantry Regiment. Colonel Plessman. 1st and 2nd Battalions and artillery company.	43	1439	19	59
1st Polish Foot Artillery Regiment; 6th Company.	7	221	20	200
1st Polish Horse Artillery Regiment. 1st Company.	5	161	108	106
1st Polish Sapper Battalion; 4th Company.	4	125	10	6
Totals	**359**	**10540**	**265**	**649**

Artillery Materiel of X Corps

Cannon	4 x 12 pdr, 42 x 6 pdr.
Howitzers	14 x 24 pdr.
Affuts de rechange	
Cannon	1 x 12 pdr, 6 x 6 pdr.
Howitzers	2 x 24 pdr.

Ammunition caissons

12 pdr	8		
6 pdr	38		
Howitzer	35		
Infantry	28		
Ammunition carts	30		
Cartridges		Canister 12 pdr	520
		Canister 6 pdr	7175
		Canister howitzer	2230
		Ball 12 pdr	240
		Ball 6 pdr	2590
		Ball howitzer	760
Infantry	357600		
Cavalry	200000		
Four-pontoon bridging wagons	8		

The Area of Operations of X Corps

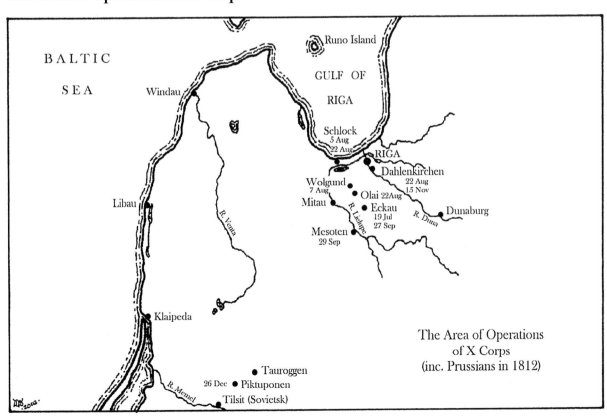

The Area of Operations
of X Corps
(inc. Prussians in 1812)

Prussian Uniforms

Infantry

Each infantry regiment had two musketier battalions and a fusilier (or light) battalion each of four companies, and two grenadier companies.

Musketier Privates

Black felt shako with white top band and black-within-white pompon; black leather chinstrap. The front was decorated with the uncrowned royal cipher FWR in brass. For parades, white cords and thin, black plumes were worn. The double-breasted, dark blue coat had two rows each of eight brass buttons, dark blue cuff flaps with three buttons and two buttons in the small of the back. The bottom cuff flap button was always worn open. The turnbacks were red and plain. Collars and cuffs were in the colour of the province in which the regiment was raised. These were: East Prussia – brick red, West Prussia – crimson, Pommerania – white, Brandenburg – poppy red, Silesia – white. The Colberg Regiment had white facings. The shoulder straps of the first regiment in each province were white, red for the second, yellow for the third and light blue for the fourth. The buttons on the shoulder straps bore the company number in Arabic numerals. Breeches were grey, the short, black gaiters had black leather buttons. Belts were white with brass buckles, the cartridge pouch had a round brass plate with the eagle on it. The brass-hilted sabre was borne in a brown leather sheath on the waist belt. On campaign the grey greatcoat – if not worn – was carried rolled and strapped to the top of the brown calfskin pack. The sabre strap and tassel were white for all companies; the 1st Battalion also had white crowns and bodies to the tassel. Company identity was shown by the colour of the wreath: 1st – white; 2nd – yellow; 3rd – light blue; 4th – red.

In the 2nd Battalion the crown and wreath were in the company colours as shown below: 1st – green; 2nd – yellow; 3rd – light blue; 4th – red.

The fusilier battalion had the same colours as the 2nd Battalion, but the body of the tassel was also in the company colour.

Above *Sword knots. Special black and white knot worn by privates for distinguished service in the 1806–7 campaign.*

Musketier NCOs

As for privates but with gold top band to shako, gold braid to the top of the cuffs and to the front and bottom of the collar, white gloves and a black and white sabre strap and tassel. Their black plumes had a white tip.

Musketier Drummers and Musicians

Swallows nests in the provincial facing colour with white lace. It is thought that Silesian and Pommeranian regiments wore poppy red swallows nests. Drums were brass, with red and white hoops and black sticks. On the body of the drum was the crowned royal cipher within trophies of arms.

Musketier Officers

Company officers wore the shako in finer construction and materials. At each side was a small Prussian eagle in gilt metal. Gold chains ran from these side eagles to the frontal pompon and to the top of the back of the shako. Their cords were silver and black as were their waist sashes.

The pompon was black and silver, and all officers wore the black and silver cockade with gold loop and button. Their coat tails reached to the back of the knee, and there were horizontal, false pocket flaps on the hips, each with two buttons. They carried swords in brown sheaths on white slings with gilt hilts and silver and black sword strap and tassel. They wore boots. In October 1808 rank badges were introduced for officers and were worn on the shoulder straps, which were in the facing colour and edged in red. A lieutenant had a single black and silver lace along the centre of the strap; a captain one at either side, and a major's strap was edged all the way round with the same lace.

Fusiliers

All details as for the musketiers except as noted below. Instead of the FWR badge they wore a black-within-white cockade, with regimental button and loop. For NCOs this loop was of brass.

Above *Prussian officers' shoulder straps 1808 to mid-1812. The outer piping is red, the field is in the regimental facing colour, the lace is silver and black. From left to right: 1st and 2nd lieutenant and staff captain; captain; field officer.*

Belts were black and worn crossed. Those armed with rifles had sword-bayonets.

Grenadiers

All details as for the musketiers except as noted below. The shako had a brass Prussian eagle plate; the shoulder strap buttons bore the company number in Roman numerals. They wore black and white sabre strap tassels.

Feldjaegers

All details as for fusiliers of line infantry except as noted below. The shako had no top band and was decorated with dark green cords and a black plume for parades. Officers had black and silver cords.

Dark green tunic and turnbacks, red collar, shoulder straps, Swedish cuffs and piping to turnbacks, yellow buttons. Grey breeches, short, black gaiters, black leatherwork.

Dragoons

All details as for musketiers except as noted below. The shako was reinforced with leather at the top and

bottom and to the sides. The cap badge was a Prussian eagle and white plumes and cords were worn for parades. NCOs' plumes had a black tip, those of officers had a black base. Trumpeters wore red plumes.

Brass chinscales were worn on campaign. The light blue, double-breasted tunic had buttons, collar, shoulder straps, Swedish cuffs and edging to the light blue turnbacks in the regimental colour. Grey overalls with buttoned sides. White belts. The old, straight swords of the 1806 era were carried at this point. The facings and buttons were as follows.

Above *Sword knots. Cavalry officer's black leather and silver sabre strap.*

Lithuanian Dragoons Nr 3 – red, yellow. 2nd West Prussian Dragoons Nr 4 – red, white. Brandenburg Dragoons Nr 5 – black, yellow.

Saddle furniture was a light blue shabraque with a piping and a wide braid in the facing colour. Over this was laid a black sheepskin saddle cover. Harness was black with fittings in the button colour.

Ulans

All details as for the dragoons except as noted below. They wore traditional lancer costume in dark blue, with red facings and yellow buttons. The czapka

Above *The eagle cap plate of line dragoons and of grenadiers of infantry. There was also a grenadier cap plate in which the eagle's wings were turned down.*

had a black base and a dark blue top and yellow piping. The 2nd Silesian Ulans had red shoulder straps; the 3rd Brandenburg Ulans had yellow shoulder straps. Belts were black. The shabraque was dark blue, edged red and had rounded rear corners. Weapons were hussar sabres and lances for the front rank; the rear rank carried carbines instead of lances. The lance pennants were dark blue over the shoulder strap colour.

Hussars

Shakos as for the dragoons, with cockade, loop and button, white cords and plumes as before. The cords of NCOs were white with black and white flounders and tassels; officers' cords were silver and black. The two Leib-Hussar regiments wore white/silver skull and cross bones badges to their shakos.

The dolman had fifteen rows of lace on the chest and three rows of buttons; the collar and cuffs were in the regimental colour as were the lace and buttons. The pelisse was in the same colours as the dolman.

Privates of all line regiments wore white fur trim to the pelisse; NCOs and officers had black fur trim.

Trumpeters had swallows nests in the collar colour.

Officers' sashes had silver and black cords with silver barrels, the men had cords in the dolman collar with barrels and other fittings in the lace colour.

Regiment	Dolman and Pelisse	Collar and Cuffs	Buttons and Lace
1st Leib	black	red	white
2nd Leib	black	black	white
Brandenburg	dark blue	red	white
Pommeranian	light blue	black	yellow

Weapons were the British M1794 pattern sabre in a steel sheath, with black fist strap. The sabretasche was red with crowned royal cipher and edging in the button colour, except for the two Leib-Hussar regiments and the Pommeranians, which had plain black leather lids. Carbines were carried on black bandoliers; the best shots had rifled weapons. The men's pouch lids were plain, except in the Leib-Hussar regiments where silver stars were worn. Officers of the line regiments wore the crowned royal cipher.

The shabraque was in the dolman colour, with wolf's tooth edging in the collar colour and lace in the regimental colour. It had a long rear corner. Harness was black with fittings in the regimental button colour and of Hungarian style.

Regimental distinctions were as shown below; the 1st Leib-Hussars had white shoulder straps, the 2nd had red ones.

Foot Artillery

As for musketiers except as noted below. Yellow top band to shako, brass, three-flamed grenade badge; black collars and cuffs edged red. Shoulder straps in the provincial colour. Black belts.

Horse Artillery

As for the foot artillery but with dragoon shako, white plumes, yellow cords, brass chinscales. Dark blue turnbacks edged in red-black-red lace. Dragoon boots.

Pontonniers

As for the foot artillery.

Engineers

As for the artillery with black velvet facings, white buttons, black shoulder straps edged red.

Colours and Standards

It is clear that various designs of colours were carried in 1812. Each regiment had a sovereign's colour and a regimental colour. Each musketier battalion was entitled to two colours. On the old colours the royal ciphers were FR; on the new version they were FWR. On the old version the scroll bore 'PRO GLORIA ET PATRIA'.

1st East Prussian IR Nr 1

Old style colours of the IR Ruechel Nr 2 from the 1806 era.

Sovereign's colour. Cloth and scroll white, centre black, emblems and eagle gold. This colour was not carried in 1812.

Regimental colour; this colour was carried in 1812. Cloth and scroll black, centre white, emblems gold, black eagle.

1st Pommeranian IR Nr 2

The old IR Ruits Nr 8; they carried old colours dating from the time of Frederick the Great. Sovereign's colour. Cloth and scroll white, centre and flame cross black, emblems gold, eagle gold. Regimental colour. Cloth and scroll black with white flame cross, white centre, emblems gold, eagle black. In 1812, this colour was carried by the IR Nr 1.

Above *Plain pattern old style infantry colour carried by various regiments in 1812.*

Above *Officer, Hussar Regiment Erzherzog Joseph Nr 2.*

Top right *A group of various Austrian infantry officers and men. Note the rank braiding to the officers' shakos and the wide, silver decoration to the thighs and side seams of the field officer of Hungarian infantry in the central group. A plate by Theodor Weigl, Vienna.*

Middle right *A group of Austrian cavalry officers from various regiments. Note the imperial cipher FI on the helmet plates and the forage cap of the groom holding the horse on the left. A plate by Theodor Weigl, Vienna.*

Bottom right *Officers and men of various Austrian hussar regiments. From left to right they are: trooper, 8th Regiment (poplar green dolman and pelisse, light red breeches); officer, 3rd Regiment (ash grey shako, dark blue dolman, breeches and pelisse); officer, 5th Regiment (red shako, dark green dolman and pelisse, crimson breeches); officer, 4th Regiment (light blue shako, poplar green dolman and pelisse, light red breeches); trooper, 9th Regiment (black shako, dark green dolman and pelisse, crimson breeches); officer, 3rd Regiment (ash grey shako, dark blue uniform).*

Far left *Trooper, Brandenburg Hussars, parade dress; Trumpeter, Silesian Kuerassiers, service dress.*

Left *Private, Garde-Jaegers, parade dress. Musician, Silesian Grenadier Battalion.*

Far left *Musketeer, 2nd Silesian Infantry Regiment, parade dress. Fusilier, Leib-Infantry Regiment, parade dress.*

Left *Gunner, Silesian artillery brigade. Pioneer, marching order.*

Right *Trooper, Brandenburg Kuerassier Regiment. Trooper, Normal-Eskadron, parade dress.*

Far right *Trooper, Guards' Ulan-Eskadron, parade dress. Trooper, Brandenburg Ulan Regiment, parade dress.*

Top left *Officer of* Nizam-Jedid. *This regiment functioned as palace guard when in Istanbul.*
Top centre *Private of* Nizam-I-Jedid.
Top right *Gunner.*
Bottom left *Private, Anatolian* Sekhan.
Bottom right *Albanian mercenary.*

These are taken from Military Costume of Turkey (XVIII Century), *published in 1818 by T. McLean in London.*

Above *The old-style colour of IR Courbiere Nr 58, carried by the 2nd West Prussian IR Nr 7. White cloth and scroll, yellow corners and centre, silver embroidery, black eagle.*

2nd East Prussian IR Nr 3

M1810 pattern colours. Sovereign's colour. Cloth and scroll white, centre black, emblems and eagle gold. Regimental colour. Cloth and scroll white, centre black, emblems and eagle gold.

3rd East Prussian IR Nr 4

M1810 pattern colours. Sovereign's colour. Cloth and scroll white, centre black, emblems and eagle gold. Regimental colour. Cloth and scroll white, centre black, emblems and eagle gold.

4th East Prussian IR Nr 5

Old style colours of the IR Diericke Nr 16 from the 1806 era. Sovereign's colour. Cloth white with upright orange flame cross and white scroll, centre orange, Emblems gold, eagle black. Regimental colour. Orange cloth and scroll, white upright flame cross, white centre, emblems gold, eagle black.

1st West Prussian IR Nr 6

Old style colours of the IR Reinhart Nr 52 from the 1806 era. Sovereign's colour. Cloth and scroll white, poppy red upright flame cross, dark green centre, emblems silver, black eagle. Regimental colour. Cloth and scroll dark green, poppy red flame cross, white centre, emblems silver, black eagle.

2nd West Prussian IR Nr 7

Old style colours of the IR Courbiere Nr 58 from the 1806 era. Sovereign's colour. Cloth and scroll white, yellow corners and centre, silver emblems and black eagle. Regimental colour. Cloth and scroll light blue, yellow corners and centre, silver emblems and black eagle.

Leib-Infantry Regiment Nr 9

M1810 pattern colours. Sovereign's colour. Cloth white, narrow black corner piles scroll light blue, centre orange with black eagle, emblems gold. Regimental colour. Cloth black, narrow white corner piles, otherwise as above.

Below *Sovereign's colour, Colberg IR Nr 10, showing both the 1808 and the 1816 versions.*

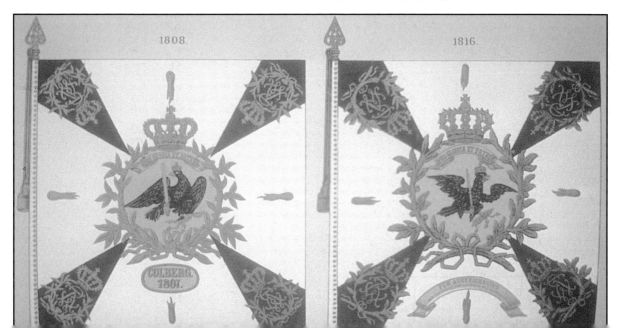

Colberg IR Nr 10

The old IRs Nrs 8 and 9; M1808 pattern colours. Sovereign's colour. Cloth white with black corner piles, orange centre, light blue scroll, black eagle, gold emblems. Below the centre was a light blue label edged in gold and bearing COLBERG in gold. Regimental colour. Cloth black with white corners, otherwise as above.

1st Silesian IR Nr 11

Old colours of the IR Pelchrzim Nr 38. No sovereign's colour; only regimental colours were carried. Cloth and scroll red, centre white, emblems gold, black eagle.

2nd Silesian IR Nr 12

Old colours of the IR Alvensleben Nr 33. No sovereign's colour; only regimental colours were carried. Cloth and scroll cornflower blue, centre white, emblems silver, black eagle.

Below Old style colours. These were carried in 1812 by the following regiments. The old-style colour of IRs Ruits Nr 8 as carried by the 1st Pommeranian IR Nr 2. The sovereign's colour was white with a black flame cross and centre, gold emblems and eagle. Regimental colours were black with white centre and flame cross, black eagle, gold emblems. The old-style colour of IR Diericke Nr 16, carried by the 4th East Prussian IR Nr 5. The sovereign's colour was white with orange centre and flame cross, black eagle, gold emblems. The regimental colour was orange with white centre and flame cross, black eagle, gold emblems. The old-style colour of IR Reinhart Nr 52, carried in 1812 by the 1st West Prussian IR Nr 6. The sovereign's colour was white with dark green centre, white scroll, black eagle, poppy red flame cross, silver emblems. The regimental colour was dark green with white centre, dark green scroll, poppy red cross, silver emblems.

Cavalry Standards

Only Kuerassiers and dragoons carried standards at this time. The scale was one per squadron; the 1st Squadron carrying the white, sovereign's standard. Dragoons carried either swallow-tailed guidons or square standards. On the old standards and guidons the royal ciphers were FR; the scroll bore 'PRO GLORIA ET PATRIA'.

1st West Prussian Dragoons Nr 2

These were the guidons of the old Dragoon Regiment Auer Nr 6.

Sovereign's guidon: white cloth, dark blue centre, gold embroidery.

Regimental guidon: dark blue cloth, silver centre, gold embroidery.

Lithuanian Dragoons Nr 3

These were the guidons of the old Dragoon Regiment Baczko Nr 7.

Sovereign's guidon: white cloth with red corner flames, black centre, gold embroidery.

Regimental guidon: black cloth, red corner flames, silver centre, gold embroidery.

2nd West Prussian Dragoons Nr 4

These were the old guidons of the Dragoon Regiment Esebeck Nr 8. No sovereign's guidon was carried.

Regimental guidon: black cloth, red corner flames, silver centre, gold embroidery.

Below Dragoon old pattern standard as carried in 1812.

Brandenburg Dragoons Nr 5

This was a newly raised unit and was presented with four regimental guidons of the disbanded Dragoon Regiment Koeningin Nr 3. No sovereign's guidon was carried.

Regimental guidon: black cloth, silver centre, gold embroidery.

Below *Old-style, swallow-tailed, regimental dragoon guidon of the Regiment von Baczko Nr 7. It was black with red cross and corner medallions, silver central disc, gold emblems and fringes.*

Section 8

The Turkish Army

Prior to the suppression of the Janissaries in 1826, any mobilised army of the Ottoman Empire contained not only the paid professionals but unpaid irregulars both in the infantry and the cavalry.

These paid professional soldiers had been established in 1326, long before those set up in 1449 by Charles VII of France.

The infantry included the *Capou-Khoulis*, originally slaves, and they were divided into various corps (*Odjaks*) as follows.

Janissaries (the infantry), *Ajani-Oglanlar* (novices), *Djebedjis* (armourers), *Topjis* (artillery gunners), *Top-Arabadjis* (artillery conductors), *Khoumbaradjis* (bombardiers) and *Sakkas* (water carriers).

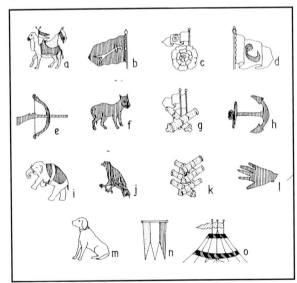

Above *Various* Janissary Ortah *badges.*

a 1st Ortah	f 15th Ortah	k 18th Ortah
b 3rd Ortah	g 16th Ortah	l 24th Ortah
c 44th Ortah	h 31st Ortah	m 71st Ortah
d 48th Ortah	i 79th Ortah	n 94th Ortah
e 82nd Ortah	j 50th Ortah	o 2nd Ortah

The *Capou-Khoulis* of the cavalry were reinforced in time of war by mounted volunteers known as *Akindjis*. There was very little uniformity of costume in the army of this era, but the various *Janissary Ortahs*, or regiments, all wore the white felt *Beurk*, or tall hat. Each had their own standard with an individual badge. This badge was also worn on the great, round tent which was the 'regiment's' field headquarters. An *Ortah* was not always the same size; it could be from 100 – 3,000 men, divided into *Odas*.

The 16th and 18th *Janissary Ortahs* always acted as escorts to the artillery in the field and wore badges of cannon barrels. The 64th, 68th and 71st *Ortahs* were riflemen. The 55th *Ortah* was responsible for the weapon training of all *Janissary* units; they wore cylindrical turbans. The 99th *Ortah* was a military band. The 101 senior *Janissary Ortahs* were collectively known as *Djemaats* and their commanders wore red boots. They were employed in the border fortresses.

At their peak, the *Janissaries* had 196 *Ortahs*. Each *Ortah* was commanded by a *Tchorbadji*, who wore yellow boots as a sign of his status.

Most *Janissary* units wore dark blue costumes. The commander of a company-sized unit (100 men) was known as a *Yuzbashi* and wore a spray of feathers in a gilt holder at the front of his hat.

In 1807 the *Janissaries* in Istanbul revolted and murdered Sultan Selim and installed his cousin Mahmud II in his place. Mahmud introduced European officers, many of them French, into his armed forces to bring them up-to-date in drill, tactics and weapons.

No orders of battle are known to exist for the Turkish armies which fought against the French in Egypt and Syria or against the Russians or Austrians in the Balkans, Romania or Bulgaria, but they made frequent use of Albanian mercenaries.

Adam, Albrecht. '*Croquis Pittoresques Dessines d'apres Nature dans la Russie en 1812*'. Munich

Bibliography

Adam, Albrecht, *Croquis Pittoresques Dessines d'après Nature dans la Russie en 1812*, Munich.

Anon., *Russian Hussars of the 1812 Epoc*h (published in Russian), Moscow, 1990.

Anon., 1812–1814 (published in Russian), Moscow: Terra, 1992.

Anon., 'Das k. k. oesterreichischen Auxiliarkorps unter Fuerst Schwarzenberg 1812', *in Streffleur's Militärische Zeitschrift*, Vol. II., Book 10, October 1912.

Baden-Hochberg, Wilhelm Markgraf von, *Denkwürdigkeiten*, bearbeitet von Karl Obeser, Heidelberg, 1906.

Barschewisch, Hauptmann von, *Geschichte des Grossherzoglich Badischen Leib-Grenadier-Regiments 1803–1871*, Karlsruhe, 1893.

Bezomosny, V M; Vasiliev, A A; Gorschman, A M; Parchajeff, O K and Smirnoff, A A, *The Russian Army 1812–1815*, (published in Russian), Moscow, 2000.

Bogdanowitsch, Generalmajor M, *Geschichte des Feldzuges von 1812*, Leipzig, 1863.

Borodino 1812, Moscow: Izdatelsvo Misl, 1987.

Chandler, D G, *The Campaigns of Napoleon*, London: Weidenfeld & Nicolson, 1967.

Clausewitz, General Carl von, *The Campaign of 1812 in Russia*, London: John Murray, 1843; London: Greenhill Books, 1992.

Ditfurth, Maximilian, Freiherr von, *Die Schlacht bei Borodino am 7. September 1812*, Marburg, 1887.

Duffy, Christopher, B*orodino. Napoleon Against Russia 1812*, London: Sphere, 1972.

du Four, Faber, *Blätter aus meinem Portefeul 1812*, Leipzig, 1897.

Duroff, V A, Russian and Soviet Military Awards, Moscow: Order of Lenin State History Museum, 1990.

Fabry, G, *La Campagne de Russe en 1812*, Paris, 1812.

Fiebig, E, *Unsterbliche Treue*, Berlin, 1936.

Gebler, KK Feldmarschallleutnant Wilhelm Edler von, *Das KK Oestereichisches Auxiliarcorps im Russischen Feldzug 1812*, Vienna, 1863.

George, Hereford B, *The Moscow Expedition*, Oxford, 1904.

Gerdes, A, *Die Geschichte der Truppen Bergs und Westfalen 1812 in Russland*, Langendreer, 1914.

Gerhardt, O, *Die Württemberger in Russland 1812*, Stuttgart, 1937.

Heilmann, 'Die Bayerische Division Preysing im Feldzuge von 1812', in *Jahrbuch für die Deutsche Armee und Marine*, Vol. 17.

Hildebrand, Bernhard, *Drei Schwaben unter Napoleon*, Stuttgart, 1968.

Hohenhausen, Leopold von, *Biographie des Generals von Ochs*, Kassel, 1827.

Holzhausen, P, *Die Deutschen in Russland*, Berlin, 1912.

Jany, Curt, *Geschichte der Preussischen Armee vom 15. Jahrhundert bis 1914*, Osnabrück, 1967.

Johnson, William E, *The Crescent Among the Eagles. The Ottoman Empire and the Napoleonic Wars 1792–1815*, Ocean Springs, MS: privately published, 1994.

Kausler, Franz von and Woerl, J E, *Die Kriege von 1792–1815 in Europa und Aegypten mit Besondere Rücksicht auf die Schlachten Napoleons und seiner Zeit*, Karslruhe and Freiburg, 1842.

Kraft, Heinz, *Die Württemberger in den Napoleonischen Kriegen*, Stuttgart, 1865.

Leyh, Max, D*ie Feldzüge des Königlich Bayerischen Heeres unter Max I Joseph von 1805 bis 1815*, Munich: Max Schick Press, 1935

Lossberg, Friedrich W von, *Briefe in die Heimat Geschrieben während des Feldzugs 1812 in Russland*, Berlin, 1912.

Lünsmann, Fritz, *Die Armee des Königsreichs Westfalen*, Berlin, 1935.

Malibran, A and Chelminski, J, *L'Armée du Duché de Varsovie de 1807 à 1815*, Paris, 1913.

Morgenstern, Oberst Franz, *Kriegserrinerungen aus Westfälischer Zeit*, Wolfenbüttel, 1912.

Pfister, A, *König Friedrich von Württemberg*, Stuttgart, 1888.

Pivka, Otto von, *Armies of the Napoleonic Era*, Newton Abbott: David & Charles, 1979.

Pivka, Otto von, *Armies of 1812*, Cambridge: Patrick Stephens, 1977.

Preysing-Moos, Generalmajor Maximilian, Graf von, *Tagebuch 1812*, Munich, 1912.

Prussian General Staff, *Kriegsgeschichtliche Einzelschriften*, Heft 24, 'Die Theilnahme des Preussischen Huelfkorps an dem Feldzuge gegen Russland im Jahre 1812', Berlin, 1898.

Prussian War Ministry, *Fahnen und Standarten der Preussischen Armee seit dem Jahre 1807*, Berlin, 1889.

Rehtwisch, Theodor, *1812–1815. Geschichte der Freiheitskriege*, 1908.

Roeder, Franz, *Der Kriegszug Napoleons gegen Russland im Jahre 1812*, Leipzig, 1848.

Roos, Heinrich von, *Mit Napoleon in Russland*, Stuttgart, 1912.

Roth von Schreckenstein, Generalleutnant Freiherr, *Die Kavallerie in der Schlacht an der Moskwa am 7. September 1812*, Münster, 1855.

Schubert, F von, *Unter dem Doppeladler: Erinnerungen eines Deutschen im Russischen Offiziersdienst 1789–1814*, Stuttgart, 1962.

Smirnoff, Alexander, 'The Russian Defence Against Napoleon in 1812', Army Quarterly Journal, October 1928.

Smith, Digby, *Borodino*, The Windrush Press, 1998.

Smith, Digby, *The Greenhill Napoleonic Wars Data Book*, London: Greenhill Books, 1998.

Stadlinger, L J von, *Geschichte des Württembergischen Kriegswesens von der Frühesten bis zur Neuesten Zeit*, Stuttgart, 1856.

Stein, F von, *Geschichte des Russischen Heeres vom Ursprunge desselben bis zur Thronbesteigung des Kaisers Nikolai I Pawlowitsch*, Leipzig, 1895.

Thiers, Louis A, *The Moscow Expedition*, Oxford, 1904.

Tolstoy, L N, *War and Peace*, Jena, 1907.

Vaudoncourt, *Mémoires pour servir à l'Histoire de la Guerre entre la France et la Russe en 1812, avec un Atlas Militaire*, London: Deboffe, Egerton, Dulau & Co., 1815.

Wöllwarth, Generalleutnant, *A Short Report on the Occurrences from the Time of Marching out of the Kingdom until the Bivouac by Minkupie, two Marches away from the Nieman*, June 1812.

Württemberg, Eugen, Herzog von, *Aus dem Feldzuge des Jahres 1812 in Russland*, Breslau, 1846.

'Württemberger im Russischen Feldzug 1812', in Württembergische Volksbücher, Stuttgart, 1911.

Zvegvintsoff, V, *Drapeaux et Etandardes de l'Armée Russe 1500–1914*.

Index

This index is organised by national armies and includes all regiments present in Russia and all commanders down to and including brigade level.

THE GRANDE ARMÉE

THE FRENCH ARMY
THE IMPERIAL GUARD
THE OLD GUARD
1er Grenadiers 40, 100,
2e Grenadiers 40, 100,
3e Grenadiers 40, 68, 70, 100,

1er Chasseurs 40, 100,
2e Chasseurs40, 100,

Sailors 43, 104,

Mamelukes 42, 48, 52, 101,
Grenadiers a Cheval 41, 48, 51, 101,
Chasseurs a Cheval 41, 48, 51, 101,
Dragoons 41, 48, 51, 101,
1er Chevau-legers 41, 101,
2e Chevau-legers 41, 68, 70, 101,
3e Chevau-legers 41,
Gendarmerie d'Elite 48, 51, 52, 101,
Artillerie a Cheval 42, 101,

Artillerie Ouvriers 101, 104,
Artillerie 42,
Artillerie a Pied 101,
Engineers 43,
Artillerie-Train Bn 43, 101, 104,

Pontonniers 104,

Flanquers-Chasseurs 41, 99,
Flanquer-Grenadiers 41,
Fusiliers Chasseurs 99,
Fusiliers Grenadiers 99,

1er Tirailleurs 41, 99,
2e Tirailleurs 41,
3e Tirailleurs 41,
4e Tirailleurs 41,
5e Tirailleurs 41, 99,
6e Tirailleurs 41, 99,

1er Voltigeurs 41, 99,
2e Voltigeurs 41,
3e Voltigeurs 41,
4e Voltigeurs 41,
5e Voltigeurs 41, 99,
6e Voltigeurs 41, 99,

Artillerie a Cheval 101,
Artillerie a Pied 99, 104,
Artillerie-Train 99, 104,

FOREIGN REGIMENTS
Legion of the Vistula 75, 77, 100,

LINE INFANTRY 43,
2e IR 113, 155,
3e IR 148, 155,
4e IR 117, 155,
5e IR 146, 155,
6e Provisional IR 145,
7e Provisional IR 145,
8e IR 145, 155,
8e Provisional IR 145,
9e IR 122, 155,
9e Provisional IR 145,
10e Provisional IR 146,
11e IR 146, 155,
11e Provisional IR 146,
12e IR 105, 155,

12e Provisional IR 146,
13e Provisional IR 146,
14e IR 145, 155,
17e IR 105, 155,
18e IR 117, 155,
19e IR 112, 155,
21e IR 105, 155,
24e IR 145, 155,
25e IR 108, 155,
27e IR 146, 155,
28e IR 145, 155,
29e IR 148, 155,
30e IR 105, 155,
33e IR 105, 155,
35e IR 122, 155,
36e IR 143, 155,
37e IR 113, 155,
43e IR 145, 155,
44e IR 142, 155,
45e IR 145, 155,
46e IR 116, 155,
48e IR 105, 155,
50e IR 146, 155,
51e IR 142, 155,
53e IR 122, 155,
54e IR 145, 155,
55e IR 142, 155,
56e IR 112, 155,
57e IR 108, 155,
59e IR 145, 155,
61e IR 108, 155,
63e IR 146, 155,
65e IR 145, 155,
72e IR 117, 155,
76e IR 146, 155,
79e IR 146, 155,

84e IR 121, 155,
85e IR 107, 155,
88e IR 145, 155,
92e IR 121, 155,
93e IR 117, 155,
94e IR 145, 155,
95e IR 145, 155,
96e IR 146, 155,
105e IR 148, 155,
106e IR 121, 155,
108e IR 107, 155,
111e IR 108, 155,
113e IR 148, 133,
123e IR 114, 146, 155,
124e IR 113, 146, 155,
125e IR 142, 146, 155,
126e IR 142, 155,
127e IR 106, 155,
128e IR 112, 155,
129e IR 117, 146, 155,
131e IR (Ile de Walcheren) 147, 155,
132e IR (Ile de Re) 147, 155,
133e IR (de la Mediterranee) 147,
155,
IR Belle-Ile 147,
Bataillon de Neuchatel 57,

LIGHT INFANTRY 44,
4e IR 155,
6e IR 145, 155,
7e IR 105, 155,
8e IR 121, 155,
10e IR 142, 155,
11e IR 113, 155,
13e IR 105, 155,
15e IR 105, 155,
16e IR 145, 155,
18e IR 122, 155,
21e IR 145, 155,
24e IR 116, 155,
25e IR 145, 155,
26e IR 112, 155,
28e IR 145,
29e IR 142, 155,
33e IR 107, 155,
35e IR 155,
39e IR 145, 155,

FOREIGN REGIMENTS 54,
1st Foreign Regiment 54,
2nd Foreign Regiment 54,

3rd Foreign Regiment 54,
4th Foreign Regiment 54,

1st Croatian Infantry R. 55, 121,
2nd Croatian Infantry R. 55,
3rd Croatian Infantry R. 55, 113,
4th Croatian Infantry R. 55,
5th Croatian Infantry R. 55,
6th Croatian Infantry R. 55,

1st Illyrian Infantry R. 55,
2nd Illyrian Infantry R. 55, 117,

Regiment Joseph Napoleon (Spanish)
56, 68, 69, 105, 122,

Portuguese Legion 55, 68, 70,
1st Infantry R. 117,
2nd Infantry R. 117,
3rd Infantry R. 112,
Cavalry R. 55,

1st Swiss IR. 56, 113,
2nd Swiss IR. 56, 113,
3rd Swiss IR. 56, 113,
4th Swiss IR. 56, 113,

CARABINIERS 44,
1er R 151, 155,
2e R 151, 155,

CUIRASSIERS 44,
1er R 151, 155,
2e R 149, 155,
3e R 149, 155,
4e R 114, 155,
5e R 151, 155,
6e R 149, 155,
7e R 114, 155,
8e R 151, 155,
9e R 149, 155,
10e R 151, 155,
11e R 149, 155,
12e R 149, 155,
14e R 114, 155,

DRAGOONS 45, 68, 69,
1er Provisional R 145,
2e R 145, 155,
5e R 145, 155,
7e R 152, 155,

12e R 145, 155,
13e R 145, 155,
17e R 145, 155,
19e R 145, 155,
20e R 145, 155,
23e R 152, 155,
28e R 152, 155,
30e R 152, 155,

CHEVAU-LEGERS 46, 68, 69,
1er R 149, 155,
2e R 151, 155,
4e R 151, 155,
5e R 149, 155,
6e R 118, 155,
9e R 149, 155,

CHASSEURS A CHEVAL 45,
1er R 110, 155,
2e R 110, 155,
3e R 110, 155,
4e R 118, 155,
6e R 152, 155,
7e R 115, 155,
8e R 115, 152,
9e R 125, 155,
11e R 150, 155,
12e R 148, 150, 155,
16e R 149, 155,
19e R 125, 155,
20e R 115, 155,
23e R 115, 155,
24e R 115, 155,
25e R 152, 155,
28e R 118, 155,

HUSSARS 45,
5e R 150, 155,
6e R 152, 155,
7e R 149, 155,
8e R 149, 155,
9e R 150, 155,
11e R 118, 155,

HORSE ARTILLERY 47, 48, 52, 106,
108, 112, 113, 114, 115, 119, 122,
126, 149, 151,

FOOT ARTILLERY 47, 105, 106,
107, 109, 110, 112, 113, 114, 115,
116, 119, 122, 126, 142, 145, 148,

ARTILLERY TRAIN 47, 105, 106, 108, 109, 110, 112, 113, 114, 115, 116, 118, 122, 126, 142, 145,

ARTILLERY PARK 47, 126,

THE ARMY OF THE GRAND DUCHY OF BADEN
1st Division, I Corps; 26th Division, IX Corps, 31st Light Cavalry Brigade.

LINE INFANTRY 48,
1st Regiment Grossherzog. 33, 143,
2nd Regiment vacant. 33, 105,
3rd Regiment Graf Wilhelm von Hochberg. 33, 143,

LIGHT INFANTRY 48,
1st Jaeger Bn von Lingg. 33, 143,

CAVALRY
Hussars von Geusau. 33, 48, 144,

ARTILLERY. 34, 48, 143,

THE ARMY OF THE KINGDOM OF BAVARIA
VI Corps

LINE INFANTRY 48, 50,
1st Regiment Koenig. 36, 130,
2nd Regiment Kronprinz. 36, 130,
3rd Regiment Prinz Carl. 36, 131,
4th Regiment Sachsen-Hildburghausen. 36, 130,
5th Regiment Preysing. 36, 131,
6th Regiment Herzog Wilhelm. 36, 131,
7th Regiment Loewenstein. 36, 131,
8th Regiment Herzog Pius. 36, 130,
9th Regiment Ysenburg. 36, 130,
10th Regiment Junker. 36, 130,
11th Regiment Kinkel. 36, 131,
13th Regiment (vacant). 36, 192,

LIGHT INFANTRY
1st Battalion. 36, 130,
2nd Battalion. 36, 130,
3rd Battalion. 36, 130,
4th Battalion. 36, 131,

5th Battalion. 36, 131,
6th Battalion. 36, 130,

CAVALRY 48, 50,
1st Chevau-Legers (vacant). 37, 152,
2nd Chevau-Legers Taxis. 37, 152,
3rd Chevau-Legers Kronprinz. 37, 131,
4th Chevau-Legers Koenig. 37, 131,
5th Chevau-Legers Leiningen. 37, 131,
6th Chevau-Legers Bubenhofen. 37, 131,

ARTILLERY. 37, 48, 50, 131,

THE TROOPS OF THE GRAND DUCHY OF KLEVE-BERG
26th Division, IX Corps, 30th Light Cavalry Brigade.

LINE INFANTRY 48, 51,
1st Regiment. 38, 143,
2nd Regiment. 38, 143,
3rd Regiment. 38, 143,
4th Regiment. 38, 143,

CAVALRY
2nd Chevau-legers. 39, 144,
ARTILLERY. 39, 143,
SAPPERS 104,

THE ARMY OF THE GRAND DUCHY OF FRANKFURT
34th Division, XI Corps

LINE INFANTRY
2nd Regiment 57, 58,

THE ARMY OF THE GRAND DUCHY OF HESSEN-DARMSTADT 58, 68, 70,
4th Division I Corps, 34th Division XI Corps, 30th Light Cavalry Brigade

GUARD
Leib-Garde Inf Regt. (Delaborde`s 2nd Div, YG as of 12 Aug) 58,
Chevau-legers 58, 144,

LINE INFANTRY 58,
Leib-Regiment 107,

LIGHT INFANTRY 58,
1st Regiment 148,

ARTILLERY 58,

THE ARMY OF THE KINGDOM OF ITALY 59, 68, 71, 72,
IV Corps

ROYAL GUARD 59,
Gardes d'Honneur 60, 125,
Velites 60, 125,
Infantry R. 125,
Conscripts Inf R. 125,
Dragoons 125,
Dragoons Regina 60, 125,
Artillery 125,
Sappers 125,

LINE INFANTRY 60,
2nd Regiment 122,
3rd Regiment 122,
Dalmatian IR. 60, 122,

LIGHT INFANTRY 60,
1st Regiment 122,
3rd Regiment 122,

CAVALRY 60,
2nd Chasseurs a Cheval 126,
Chasseurs a Cheval 126,

ARTILLERY 61, 122, 126,

MECKLENBURG-SCHWERIN
Infantry Regiment 62, 68, 72, 109,
5th Division, I Corps

MECKLENBURG-STRELITZ
Infantry Bn 62, 68, 72, 106,
3rd Division, I Corps

THE ARMY OF THE KINGDOM OF NAPLES 63,
33rd Division, XI Corps

GUARD 63,
Marines 147,
Velites a Pied 147,
Gardes d'Honneur 147,
Velites a Cheval 147,

LINE INFANTRY 64,
5th Regiment 147,
6th Regiment 147,
7th Regiment 147,

CAVALRY 64,

ARTILLERY 64, 147,

4th REGIMENT, CONFEDERATION OF THE RHINE 64,
34th Division, XI Corps 148,

5th REGIMENT, CONFEDERATION OF THE RHINE 65, 72, 77,
34th Division, XI Corps 148,

6th REGIMENT, CONFEDERATION OF THE RHINE 66, 73, 77,
34th Division, XI Corps 148,

THE ARMY OF THE KINGDOM OF PRUSSIA

LINE INFANTRY
1st Combined Infantry Regiment. 191,
2nd Combined Infantry Regiment. 191,
3rd Combined Infantry Regiment. 191,
5th Combined Infantry Regiment. 191,
6th Combined Infantry Regiment. 191,
Leib-Infantry Regiment. 191, 198,
Silesian Grenadiers. 198,
2nd Silesian Infantry Regiment. 198,

LIGHT INFANTRY
Garde-Jaeger. 198,

East Prussian Feld-Jaeger Battalion. 191,

CAVALRY
Garde-Ulanen. 199,
Brandenburg Kuerassiers. 199,
Silesian Kuerassiers. 198,

1st Combined Dragoons. 192,
2nd Combined Dragoons. 192,

Brandenburg Hus-R. 196, 198,
1st Combined Hussars. 192,
2nd Combined Hussars 149, 192,
3rd Combined Hussars. 192,
1st Leib-Hus-R. 196,
2nd Leib-Hus-R. 196,
Normal-Eskadron. 199,
Pommeranian Hus-R. 196,

Brandenburg Ulans. 199,
Combined Ulans 150, 192,

ARTILLERY. 192, 198,
PIONEERS. 198,

THE ARMY OF THE KINGDOM OF SAXONY 66,
VII Corps
GUARD
Garde du Corps 67, 73, 137, 153,

LINE INFANTRY 67, 74, 77,
Grenadier Bn Anger 136,
Grenadier Bn von Brause 136,
Grenadier Bn von Liebenau 135,
Grenadier Bn von Spiegel 136,
Regiment Koenig 136,
Regiment von Niesemueschel 136,
Regiment Prinz Anton 135,
Regiment Prinz Clemenz 135,
Regiment Prinz Friedrich 135,
Regiment Prinz Maximilian 148,

LIGHT INFANTRY 67, 74, 77,
1st Regiment. 135,
2nd Regiment. 136,

CAVALRY 67,
Kuerassier-Regiment (vacant) von Zastrow 78, 137, 153,
Prinz Albrecht Chevau-legers 152,
Prinz Clemenz Ulans 73, 77, 136,
Prinz Johann Chevau-legers 137, 144,
Von Polenz Chevau-legers 136,
Hussars 73, 77, 136,

ARTILLERY 79, 75, 77, 135, 136, 137, 153,

THE ARMY OF THE GRAND DUCHY OF WARSAW 79,
V Corps.

LINE INFANTRY 75, 76, 77, 80, 82,
1st Regiment 127,
2nd Regiment 127,
3rd Regiment 127,
4th Regiment 144,
5th Regiment. 192,
6th Regiment 127,
7th Regiment 144,
8th Regiment 127,
9th Regiment 144,
10th Regiment. 192,
11th Regiment. 192,
12th Regiment 127,
13th Regiment 127,
14th Regiment 127,
15th Regiment 127,
16th Regiment 127,
17th Regiment 127,

CAVALRY 76, 77, 79, 80, 81,
1st Chasseurs a Cheval 127,
2nd Lancers 153,
3rd Lancers 153,
4th Chasseurs a Cheval 127,
5th Chassuers a Cheval 127,
6th Lancers 149,
7th Lancers 125, 153,
8th Lancers 149,
9th Lancers 110,
10th Hussars 150,
11th Lancers 153,
12th Lancers 127,
13th Hussars 127,
14th Cuirassiers 153,

15th Lancers 153,
16th Lancers 153,

ARTILLERY 82, 127, 128, 153, 193,
SAPPERS. 193,

*THE ARMY OF THE KINGDOM OF
WESTFALIA* 83,
VIII Corps

GUARD 83, 92, 93,
Garde du Corps (left VIII Corps with
King Jerome in July) 92, 95,
Grenadier-Garde Bn 92, 94, 140,
Chasseurs-Carabiniers Bn 140,
Garde-Jaeger-Bn 92, 94, 140,
Chevau-legers Regiment. 92, 94,
Artillery 76, 77, 83,

LINE INFANTRY 84,
1st Regiment 141, 193,
2nd Regiment 140,
3rd Regiment 140,
4th Regiment 148,
5th Regiment 140,
6th Regiment 140,
7th Regiment 140,
8th Regiment 141,

LIGHT INFANTRY 84, 92, 94,
1st Battalion 140,
2nd Battalion 140,
3rd Battalion 140,

CAVALRY 84,
1st Kuerassiers 92, 94, 153,
2nd Kuerassiers 153,
1st Hussars 92, 93, 141,
2nd Hussars 92, 93, 141,

ARTILLERY 84, 92, 94, 140, 141,
153,

*THE ARMY OF THE KINGDOM OF
WUERTTEMBERG* 85
25th Division, III Corps.

LINE INFANTRY 87,
1st Regiment Prinz Paul. 117,

2nd Regiment Herzog Wilhelm 117,
4th Regiment (vacant) von
Franqemont.117,
6th Regiment Kronprinz. 117,

LIGHT INFANTRY 87,
1st Jaeger Bn. Koenig. 117,
2nd Jaeger Bn. 117,
3rd Light Inf Bn. 117,
4th Light Inf Bn. 117,

CAVALRY 86, 87, 92, 96,
1st Chevau-legers Herzog Heinrich.
14, 118,
2nd Leib-Chevau-legers 14, 91, 118,
3rd Jaeger zu Pferde Herzog Louis.
14, 15, 150,
4th Jaeger zu Pferde Koenig. 14, 118,

ARTILLERY 88, 89, 92, 96, 119,

*THE ARMY OF THE GRAND DUCHY
OF WUERZBURG* 90,
(aka 1st Regiment, Confederation of
the Rhine)
34th Division, XI Corps.

LINE INFANTRY 90, 92, 96,
Chevau-leger Regiment 92, 96,

**THE ARMIES OF NAPOLEON'S
OPPONENTS**

THE ARMY OF IMPERIAL RUSSIA

THE IMPERIAL GUARD
Finlandski Jaeger R. 163,
Izmailovski Life Guards. 163,
Litovski Life Guards. 163,
Life Guards Jaeger Bn. 163,
Preobrazhenski Life Guards. 163,
Semenovsky Life Guards. 163,
Life Guards Jaeger Bn. 163,
Chevalier Guards. 163, 175,
Horse Guards. 163, 175,
Life Guard Dragoons. 163, 176,
Life-Guard Hussars. 163, 182,
Life Guard Ulans. 163, 183,

Life-Guard Cossacks. 163,

LINE INFANTRY
GR = GRENADIER REGIMENT, G
Bn = GRENADIER BATTALION.
IR = INFANTRY REGIMENT
Alexopolski IR. 164,
Apscheronski IR. 166,
Arakchejeff GR. 162,
Archangelgorodski IR. 167,
Astrakhanski GrenR. 165,
Azovski IR. 168,
Bialostockski IR. 167,
Bieleff IR. 169,
Bieloserski IR. 162,
Brestski IR. 162,
Brianski IR. 168,
Butyrski IR. 163,
Caucasus IR. 169,
Chernigoffski IR. 162,
Combined GBns, 1st Gren Div. 163,
Combined GBns, 4th Div. 163,
Combined GBns, 9th Div. 165,
Combined GBns, 15th Div. 165,
Combined GBns, 17th Div. 163,
Combined GBns, 18th Div. 165,
Combined GBns, 23rd Div. 163,
Combined GR. 162,
Count Arakchejeff Grenadier R. 162,
Depot Bns, 1st Gren Div. 169,
Depot Bns, 2nd Gren Div. 169,
Depot Bns, 3rd Div. 169,
Depot Bns, 4th Div. 168,
Depot Bns, 5th Div. 168,
Depot Bns, 7th Div. 169,
Depot Bns, 9th Div. 169,
Depot Bns, 11th Div. 169,
Depot Bns, 12th Div. 166,
Depot Bns, 14th Div. 168,
Depot Bns, 15th Div. 166,
Depot Bns, 17th Div. 168,
Depot Bns, 18th Div. 166, 169,
Depot Bns, 23rd Div. 169,
Depot Bns, 24th Div. 169,
Depot Bns, 26th Div. 169,
Depot Bns, 27th Div. 169,
Dnieprovski IR. 165,
Estlandski IR. 161,
Fanagorski GR. 165,
Galitzki IR. 168,
Kabardinsk IR. 169,

Kalugski IR. 161,
Kamchatski IR. 167,
Kaporski IR. 162,
Kazan IR. 169,
Kexholm IR. 162,
Kherson IR. 169,
Kievski GrenR. 165,
Koliwanski IR. 166,
Koslovski IR. 166,
Kostromski IR. 165,
Krementchugski IR. 162,
Krimski IR. 167,
Kura IR. 166,
Kurski IR. 167,
Ladogaski IR. 164,
Leib Grenadier R. 162,
Libauski IR. 163,
Litovski IR. 168,
Little Russia GR. 165,
Mingrelski IR. 167,
Minski IR. 162,
Mogilevski IR 161,
Moscow GR. 165,
Moscow IR. 163,
Muromski IR. 162,
Navaginski IR. 161,
Narvaski IR. 164,
Nascheburgski IR. 166,
1st Naval IR. 168,
2nd Naval IR. 168,
3rd Naval IR. 168,
Neuschlotski IR. 168,
Nevaski IR. 168,
New Ingermannland IR. 164,
Nishegorodski IR. 164,
Nizovski IR. 168,
Ochotski IR. 167,
Odessa IR. 165,
Olonetski IR. 168,
Orelski IR. 164,
Pavloff GR. 162,
Permski IR 161,
Pernovski IR. 162,
Podolski IR. 168,
Polotski IR. 162,
Poltawaski IR. 164,
Pskoffski IR. 163,
Revalski IR. 162,
Rialski IR. 162,
Riashki IR. 166,
Riasanski IR. 162,

St Petersburg GR. 162,
Saratovski IR. 168,
Schirwanski IR. 163,
Schluesselburgski IR. 167,
Selenginski IR. 162,
Sevastopol IR. 169,
Sibirski GR. 165,
Simbirski IR. 165,
Sievski IR 161,
Smolenski IR. 164,
Sophiiski IR. 163,
Staroi-Ingermannlandski IR. 167,
Staroi-Okolski IR. 167,
Susdal IR. 169,
Tauride GR. 162,
Tambovski IR. 165,
Tarnopol IR. 165,
Tenginski IR. 161,
Tiflis IR. 169,
Tobolski IR. 162,
Tomski IR. 163,
Troitsk IR. 169,
Tulski IR. 161,
Ufimski IR. 163,
Uglitsch IR. 168,
Ukrainski IR. 167,
Veliki-Lutzk IR
Vitebski IR. 166,
Vladimirski IR. 165,
Voroneschski IR. 168,
Wiatkaski IR. 167,
Wiborgski IR. 167,
Wilmannstrandski IR. 162,
Wilna IR. 165,
Wolhynski IR. 162,
Yakutski IR. 166,
Yaroslavski IR. 168,
Yekaterinburgski IR. 162,
Yekaterinoslaff GR. 162,
Yeletzki IR. 162,

JAEGER REGIMENTS
1st. 162,
2nd. 168,
3rd. 168,
4th. 162,
5th. 164,
6th. 164,
7th. 168,
8th. 167,
9th. 169,

10th. 166,
11th. 163,
12th. 168,
13th. 166,
14th. 166,
15th. 169,
16th. 169,
17th. 169,
18th. 162,
19th. 163,
20th. 162,
21st. 162,
22nd. 168,
23rd 161,
24th 161,
25th 161,
26th 161,
27th. 168,
28th. 165,
29th. 167,
30th. 162,
31st. 168,
32nd. 165,
33rd. 162,
34th. 162,
35th. 168,
36th. 163,
37th. 167,
38th. 166,
39th. 167,
40th. 163,
41st. 164,
42nd. 164,
43rd. 168,
44th. 168,
45th. 167,
46th. 169,
47th. 168,
48th. 162,
49th. 165,
50th. 165,

KUERASSIER REGIMENTS
Chevalier Guard 161, 175,
Astrakhan. 175,
Gluchovski. 165, 175,
Leib-KuerR Her Majesty. 163, 175,
Leib-KuerR His Majesty. 163, 175,
Little Russia. 165, 175,
Military Order. 165, 175,
Novgorodski. 165, 175,

Pskoff. 175.
Starodub. 175,
Yekaterinoslav. 165, 175,

DRAGOON REGIMENTS
Arsamaski. 166, 176, 181,
Borissoglebsk. 169, 176,
Charkovski. 165, 181,
Composite regiment. 168,
Courland. 164, 176,
Dorpatski. 167, 176, 181,
Finland. 168, 181,
Ingermannlandski. 164, 176,
Irkutski. 164, 176,
Kazanski. 163, 176,
Kargopolski. 164, 176,
Kievski. 165, 176,
Kinburnski. 167, 176,
Livland. 167, 169, 176, 181,
Mittau. 168, 169, 176,
Moscow. 164, 176,
Narwa. 169, 176,
New Russian. 165,
Nezhinski. 163, 176, 181,
Nischegorod. 176,
Novgorod. 176,
Orenburgski. 164, 181,
Pskoffski. 164, 181,
Pereslavski. 167, 181,
Riga. 169, 181,
St Petersburg. 167, 181,
Serpuchoffski. 166, 181,
Sibirski. 164, 181,
Sieverski. 167, 181,
Smolenski. 167, 181,
Starodubski. 166, 181,
Taganrogski. 166, 169, 181,
Tchernigoffski. 165, 181,
Tiraspolski. 167, 181,
Twerskoi. 166, 181,
Vladimirski. 166, 169, 176,
Yamburg. 181,
Zhitomirski. 166, 176,

HUSSAR REGIMENTS
Achtirski. 165, 182,
Alexandriaski. 166, 182,
Bielorussi (White Russian). 167, 182,
Grodno. 182,
Isumski. 164, 182,
Lubno. 166, 182,

Mariupolski. 164, 182,
Olviopol. 168, 182,
Pavlogradski. 165, 182,
Ssumski. 164, 182,
Yelisabethgrad. 163, 182,

ULAN REGIMENTS
Litovski. 165, 183,
Orenburg. 183,
Polish. 164, 183,
Serpuchoff. 183,
Siberia. 183,
Taganrog. 183,
Tartar. 166, 183,
Tchugujevski. 167, 183,
Vladimir. 183,
Volhynski. 168, 183,
Yamburg. 183,
Zhitomir. 183,

TARTAR REGIMENTS
Evpatoriaski. 166,
Perekop. 164,
Simferopol. 164,

BASCHKIRS
1st Regiment 164,
2nd Regiment 164, 166.

COSSACK REGIMENTS
1st Bug Regiment. 164,
2nd Bug Regiment. 164,

DON COSSACK PULKS.
Andrianoff II. 164,
Ataman. 164,
Barabanchikoff II. 166,
Bichaloff I. 165,
Charitnoff VII. 164,
Chernozuboff VII. 164,
Denisoff VII. 164,
Diatzkin. 165,
Grekoff IV. 167,
Grekoff VI 161,
Grekoff VIII. 167,
Grekoff XVIII. 164,
Grekoff XXI. 165,
Illowaiski V. 164,
Illowaiski X. 165,
Illowaiski XI. 165,
Janoff. 166,

Karpoff II. 165,
Kireev II. 168,
Kommissaroff I. 165,
Kutainikoff IV. 167,
Lukovkina II. 168,
Melnikoff III. 164, 167,
Melnikoff IV. 165,
Melnikoff V. 167,
Pantelejeff II. 167,
Platoff IV 161,
Platoff V. 165,
Poschilin. 168,
Rodianoff 161,
Selivan 161,
Sissojeff III. 165,
Tsickileff. 166,
Turtsaninoff. 168,
Vlassoff II. 166,
Vlassoff III. 164,

Tjeptjarski Cossacks 1st Regiment.
164,

KALMUCKS
1st Regiment. 166,
2nd Regiment. 166,

HORSE ARTILLERY. 161, 163, 164,
165, 166, 167,

FOOT ARTILLERY. 161, 162, 163,
164, 165, 166, 167, 168,

ENGINEERS / SAPPERS. 161, 164,
165, 166, 168,

PONTONNIERS. 161, 164, 165, 166,
168,

THE ARMY OF IMPERIAL AUSTRIA
Stabs-Ingenieure

LINE INFANTRY
Grenadier Bn Nr 15 Kirchenbetter.
184,
Grenadier Bn Nr 14 Przeczinski. 184,
IR Nr 1 Kaiser. 187,
IR Nr 2 Hiller. 184, 187,
IR Nr 9 Czartoriski. 184, 187,
IR Nr 12 Liechtenstein. 187,

IR Nr 19 Alvintzy. 184, 187,
IR Nr 30 de Ligne. 184, 187,
IR Nr 32 Esterhazy. 184, 187,
IR Nr 33 Colloredo. 184, 187,
IR Nr 34 Davidovich. 184, 187,
IR Nr 37 Weidenfeld. 187,
IR Nr 39 Duka. 184, 187,
IR Nr 41 Kottulinski. 184, 187,
IR Nr 48 Simbschen. 184, 187,
IR Nr 58 Beaulieu. 184, 187,
IR Nr 60 Gyulai. 187,

BORDER INFANTRY

Grenz IR Nr 16 Warasdiner-St
Georger. 184, 187,

LIGHT INFANTRY

5th Jaeger Bn. 184,
7th Jaeger Bn. 184,

DRAGOONS

Regiment Nr 4 Levenehr. 184, 188,
Regiment Nr 6 Riesch. 184, 188,
Stabs-Dragoner. 184,

CHEVAU-LEGERS

Regiment Nr 2 Hohenzollern. 184,
188,
Regiment Nr 3 O'Reilly. 184, 188,

HUSSARS

Regiment Nr 1 Kaiser. 184, 189,
Regiment Nr 3 Ferdinand d'Este. 197,
Regiment Nr 4 Hessen-Homburg.
184, 189, 197,
Regiment Nr 5 Radetzky. 197,
Regiment Nr 6 Blankenstein. 184,
189,
Regiment Nr 8 Kienmayer. 184, 189,
197,
Regiment Nr 9 Frimont. 197,

FOOT ARTILLERY. 184, 187,
ENGINEERS. 188,
SAPPERS AND MINERS. 188,
PIONIERS. 184, 187,
PONTONIERS. 184, 187,

THE ARMY OF THE OTTOMAN EMPIRE

INFANTRY. 204,
CAVALRY. 204,
ARTILLERY. 204,

THE COMMANDERS

Alexander I, Emperor of Russia. 23,
Andrianoff II. 164,
Anthing, C-H-G, GdB. 148,
Arackchejeff, Count, 163,
Ataman. 164,
Auerstaedt, Duke of, see Davout.
Augereau, C-P-F, Duke of Castiglione,
Marshal. 145, 158,
Aximatowski, W. GdB. Commanded
1st Brigade, 17th (Polish) Division
early in the campaign; not listed there.
Bachmetieff I, MG. 162,
Bachmetieff II, MG. 162,
Baggovut, K F, LG. 162,
Bagration, P I, Prince, GoI. 23, 157,
164,
Barabanchikoff II. 166,
Barclay de Tolley, M A, GoI. 156, 161,
Beckers, GM. 130,
Belliard, A-D. GdD. CoS to Murat. 21,
Belluno, Duke of, see Victor.
Below, von, Col. 191,
Berg, G M, MG. 161,
Berthier, Alexander, GdD, CoS to
Napoleon. 18, 22, 57,
Beurmann, GdB. 118,
Bezler, Captain. 17,
Billard, P-J, GdB 142,
Bianchi, V F F Freiherr, FML. 184,
Bichaloff I. 165,
Bieganzki, L. GdB. Commanded 1st
Brigade, 18th (Polish) Division; not
listed there.
Billard, P-J, GdB. 142,
Blanmont, M-P-I, GdB. 142,
Bordesoulle, E, GdB. 110,
Borosdin I, M M , LG. 165,
Breissand, J, GdB. 145,
Breuning, Lt. 18,
Bronikowski, M. GdB. Commanded a

brigade in the 28th (Polish) Division;
not listed there.
Broussiere, J-B, GdD. 122,
Bruyeres, P-J, GdD. 149,
Bulatoff, M L, MG. 167,
Burthe, A, GdB. 150,
Camus, L, GdB. 12th Div, IX C. 142,
Castex, B-P, GdB. 115,
Castiglione, Duke of, see Augereau.
Caulaincourt, A-A-L, Duke of Vicenza,
GdD. 20, 22, 23, 24,
Charitnoff VII. 164,
Chastel, L-P-A, GdD. 152,
Chernozuboff VII. 164,
Chlopicki, J. GdB. Commanded a
brigade in the 28th (Polish) Division;
not listed there.
Clamus GdB 142,
Claparede, M-M, GdD. 100,
Compans, J-D, GdD. 108,
Constantine Pavlovich, Grand Duke.
163,
Corbineau, J-B-J, GdB. 115,
Crais, War Commissary. 15, 18,
Daendels, H-W, GdD. 143,
Damas, F-E, GM. 140, 143,
Danzig, Duke of, see Lefebvre.
Davout, L-N, Marshal. 13, 18, 25, 27,
28, 31, 105, 155,
D'Auvray, MG. 156,
Defrance, J-M-A, GdD. 151,
Delaborde, H-F, GdD. 99,
Delaitre, A-C-B, GdB. 144,
Delzons, A-J, GdD. 121,
Denisoff VII, 164,
Depreradovitch, N I, MG. 163,
Deroy, GdD. 130,
Dessaix, J-M, GdD. 107,
Destrees, F, GdD. 33rd Div XI C 147,
Diatzkin. 165,
Dochturoff, D S, GoI. 163,
Dombrowski, J-H, GdD. 28, 127, 158,
Dommanget, J-B, GdB. 152,
Doumerc, J-P, GdD. 114,
Duka, I M, MG. 165,
Durutte, P-F-J, GdD. 28, 147,
Dziewanowski, D. GbB. Commanded
the 19th Light Cavalry Brigade, 17th
(Polish) Division; not listed there.
Elchingen, Duke of, see Ney.
Ertell, F F, LG. 169,

Essen, P K, LG. 167,

Eugen von Wuerttemberg, Prince. 162,

Eugene de Beauharnais, Viceroy of Italy, GdD. 25, 31, 158,

Fournier-Sarlovese, F, GdB. 144,

Frelich, GM. 184,

Friant, L, GdD. 105,

Friedrich, Crown Prince of Wuerttemberg. 17, 18, 19,

Frimont, J M, Fuerst, FML. 184,

Funck, GdD 136, 137,

Gablenz 136,

Gamen, A J, MG. 168,

Gauthrin, P-E, GdB. 152,

Gerard, F-J, GdB. 152,

Gerard, M-E, GdD. 105,

Girard, J-B, GdD. 144,

Girardin, D`Ermenonville, A-L-R, GdB. 110,

Gourgaud, ADC to Napoleon. 23,

Gouvion St-Cyr, L, Marshal. 28, 130, 156, 157,

Grabowski, M. GdB. Commanded 2nd Brigade, 18th (Polish) Division; not listed.

Grandjean, C-L-D, GdD. 192,

Grawert J A R von, GoI 155, 191,

Grekoff IV. 167,

Grekoff VI. 161,

Grekoff VIII, 167,

Grekoff XVIII. 164,

Grekoff XXI. 165,

Gros, J-L, GdB. 100,

Grouchy, E, GdD. 152,

Gudin de la Sablonniere, C-E, GdD. 105,

Harditsch, Lt-Col. 18,

Hessen-Homburg, P, Prinz, GM. 184,

Heudelet de Bierre, E, GdD. 145,

Hochberg, Wilhelm, Graf von, GdD. 143,

Horn, H W, Col. 156, 191,

Huehnerbein, F H K G, Freiherr, Col. 192,

Husson, P-A, GdD. 145,

Illowaiski V. 164,

Illowaiski X, 165,

Illowaiski XI. 165,

Jacquinot, C-C, GdB. 149,

Janoff. 166,

Jeanneret, Col. 192,

Jerome, King of Westfalia. 140,

Junot, J-A, Duke of Abrantes. 31,

Kamienicki, GdD. 127,

Kantakuzen, MG. 163,

Karl, Prince von Mecklenburg, MG. 165,

Kapsevich, P M, LG. 163,

Karpoff I, A A, MG. 165,

Karpoff II. 165,

Kazoffskoi, P D, MG. 161,

Kireev II. 168,

Kleist, von, MG. 191,

Klengel, GdB 136, 155,

Kniaziewicz, K. GdD. Commanded 18th (Polish) Division later in the campaign; not listed there.

Knorring, I F, MG. 165,

Kolubakin, I M, MG. 164,

Kommissaroff I. 165,

Konnovnitzin, P P, LG. 155, 162,

Korff, F K, Baron, GAdjt. 164,

Kossecki, F. GdB. Commanded 1st Brigade, 17th (Polish) Division later in the campaign; not listed there. 158,

Kraczinsky, General, commander, 1st Polish Lancers of the Guard 16, 17, 18,

Krazinsky, Izydor, GdB. Commanded a brigade in the 16th (Polish) Division; not listed there.

Kutainikoff IV. 167,

Kutuzov, Mikhail Illarionovich Golenischchev, Prince, GoI. 23, 157, 158, 159,

Lacuee Cessac. 11,

La Houssaye, A, GdD. 152,

Lambert, K O, Count, MG. 158, 166,

Langeron, A F, GoI. 167,

Latour-Maubourg, M-V-N, GdD. 31, 153,

Lavroff, N I, LG. 163,

Lecchi, GdD. 125,

Lecoq, E von, GL. 135,

Ledru des Essarts, F, GdD. 116,

Lefebvre, F-J, Marshal, Duke of Danzig. 100,

Legrand, C-J-A, GdD. 112,

Lagrange, GdD. 31st Div, XI C 146,

Legras, GM. 140,

Lepel, Baron, GM. 153,

Lichacheff, P G, MG. 163,

Liechtenstein, A, Fuerst GM. 184,

Lieders, N I, MG. 168,

Lieven, I A, MG. 167,

Lilienberg, GM. 184,

Lingg, GM. Berg. 143,

Loewis, MG 155, 156,

Loison, L-H, GdD. 28,

Lorge,J-T-G, GdD. 153,

Lukovkina II. 168,

Macdonald, J-E-J-A, Duke of Tarento, Marshal. 28,

Massenbach, von, LG. 191,

Mayer, GM. 184,

Melnikoff III. 164, 167,

Melnikoff IV. 165,

Melnikoff V. 167,

Merle, P-H-V, GdD. 113,

Mielzynski, S. GdB. Commanded 1st Brigade, 16th (Polish) Division early in the campaign; not listed there.

Miloradovich, GoI. 157, 158,

Minucci GM. 130,

Mohr, J F, Freiherr, GM. 184,

Montbrun, L-P, GdD. 15,

Morand, C-A-L-A, GdD. 105,

Morand, J, GdD. 148,

Mortier, A-E-C-J, Marshal. 26, 31, 99,

Mourier, P, GdB. 118,

Muenchingen, Lieutenant. 17,

Murat, Joachim, King of Naples. 19, 21, 155, 157,

Nansouty, E-M-A-C, GdD. 149,

Napoleon I, Emperor of the French. 7, 10, 11, 12, 13, 16, 17, 18, 19, 20, 21, 22, 23, 24, 25, 26, 27, 28, 30, 32, 53, 54, 156, 157, 158, 159,

Nazimoff, F V, MG. 166,

Neveroffsky, D P, MG. 156, 165,

Ney, M, Duke of Elchingen, Marshal. 15, 17, 18, 19, 31, 116, 156,

Niemojewski, W. GdB. Commanded a Polish cavalry brigade, I Cavalry Corps; not listed there.

Nienwiewski, GdB. 149,

Nostitz, von, GM. 135,

Ochs, A L von, GL. 140,

Olsuffieff, E D, LG. 162,

Orloff-Denisow, LG, 158,

Ornano, P-A, GdB. 125,

Osten-Sacken, F V, LG. Baron. 158, 165, 166,

Oudinot, N-C, Marshal, Duke of Reggio. 18, 112, 156, 159,

Pahlen, P P, Count, LG. 164,

Pakosch, K. GdB. Commanded 2nd Brigade, 17th (Polish) Division late in the campaign; not listed there.

Palm, Lt-Col. 18,

Pantjeleff II. 167,

Partouneaux, L, GdD. 24, 142,

Paskewitch, I F, LG. 164,

Paszkowski, F, GdB. Commanded a brigade in the 16th (Polish) Division; not listed there.

Paulucci, MG. 169,

Pflacher, GM. 184,

Pinot, GdD. 20, 122,

Piotrowski, M. GdB. Commanded 2nd Brigade, 17th (Polish) Division early in the campaign; not listed.

Pire, H-M-G, GdB. 149,

Platoff, M I, GoC. 164,

Platoff IV. 161,

Platoff V. 165,

Poniatowski, J-A, GdD. 31, 127,

Poschilin. 168,

Potocki, S. GdB. Commanded 2nd Brigade, 18th (Polish) Division later in the campaign; not listed there.

Preysing, M, Graf von, GM. 130,

Rachmanoff, V S, MG. 168,

Radziwill, M. GdB. Commanded a brigade in the 28th (Polish) Division; not listed.

Raglovich, GM. 130,

Rajevsky, N N, LG. 155, 164,

Rapp, Jean, GdD. 28,

Raumer, Col. 191,

Razout, J-N, GdD. 117,

Rechberg, GM. 130,

Reggio, Duke of, see Oudinot.

Repnin-Volkonski, N G, MG. 161,

Reynier, J-L-E, GdD. 28, 135,

Rodianoff. 161,

Roguet, F, GdD. 99,

Rosen, F F, MG. 168,

Rosen, G V, MG. 163,

Rozniecki, A. GdD. 153,

Rutcheff, MG. 169,

Sabanieff, I V, LG. 168,

St Genies, J-M-N, GdB.

St Germain, A-L, GdD. 149,

Sahr, GdB 136, 137,

Salm, Graf. 16,

Sazonoff, I T, MG. 161,

Scheeler, C F W, GdD. 117,

Scherbatoff, A G, Prince, MG. 165,

Schewitsch, E I, MG. 163,

Schoenlin, Over Commissary 15,

Schramm, J-A, GdB. 148,

Schuvaloff, P A, Count, LG. 162,

Schwarzenberg K P, Fuerst, FM. 28, 156, 158, 184,

Sebastiani de la Porta, H-F-B, GdD. 28,

Segur de, Philip, Count. 11, 12, 13, 14, 19, 24, 25, 28, 29, 30, 31,

Seidewitz, GM. 130,

Selivan. 161,

Siebein, GM. 130,

Siegenthal, H Freiherr, FML. 184,

Sievers I, K K, Count, MG. 165,

Sissojeff III. 165,

Sorokin, M M, MG. 166,

Steindel, von, GM. 135,

Steinheil, F F, Count, LG. 157, 168,

Stroganoff, P A, MG. 162,

Stutterheim, FML, Baron. 184,

Subervie, J-G, GdB. 150,

Sulkowski, A. GdB. Commanded 20th Light Cavalry Brigade, 18th (Polish) Division; not listed there.

Tchichagoff, P V, Admiral. 159, 167,

Tharreau, GdD. 140,

Thielmann, J A, Freiherr von, GL. 137, 153,

Tormassoff, A P, GoC. 155, 156, 165, 166,

Trautenberg, FML. 184,

Treviso, Duke of , see Mortier.

Tsikileff. 166,

Turno, K. GdB. Commanded a brigade in the 4th (Polish) Light Cavalry Division, IV Cavalry Corps; not listed there.

Turtsaninoff. 168,

Tutchkov I, LG. 156, 162,

Tyszkiewicz, T. GdB. Commanded a cavalry brigade in the 16th (Polish) Division; not listed there.

Udom, E E, MG. 166,

Uvaroff, F P, LG. 163,

Valence, J-B-C-M-A, GdD. 149,

Vassiltchikov, MG. 164,

Verdier, J-A, GdD. 113,

Victor, C-V, Marshal. 28, 31, 142, 157, 158,

Villata, GdB. 125,

Vincenti, GM. 130,

Vlassoff II. 166,

Vlassoff III. 164,

Voinoff, A L, LG. 167,

Wachtenburg, GM. 184,

Walther, F-H, GdD. 101,

Watier de St Alphonse, P, GdD.

Wellington, Duke of. 24,

Wickenberg, GM. 140,

Wittgenstein, P X, LG. 156, 157, 158, 161,

Woellwarth, F A W, GL. 14,

Wrede, K P, GL. 130,

Wrede, GM. 184,

Wuerttemberg, Eugen, Duke, GM. 162,

Yorck, J D L von, GL. 157,

Zass, A P, Baron, LG. 167,

Zayonchek (Zajaczek), J, GdD. 127,

Zechmeister, GM. 184,

Zoltowski, E. GdB. Commanded 2nd Brigade, 17th (Polish) Division later in the campaign; not listed there.